MW00988524

GOD AND THE IRS

Seventy-five percent of Americans claim religious affiliation, which can impact their taxpaying responsibilities. In this illuminating book, Samuel D. Brunson describes the many problems and breakdowns that can occur when tax meets religion in the United States, and shows how the US government has too often responded to these issues in an unprincipled, ad hoc manner. *God and the IRS* offers a better framework to understand tax and religion. It should be read by scholars of religion and the law, policymakers, and individuals interested in understanding the implications of taxation on their religious practices.

Samuel D. Brunson teaches tax and business law at Loyola University Chicago. He has published extensively on federal income tax. In addition, he blogs regularly about tax and religion and, often, both together. When he is not writing about tax or religion, you can often find him listening to jazz, playing piano, or rock-climbing with his family. Professor Brunson sits on the boards of two nonprofit organizations and is on the organizing committee of the J. Reuben Clark Law Society Faculty Group.

God and the IRS

ACCOMMODATING RELIGIOUS PRACTICE IN UNITED STATES TAX LAW

SAMUEL D. BRUNSON

Loyola University Chicago School of Law

CAMBRIDGE
UNIVERSITY PRESS

University Printing House, Cambridge CB2 8BS, United Kingdom

One Liberty Plaza, 20th Floor, New York, NY 10006, USA

477 Williamstown Road, Port Melbourne, VIC 3207, Australia

314–321, 3rd Floor, Plot 3, Splendor Forum, Jasola District Centre, New Delhi – 110025, India

79 Anson Road, #06–04/06, Singapore 079906

Cambridge University Press is part of the University of Cambridge.

It furthers the University's mission by disseminating knowledge in the pursuit of education, learning, and research at the highest international levels of excellence.

www.cambridge.org
Information on this title: www.cambridge.org/9781107176300
DOI: 10.1017/9781316816875

First published 2018

Printed in the United States of America by Sheridan Books, Inc.

A catalogue record for this publication is available from the British Library.

ISBN 978-1-107-17630-0 Hardback
ISBN 978-1-316-62955-0 Paperback

Cambridge University Press has no responsibility for the persistence or accuracy of URLs for external or third-party internet websites referred to in this publication and does not guarantee that any content on such websites is, or will remain, accurate or appropriate.

To Jamie, Jane, Mary, and Miles

Contents

Acknowledgments

In writing this book, I benefited from the support, encouragement, and ideas of several friends and colleagues. Without their help, this book would not have been possible.

In particular, I owe a debt of gratitude to the Loyola University Chicago School of Law for its generous support of my research and writing.

I also want to especially thank Bart Davis and Robert P. Lunt, who were generous enough to share personal reminiscences of *Davis* v. *United States* with me.

In addition, Michael Austin, Kevin Barney, Adam Chodorow, Bobby Dexter, Steve Evans, Jeffrey L. Kwall, Roberta R. Kwall, Ira C. Lupu, Jonathan Stapley, and Alex Tsesis have generously read part or all of the manuscript and given me invaluable suggestions and reactions.

I presented portions of the book at the Mid-American Jesuit Faculty Workshop, the Association of Mid-Career Tax Professors Conference, and the Midwest Mormon Studies Working Paper Group, as well as to the faculty of the University of Utah's S.J. Quinney College of Law, and received valuable feedback from each of those groups.

Finally, I want to thank my wife and children for their support and encouragement throughout the time I spent writing this book.

Introduction

On Thanksgiving 2014, as I stepped away briefly from the day's festivities, I joined a Twitter argument about Kent Hovind.[1] I knew very little about Hovind, but I knew that he had been convicted of and jailed for tax evasion and other financial crimes. And I knew that he had a fervent body of supporters who believed that his conviction for various financial crimes was just a cover for what the government viewed as his true crime: promoting creationism.[2]

Hovind had spent his professional life as a minister of sorts. In 1989, he established Creation Science Evangelism, a ministry devoted to the promotion of creationism and opposition to evolution. To promote creationism, Hovind lectured domestically and internationally. In addition, he sold creationism-related merchandise through his ministry.

In 2001, Hovind took his creationist ambitions to a new level. Not content to merely lecture, he opened Dinosaur Adventure Land ("Where Dinosaurs and the Bible Meet!"), a seven-acre theme park and museum in Pensacola, Florida. As children enjoyed dinosaur-themed rides and created their own miniature Grand Canyons, they also learned that dinosaurs coexisted with humans – in fact, according to Dinosaur Adventure Land, a pair survived the Flood on Noah's Ark.[3]

Though creationism was Hovind's professional passion, it was far from his only interest. Hovind was also deeply dedicated to not paying taxes.

A loose community of dedicated tax protestors exists in the United States.[4] These tax protestors have come up with elaborate reasons why the US tax law is invalid or, at least, does not apply to them. They share their secrets with other tax protestors, assuring each other that the government has no legal authority to collect taxes from them. The tax protestors' arguments are utterly frivolous. Still, enough taxpayers believe them (or, at least, find it convenient to claim to believe them) that every year the IRS releases a list of frivolous tax arguments. Along with the list, the IRS warns taxpayers that if they refuse to pay their taxes and defend their noncompliance using those frivolous arguments, they will face significant financial penalties and even jail time.[5]

Hovind was as dedicated a tax protestor as any. He did not file a single federal tax return between 1989 and 1996.[6] The IRS noticed and demanded that Hovind provide them with certain financial records. He refused. In fact, in his attempts to impede the IRS's investigation, Hovind went so far as to file a lawsuit against the IRS, demanding that the court order the IRS and its agents to stop contacting and harassing him and that it order the IRS to stay off his property.[7]

Eventually Hovind shifted from merely employing frivolous tax arguments to selling them, too: in addition to its creationist merchandise, his Christian Science Evangelism began to sell books and videos that taught customers how they could avoid paying taxes, based on his tax protestor arguments.[8]

Although Hovind has proven remarkably dedicated to evading taxes, for the most part, he has not been imaginative in his tax evasion. Most of his justifications for refusing to pay taxes are entirely banal, the kinds of arguments promulgated on YouTube, in self-published books, and on sketchy websites. Tax protestors believe and trumpet these once-furtive arguments. "The federal income tax is 100 percent voluntary!"[9] they announce proudly, which means that if they choose not to pay, there is nothing the government can do.

But Hovind's flavor of tax evasion differs from most tax protestors' in one significant way: he ultimately rests his belief that he owes no taxes – at least, to the extent anything besides bald greed underlies that belief – on his status as a Christian and a minister. He believes that something about being a religious believer makes him different from the vast majority of his fellow citizens. This difference, he believes, is itself sufficient to excuse him from paying taxes. That is, in Hovind's mind, there is something about the economics of religious practice that materially alters the secular assumptions that underlie the tax law.

Hovind's understanding of the difference that frees him from the clutches of the taxation that his fellow-citizens face comprises two parts, one descriptive and one normative. Descriptively, he argues that he is a minister and, as a minister, everything he owns belongs to God. Normatively, he argues that he should not be subject to earthly taxation on money he earns doing God's work.[10]

Because I will deal with these ideas of divine ownership and divine employ later in the book, it is enough here to say that even if his economic situation, as a minister and a Christian, differs from the economic situations of nonministers and the nonreligious, the differences are immaterial in determining his tax liability. That said, in his attempt to justify his nonpayment of taxes, he has highlighted – albeit inadvertently – an important and underappreciated fact: in a number of ways, the tax law does treat religious individuals differently from those who do not practice a religion.

Under US law, religion is special. It functions within a special constitutional sphere, and scholarship on the intersection between religion and law in the United States tends to focus on that sphere. Scholars want to know if a law improperly burdens religious practice, in violation of the Free Exercise Clause of the First Amendment, or if it inappropriately favors religion, in violation of that same amendment's Establishment Clause. Scholars debate where these lines *should* fall, and courts often must resolve conflicts when religious practice collides with the state in real life.

Sometimes, the application of the Religion Clauses' goals intersect, and sometimes, upon intersecting, the goals prove incompatible. Sometimes when they intersect, an individual's right to exercise her religion will trump the Establishment Clause and requires the government to accommodate religious practices that would otherwise violate a generally applicable law. And sometimes, the Establishment Clause prevents the government from accommodating a religious practice. Courts and scholars have worked to sketch out these constitutional boundaries of accommodation, mapping both where it is required and where it is prohibited.

Even the roughly sketched contours of accommodation prove unnecessary and unhelpful in the tax context, though. In recent years, scholars and judges have pushed back against tax exceptionalism (that is, the idea that the tax law is *sui generis* and should be treated differently from other areas of law).[11] In its intersection with religion, though, tax law *is* exceptional. The government's interest in raising revenue is so compelling, courts have held, that the government is not obliged to accommodate *any* religious practice that is inconsistent with the tax law. At the same time, for reasons unique to the tax law, it is effectively impossible to challenge tax accommodations granted by Congress or the IRS.

And, surprising as it may sound, religion and the tax law do intersect in ways that implicate accommodation. At times, a person's religious practice may cause her to earn, hold, or spend money differently from other Americans, and in a way not anticipated by the tax law. The space between her religious practice and others' anticipated financial practices will sometimes prove advantageous for the religious believer, and sometimes disadvantageous. In some cases, the tax results seem appropriate. In other cases, they may offend our sense of justice.

Because the Religion Clauses are unlikely to come into play in deciding what (if anything) to do to accommodate religious practice in the tax law, tax policymaking demands an extra-constitutional analysis. The question shifts from whether the government can (or must) accommodate religion to whether the government *should* accommodate religion. And to answer that question, we must have some sort of rubric that helps us evaluate tax accommodation in a systemic way.

Currently, no such rubric exists. In this book, I intend to build an analytic framework for thinking about existing and proposed tax accommodation. I will focus almost exclusively on religious individuals rather than religious institutions. Because of this focus on religious individuals, I will not cover several (important) issues of tax and religion. For example, I will largely ignore the constitutional issues attendant to exempting churches and other religious entities from taxation. The tax treatment of churches is, of course, an important topic, and one that has been broadly addressed by scholars in other places. But the manner in which the corporate income tax applies to churches is a different question, substantively and analytically, than the question of how the personal income tax treats religious individuals.

While I will address questions of constitutionality, I will spend very little time on the constitutionality of tax law provisions that treat (or fail to treat) religious individuals differently from nonreligious individuals. Those questions are also important, of course, but the Supreme Court has recognized that the government has relatively broad (albeit not unlimited) discretion to accommodate religion.[12] Beyond the government's broad discretion, moreover, is a practical consideration: even if the government crosses that constitutional line in enacting or administering the tax law, it can be difficult, if not impossible, to establish standing to challenge the accommodation.

Of course, if I only declined to address topics, this book would be remarkably short. So what *will* it do? The book will begin by laying out, in broad strokes, how the Constitution constrains lawmaking in relation to religion, as well as the place of accommodation within that constitutional regime. It will also briefly lay out the history and process of making the modern federal income tax, and will discuss the idiosyncrasies of accommodation and the tax law.

After laying this groundwork, I will tell stories of religious taxpayers. Some of these religious taxpayers (including Hovind) have tried to use their religious status to take advantage of the tax law. Others have faced additional tax burdens as a result of their religious practices. Some stories will recount how Congress, the IRS, or the courts have decided to accommodate religious practice. Others will illustrate what happens when those institutions have decided against accommodation.

By telling the stories of the tax law's religious accommodations, I hope to get past Americans' aversion to talking about taxes. Taxes are interesting and, when they and their consequences can be laid out simply and clearly, they are even exciting. Remember Warren Buffett's famous assertion the preferential tax rate on capital gains allowed him to pay a lower tax rate than anybody else in his office, in spite of earning significantly more money than they earned?[13] With that simple story, he crystalized a tax problem in a way that Americans could easily understand. Before Buffett's example, many Americans believed that the tax law benefited the rich. But after, they had a face and a story that told them exactly *how* the rich benefited.

Tax stories risk oversimplifying, of course: in Buffett's case, while it is true that many provisions benefit the rich, others benefit the middle class and the poor. Still, taken as a whole, Congress has been captured by the wealthy, which has allowed the wealthy to have inordinate influence over the contours of the tax law. Because Buffett reduced what could have been a complicated and offputting tax policy discussion (horizontal equity! vertical equity! progressivity! fairness!) down to a relatable and comprehensible narrative, he provided a framework that reformers can use to inveigh against specific provisions of the tax law that provide an outsize benefit to the rich. For example, this framework has allowed a robust conversation about the way that private equity and hedge fund managers get paid. Though the general public may not understand the details underlying *carried interest*, it can understand that hedge fund managers, who can earn hundreds of millions of dollars annually, are able to structure their compensation so that some large percentage of what they earn is taxed at the lower long-term capital gains rates rather than the higher rates potentially applicable to ordinary income.

While the stories alone may be the reason readers pick the book up, I hope they come away with more than just cocktail party anecdotes about religious tax accommodation. By setting these various stories next to each other, I intend to illustrate just how random and unprincipled the development of tax accommodation has been. The tax treatment of ministers has no relation to the tax treatment of Muslim homeowners, which in turn has nothing to do with the tax treatment of individuals who live in religious communes. Yet in each case, religious belief and practice underlie some economic decisions these individuals make, economic decisions that ultimately have tax consequences.

Tax policymakers, then, need a policy framework for thinking about religious tax accommodation. As I tell the stories of accommodation that exist, and as I illustrate how each of these tax accommodations developed entirely separately from every other accommodation, I will also develop such a framework for thinking about religious tax accommodation in a systemic way. Such a framework is hard – though not impossible – to imagine. In general, I assume that horizontal equity considerations – that similarly situated taxpayers should pay similar taxes – apply, even between the religious and the unreligious. That is, for the most part, different tax treatment of the religious and the unreligious should reflect underlying economic differences between them. Generally, matters of belief and conscience do not create economic difference.

Where tax policymakers have a coherent, consistent framework from which to create or deny tax accommodations for religious taxpayers, they can ensure consistency in the treatment of religious taxpayers. Questions of accommodation, when they arise, will fit together in a coherent, reasoned way. And the tax law will be fairer to both religious and nonreligious taxpayers.

AUTHOR'S NOTE, POST-TAX REFORM

One challenge to writing a book on the tax law is that the tax law frequently changes. In the course of writing this book, I had to remember on several occasions to update sections when, for example, a new judicial opinion was issued. The changes tended to be minor, though, and nothing that I could not integrate into the book.

And then, on December 22, 2017, as this book was in the very final editing stages and I could no longer make substantive changes to it, President Donald Trump signed H.R. 1, the most far-ranging set of amendments to the Internal Revenue Code in three decades. Fortunately for my project, Congress did not amend any of the provisions that deal specifically with taxation of religious individuals. It did, however, amend some provisions that I mentioned. For example, in the conclusion to chapter 10, I explain corporations begin paying taxes at a 35 percent rate on income in excess of $75,000, while in 2017, individuals did not hit 34 percent (the closest analogue) until they earned $417,000. That remains true, but, as of 2018, corporations will never hit a 35 percent marginal rate. Instead, corporations will pay taxes on their income at a 21 percent rate.

I mention the new rate structure parenthetically at the end of chapter 10, and I have, I believe, caught all the other peripheral changes except one: in a number of places, I illustrate tax consequences using a 25 percent marginal rate. As of 2018, the 25 percent rate has gone away, replaced by a 22 percent rate, which is followed by a 24 percent and then a 32 percent rate. Had tax reform occurred earlier in the editing stages, I would have redone the illustrations using the 22 percent rate. The math was purely illustrative, though, and because the editing is substantively done and the examples still illustrate the point, I will pretend, for purposes of my examples, that the 25 percent tax bracket still exists, and hope that you will suspend your disbelief for those same purposes.

1

Religion and the State

Few areas of American life evoke such strong feelings as religion. Approximately 75 percent of Americans identify with a particular religion, but these 75 percent are split between various Christian, Jewish, Muslim, and other denominations. Moreover, the remaining 25 percent claim no particular religious affiliation. The different religious beliefs and practices embraced by different Americans can lead to conflict.

In the modern United States, that conflict generally does not include physical violence.[1] But it does include different views of the world, including views of the government. And, while differing beliefs and practices can introduce conflict into everyday life, these interpersonal conflicts largely pale in comparison with the conflicts engendered when religion intersects with the law. Sometimes, a religious group claims that the law must conform to its beliefs. Other times, the religious group has no interest in influencing generally applicable law, but want to be excused from obeying laws that conflict with its beliefs.

These legal conflicts appear largely intractable. While the US Constitution protects individuals' rights to practice their religion, it also limits the government's ability to discriminate in favor of or against religion. The conflict between the First Amendment's Free Exercise and Establishment clauses has launched legal, academic, and popular debate, but their contours remain hazy and indeterminate.

Providing an in-depth analysis of the Free Exercise and the Establishment clauses of the Constitution is beyond the scope of this book for a couple of significant reasons. First, the output of writing on this topic is voluminous. Scholars and judges have written articles, books, and opinions detailing the Religion Clauses both at a macro and a micro level. In a single chapter, I could not hope to respond to everything that has been written, much less do justice to the various arguments.

More importantly, though, a detailed account of the Religion Clauses is unnecessary to the work I hope to do in this book. For reasons I will discuss in the next chapter, the scope of the Religion Clauses is mostly irrelevant when it comes to the intersection of tax and religion. As a practical matter, the Religion Clauses do little to demand nor restrain when it comes to the federal income tax.

That said, the US federal income tax system is part of the constitutional government, and, even where the direct effects of the Religion Clauses on the tax law are tenuous, the tax law exists within the context of the Constitution. As a result, this chapter will provide a brief overview of the Religion Clauses, looking at both when they were drafted and how they have been interpreted and applied over the more than two centuries they have existed.

CONTENT OF THE RELIGION CLAUSES[2]

The first sixteen words of the First Amendment of the Constitution make up the Religion Clauses. They read that: "Congress shall make no law respecting an establishment of religion, or prohibiting the free exercise thereof." These two clauses, read together, are meant to "prevent, as far as possible, the intrusion of either [church or state] into the precincts of the other."[3]

The Religion Clauses achieve their goal by limiting the ability of the state to help or to impede religion. The Supreme Court has explained that the Free Exercise Clause is meant to prevent the government from enacting laws that "suppress religious belief or practice."[4] And the Establishment Clause is popularly analogized to a wall separating church and state. While that metaphor does not fully capture the contours of Establishment Clause jurisprudence, it does serve as a reminder that, as the Supreme Court has explained, the Establishment Clause "forbids an established church or anything approaching it."[5]

The simplicity of the Supreme Court's description of the Religion Clauses belies their complexity and ambiguity, both in historical development and contemporary application. It serves, however, as a reasonable starting point for understanding how they operate in US law.

Even at this level of abstraction, the Religion Clauses will, in some circumstances, come into conflict with each other. Neither Clause is amenable to an absolutist reading. In evaluating religious claims, courts must both balance the religious beliefs of individual believers against the goals of the state and balance the mandate of the Establishment Clause against that of the Free Exercise Clause.[6] And that balancing adds to the complexity and uncertainty of dealing with religious practice in a pluralistic society.

ORIGINS OF THE RELIGION CLAUSES

Although the Religion Clauses are the first provisions of the First Amendment of the Bill of Rights, there is no reason to believe that protecting religion was at the forefront of the Founders' minds in drafting the Bill of Rights. In fact, Charles Pickney, a delegate from South Carolina, proposed that the Constitution include a clause preventing the legislature from passing any "law on the subject of religion." The Constitutional Convention never acted on his proposal, likely because they found it unnecessary. Because the Constitution limited the federal government to enumerated powers, the government lacked authority over religion, even without an explicit limiting provision.

Moreover, the Constitution itself addressed religious liberty. In addition to his proposal that the legislature be prohibited from passing any law on religion, Pickney proposed to ban religious test oaths for federal offices. In this, too, he broke with a number of states that required public officials to swear particular religious oaths before they could take office. The delegates at the Constitutional Convention approved this ban on religious test oaths with little debate (although the provision provoked debate in a number of the ratifying conventions).

With the test oath ban in place, Federalists argued that the lack of a bill of rights in no way jeopardized religious liberty. They argued that the federal government lacked any right to interfere with religion and, moreover, that the variety of sects and denominations that existed throughout the country was itself sufficient to protect religious liberty. Antifederalists, who opposed the strong central government anticipated by the Constitution, did not entirely disagree. While they believed that religious test oaths were inimical to the society they wanted to establish, they also believed that banning them was an important aspect of religious liberty.[7]

In spite of the ultimate agreement on religious test oaths, Antifederalists still wanted the Constitution to include an explicit bill of rights. Even though Federalists argued that the Constitution prevented the federal gxovernment from becoming involved in religion, many of their contemporaries disagreed. Antifederalists used the lack of specific guarantees, including the lack of a guarantee of religious liberty, to attack the Constitution. Others truly believed that the country needed formal protection for religious liberty, if not for the present, then at least for a potentially more contentious future. Ultimately, it is not clear how strongly Antifederalists believed in the need for providing constitutional protection for religious liberty. While they argued that the country needed to protect religious liberty, trial by jury, and freedom of the press, the protection of religious liberty was the least important in their minds. Still, their promotion of explicit protections for religious liberty ultimately put questions of religious liberty in the forefront of constitutional debate.[8]

In the end, religious liberty made its way into the nascent Bill of Rights. How? At least in part, thanks to James Madison, a Federalist who had argued against the need for a bill of rights during debates on the ratification of the Constitution. Virginia Baptists had recently faced religious persecution, and feared the ability of the federal government to limit their ability to preach or to tax them for the support of other religions. To secure his election to Congress, Madison had to assure them that their religious rights would be protected.

With the Baptists' support, Madison won his seat. Once elected, he made good on his promises, though it took time and effort. After Madison proposed amendments dealing with religion, he had to prod members of the committee reviewing the Bill of Rights to deal with them.[9]

It was not immediately obvious what form the protection would take. While Congress could look to various states for a model of protecting religious liberty, in many cases the actual protection provided by states' constitutions was limited. Sometimes the guarantees of religious liberty applied only to certain types of religions. Sometimes they only applied to a single religion. Notwithstanding their constitutional guarantees of religious freedom, most states allowed for the support of (some, at any rate) clergy with tax receipts. In short, to the extent Antifederalists wanted the Bill of Rights to limit the federal government's authority, they had few models for the Religion Clauses.[10] Ultimately, after several iterations of language and concept, Congress included our current Free Exercise and Establishment Clauses into the Bill of Rights.

CONFLICT BETWEEN CHURCH AND STATE

For the first half-century of the Constitution, it looked like the Federalists were right about the Religion Clauses' being superfluous and unnecessary. The Supreme Court did not deal with a free exercise question under the federal Constitution until 1845, when it had to adjudicate whether a municipal law prohibiting open-casket funerals violated the Free Exercise Clause.[11] Even then, the Court managed to avoid on the substantive question of free exercise, holding instead that, because Louisiana had been admitted as a state, the protections of the federal Bill of Rights did not apply to its state or local laws.[12]

It took almost twice as long before the Supreme Court addressed the Establishment Clause. And between 1899, when it first adjudicated an Establishment Clause question, and 1960, it had only addressed questions of Establishment eight times.[13]

Questions of Free Exercise

In the late nineteenth century, the Supreme Court decided the Mormon Cases, a series of decisions evaluating the permissibility of federal laws that criminalized polygamy. In the first of the Mormon Cases, the Court upheld the conviction of George Reynolds for bigamy. While bigamy laws are generally uncontroversial, Reynold's case, the Court recognized that his polygyny was based on sincere religious belief. Thus, the Court had to determine whether "those who make polygamy a part of their religion are excepted from the operation of the statute."[14] In today's language, the Court asked whether the government had to accommodate the Mormons' religious practice. If the Free Exercise Clause mandated that accommodation, the Court said, "then those who do not make polygamy a part of their religious belief may be found guilty and punished, while those who do, must be acquitted and go free."[15]

The Court determined that the Free Exercise Clause did not protect religious practice that violated laws of general applicability. While it shielded religious *belief*, allowing religious individuals to act on those beliefs where the beliefs fundamentally violated societal norms would be to put religious doctrine ahead of the law, to allow every citizen to become her own sovereign, and, ultimately, would destroy effective government.[16]

In subsequent decisions, the Supreme Court doubled down on its determination that free exercise of religion was, at least in certain cases, subservient to the government's interest in proscribing certain behaviors. In *Davis v. Beason*, decided a decade later, the Court moved beyond the belief–practice dichotomy. An Idaho law disenfranchised not only polygamists, and not only people who encouraged polygamy, but people who were members of organizations that taught or encouraged polygamy.[17] Davis was convicted of falsely stating under oath that he did not belong to such an organization. He challenged the constitutionality of the Idaho law, but the Supreme Court upheld his conviction, holding that the Free Exercise Clause was necessarily subordinate to US criminal law.[18]

Subsequent to the Mormon Cases, the Supreme Court developed a fairly well-established and relatively uncontroversial jurisprudence. Essentially, between the early twentieth century and 1993, the Court applied a balancing test when Free Exercise Clause questions arose, weighing the interests of a religious individual in engaging in particular behavior against the government's interest in limiting that behavior. The government could infringe on religious practice, but only where it had a compelling interest that underlay the infringement. Without such a compelling interest, the government had to accommodate religious practice. In other words, unless the government prevailed in a Free Exercise case, it had to carve out an exception to its generally applicable law.[19]

The law described in the Mormon Cases – that the state did not have to accommodate religious practice – remained stable for about half a century. Starting in the 1940s, though, that stability began to deteriorate incrementally, as members of the Jehovah's Witnesses won a series of Free Exercise cases. Two of the cases dealt with religiously mandated proselytizing; in New Haven, Connecticut, a Jehovah's Witness was convicted of breaching the peace and violating state solicitation law. In Pennsylvania, a group of Jehovah's Witnesses were convicted of violating ordinances that regulated door-to-door solicitation (which, incidentally, had been passed specifically in response to the proselytizing). In both cases, the Supreme Court held that the laws – which were laws of generally applicability – were unconstitutional violations of the Jehovah's Witnesses' Free Exercise rights.

A third case dealt with Jehovah's Witnesses refusing to salute the flag in public schools. Children who refused risked expulsion and their parents risked jail. In 1940, when it first looked at this question, the Court predictably followed the precedent that dated back to the Mormon Cases, and held that the government's interest in inculcating national security through a national symbol trumped the Jehovah's Witnesses' claim to free exercise. Three years later, the Court reversed itself. Technically, the reversal was founded on free speech, rather than free exercise, grounds, and thus did not overrule the previous case. Effectively, though, it did. Over the next half century, the Supreme Court ruled in a number of cases that the government had to accommodate religious practice.[20] As this period of Free Exercise jurisprudence matured, the jurisprudential test solidified: the state must show a "compelling state interest" to justify an imposition on citizens' free exercise of religion. Otherwise, the state had to accommodate the religious practice.[21]

Like the first period of Free Exercise jurisprudence, the compelling state interest test lasted about half a century. Suddenly, in the last decade of the twentieth century, that well-established jurisprudence "swirled into a remarkably confused mess."[22] In 1989, the Supreme Court heard the case of two men who had been denied unemployment benefits after being fired from their jobs for using sacramental peyote. Peyote use was a criminal offense, which, under Oregon law, would have justified the state's refusal to pay unemployment benefits. The men argued that, notwithstanding general Oregon law, for them, peyote use was sacramental, a central part of their religious practice. The state, they argued, needed to accommodate their religious beliefs in determining whether to pay unemployment benefits.

Although previous cases held that the government could not withhold unemployment benefits from individuals who had been fired for religious reasons, in 1990, the Supreme Court ruled against the men. In doing so, it held that neutral laws of general applicability were not subject to the compelling interest standard; rather, the Court held that the government did not have to accommodate religious practice provided the law was not aimed at a particular religion, or at religion in general.[23]

In response to public outcry against the Supreme Court's *Smith* decision, in 1993 Congress passed the Religious Freedom Restoration Act (RFRA) in an attempt to reinstate the pre-1990 Free Exercise standard. Under RFRA, even a neutral law of generally applicability must provide accommodations for religious practice unless the government has a compelling interest for enacting the law.[24]

The Supreme Court ruled, though, that Congress had overstepped its authority with RFRA. While it left the legislation in place as applied to the federal government, the Court held in *City of Boerne* v. *Flores* that RFRA was unconstitutional as applied to state and local governments. Congress then passed the Religious Land Use and Institutionalized Persons Act (RLUIPA). RLUIPA's scope was narrower, focusing on the religious rights of people in state-run prisons, hospitals, and other similar institutions, as well as property owners facing zoning and landmark laws. In 2005, the Court upheld the law as applied to institutionalized persons.[25]

Although RFRA did not apply to states, and RLUIPA applied only narrowly, some states wanted to provide additional protection to their citizens' religious practice. As of the end of 2016, twenty-one states had enacted so-called mini-RFRAs. These mini-RFRAs largely follow the federal law, though some differ in small ways.[26] Ultimately, then, the state of accommodation depends on both where an individual attempts to practice her religion and whether state or federal law burdens her religious practice.

Questions of Establishment

The purpose behind the Establishment Clause is relatively uncontroversial. The Antifederalists could look to the previous two centuries of religious history in Europe, where various European states adopted state religions, and some states persecuted members of unestablished sects. And the pattern of established churches replicated itself in colonial America, as various colonies embraced different (Christian) churches.[27]

Taxes may have been as salient and important as religious persecution in adopting the Establishment Clause. At least some of the early states not only had established religions, but they supported the established church with tax revenue. Such public support meant, for example, that an Episcopalian in New Hampshire would nonetheless provide financial support for New

Hampshire's established Congregational church. Notably, James Madison, who helped write the Constitution, successfully defeated a Virginia proposal that would have provided financial support for the Episcopal and Presbyterian churches in Virginia.[28]

Why would Americans have been uncomfortable with state support of religion? Certainly part of the problem was with the state's supporting *somebody else's* religion; a Congregationalist in New Hampshire, or an Episcopalian or Presbyterian in Virginia, would have objected less to such state support than, say, a Baptist in either state.

The objection did not arise solely from religious minorities, though. During the founding generation, Baptists and Deists propounded another philosophical and religious objection to establishment: that a union of religion and government ultimately degrades both. To protect religion, proponents of the corruption thesis believed, it was necessary to keep government out of religion and religion out of government.[29]

The Establishment Clause emerged out of this history and milieu. But given the lack of specificity in its drafting and the lack of recorded debate over its meaning, its exact contours have been uncertain since the beginning. Was it meant merely to prevent the support of an established church with public funds? Was it meant to prevent government from benefiting religion in any way? Was it meant to keep religion and government in entirely separate spheres?

Answering these and other basic questions about the Establishment Clause has fallen by and large to the courts. For the first century and a half of its existence, the Supreme Court barely engaged with the Establishment Clause. In 1947, though, the Court established the foundational principles that would guide Establishment Clause jurisprudence for the next fifty years. The Court found that, while the Establishment Clause required a strict separation between church and state, that it proscribed the support of all religions or favoritism toward one, and that it prohibited the use of tax dollars to support religion.

During that half century, the Supreme Court decided fifty-two Establishment Clause cases. More than half dealt with education, and the Court's decisions split, depending on what type of educational institution was at issue. The Court uniformly upheld government aid to religious institutions of higher learning. By contrast, while it permitted programs that helped ease the financial burdens of parents sending their children to religious grade schools (barely), it generally struck down government aid provided directly to religious primary and secondary schools.[30]

The Court standardized its approach to questions of religious establishment with the famous *Lemon* test. In articulating the *Lemon* test, the Court acknowledged that the complete separation of government and religion is impossible. Nonetheless, the Court explained, the Establishment Clause was meant to prevent three evils: the government's sponsorship, its financial support, and its literal involvement in religious activity. To defend against these evils, laws that benefit religion must meet three criteria: (1) they must have a secular purpose, (2) their principal effect must neither advance nor inhibit religion, and (3) they must not excessively entangle the government with religion.[31]

In many cases, the *Lemon* test has successfully demarcated the bounds of permissible government intervention into religion. On the margins, though, lines are much harder to discern. Even Supreme Court Justices have acknowledged that the line dividing permissible and impermissible government aid to religious schools was almost illusory, and that they could "only dimly perceive the lines of demarcation in this extraordinarily sensitive area of constitutional law."[32] Perhaps that lack of clarity at the edges is what led Professor Fredrick Gedicks to characterize Establishment Clause jurisprudence as "famously chaotic," and most scholars seem to agree with his assessment. That is, while the Supreme Court has developed the *Lemon* test (and a number of other tests) in looking at Establishment Clause cases, it has also proven willing to ignore those tests to come to the conclusion it wants. That is not to say there has been *no* consistency in the Supreme Court's Establishment Clause doctrine, but it is to say that such consistency appears to be the exception rather than the rule.[33]

In spite of more than seventy years of Establishment Clause jurisprudence, new questions constantly pop up, without clear answers. For example, in the beginning of 2017, President Donald Trump issued an executive order halting immigration from seven predominantly Muslim countries, then issued a new executive order reducing the number of banned countries by one. The executive order fulfilled his campaign promise to enact a Muslim ban, and opponents of the executive order latched on to those promises as evidence that the order targeted individuals on the basis of their religion. If true, several courts held, such religion-based targeting may violate the Establishment Clause.[34]

THE DISPUTED POSITION OF RELIGION

The question of religion and the law extends beyond even the disputed contours of the Religion Clauses. In recent years, scholars have begun to question whether religion should, as a normative matter, receive special treatment under the law. Professor Brian Leiter, for example, has argued that singling out religion *qua* religion for special treatment "is tantamount to thinking we ought to encourage precisely [religion's] conjunction of categorical fervor and its basis in epistemic indifference." In the end, he does not argue that religion should not be tolerated; rather, he argues that any special treatment accorded religion should be because it involves "matters of *conscience*, not matters of religion."[35]

Professor Leiter is not alone in his skepticism that religion as a category deserves special treatment. Professors Christopher Eisgruber and Lawrence Sager similarly argue that religious practice should not receive special constitutional solicitude. It is not, in their view, wrong to protect religious belief. After all, the colonies that eventually became the United States served as a refuge for persecuted religious minorities, and protection from persecution is a legitimate goal of government. The problem, in their view, is not in religious liberty; rather, it is in *privileging* religion, to the point where religious individuals do not have to follow the same playbook as others. While they are comfortable granting protection from persecution, they are uncomfortable with the idea of accommodation, because when the government accommodates religious practices, it allows religion to flourish in a way unavailable to other human pursuits. In their view, religious should naturally have the ability to flourish, but only if it does so on the same terms as other institutions.[36]

The general objection to special legal regard for religion, then, seems to comprise two main parts. First, critics argue that there is no substantive difference between religion and other moral frameworks, which can, perhaps, be represented under the umbrella of "conscience." Second, by giving special protections to religion, either religion is overly privileged or other issues of conscience are underprotected. Neither, according to these critics of the current constitutional treatment of religion, is supportable, and neither is right in a pluralistic society. By privileging religion, the government distorts citizens' decision of whether to practice religion or not, because their religious behaviors will receive more consideration and support than their nonreligious actions. Not only is this distortion inefficient, but it undercuts the government's duty (also constitutionally mandated) to refrain from favoring one religion over another, and to refrain from favoring religion over nonreligion.

It is important to understand that criticizing the current approach to legal accommodations is not inherently an anti-religious endeavor. While some of the critics may, in fact, be unsympathetic toward religion, others view accommodation as actually harmful to religion. Professor William Marshall, for instance, asserts that accommodation damages the integrity of religion. And how does it damage religion's integrity? For one thing, Professor Marshall says, it creates an incentive for individuals to frame their actions as religiously motivated, because religiously motivated actions get special consideration and accommodation. But as specious claims of religiosity pile up, it becomes more difficult to credit believers' sincere religious beliefs. In addition, he argues, claiming that religious belief needs special protection demeans religion itself. If a religion or set of religious beliefs cannot stand on its own, propping it up through accommodation conflicts with the meritocratic assumptions of contemporary American society.[37]

One response to the critics is that, even if they are right as a normative matter, the Constitution is what it is. While the sometimes-inconsistent mandates of the Free Exercise and the Establishment Clauses can conflict with one another, the Free Exercise Clause does require special solicitude to religious practice. Moreover, that special solicitude constitutionally accorded to religion exceeds the solicitude owed other forms of conscience.

But the special treatment religion receives is on sandy intellectual ground if the sole basis for its privileged treatment is that the Constitution currently privileges it. Not only is such argumentation circular, but it is unconvincing. While the long history of treating religion differently, and that this special treatment continues today, suggest that we should approach change cautiously, they do not suggest either that the current legal treatment of religion is correct or that the current treatment should stay the same.

The arguments in favor of the special treatment of religion are not limited, however, to describing the law as it currently stands. A number of scholars have argued that not only *is* religion treated differently under the Constitution, but that it *should* receive such different treatment.

For instance, Professor Jane Rutherford argues that religion is not special because of the content of religious views. Rather, it is special for structural reasons: religion plays a special role "in balancing power, providing voices for outsiders, advancing nonmarket values, and fostering individual identity and spirituality."[38]

Professor Michael McConnell also approaches the question of accommodation structurally, though the structure he explores does not focus on the balance of power. Instead, he defends accommodation by looking at the structure of the Religion Clauses themselves. True, they single out religion, but, he argues, they do so in a symmetrical manner. Sometimes the singling out provides benefits to religion, such as when a religious conscientious objector can avoid working at a munitions factory while a nonreligious objector cannot. But sometimes it works to the detriment of religion, such as when a public school teacher wants to lead her class in prayer but cannot. Professor McConnell asserts that the law certainly could choose not to single out religion for special benefits, but to maintain consistency, it would also have to refrain from singling out religion for special detriments.[39] Under Professor McConnell's telling, if the government could not accommodate religious practice, it should also lose the ability to prohibit school prayer and Ten Commandments displays on public land.

But perhaps the strongest (and most recent) normative argument for treating religion differently from nonreligion has been made separately by Professors Andrew Koppelman and Christopher C. Lund. Both acknowledge the arguments against special treatment for religion. Professor Lund notes specifically the argument that religion is not significantly different from other human values, and as such should not receive special treatment that other such values receive. And he ultimately agrees that no clean line divides religion from nonreligion. Still, he argues, religion is different *enough*. Sure, religious freedom encompasses and overlaps with conscience, with speech, and with all kinds of other human endeavors. Other rights do as well: ultimately, the rights we protect serve "a large set of overlapping values in a messy, imprecise kind of way."[40] But the messy and imprecise protections accorded religion are part of a constitutional system that protects *a lot* of imprecise, but important, human activity. And, Professor Lund argues, religion is special enough to be part of that messy and imprecise system.[41]

Professor Koppelman defends the idea of special treatment of religion from a very similar perspective. He explains that religion, in all its messiness and imprecision, is an important marker of identity for many people. And religion, he says, is a "hypergood" – a good that cannot be perfectly substituted, the value of which transcends personal preference. Impeding hypergoods "is a serious injury," and preventing this type of injury justifies special accommodation of religious practice.[42]

Still, religion is not the only cognizable hypergood, and Professor Koppelman acknowledges that no single justification for focusing on religion will prove convincing. Moreover, substituting other values may be able to capture much of the distinctiveness of religion. Still, any substitute (such as focusing on freedom of *conscience*) will ultimately be underinclusive, not capturing all of what makes religion a hypergood.

While that explains why conscience does not substitute for religion, it fails to explain why religion itself deserves special accommodation. He has two responses to that: first, the state cannot directly provide certain benefits that people want, but religion provides a good proxy. Second, religion may be a good proxy for many goods, some of which the government cannot officially endorse. In either event, using a different proxy that the government *can* directly aim for would be underinclusive.[43]

Ultimately, even though he convincingly argues that religion not only is, but that it should, be treated differently, Professor Koppelman acknowledges that such special treatment can result in unfairness. The law can – and should – attempt to minimize that unfairness, but where accommodation allows religiously motivated people to do things that nonreligious individuals cannot, there is inevitable unfairness. But given the complexity of law, not to mention the complexity of lived experience, no one rule "can protect all deeply valuable concerns, [so] more specific rules are necessary." And religious accommodations are necessary examples of these more specific rules.[44]

STRUCTURING ACCOMMODATION

Although some sort of accommodation for religious practice is *fait accompli*, the special legal treatment religion receives does not rest solely on the accident of having been enshrined in the Constitution. There are philosophical and legal policy reasons why the government should accommodate religious practices. In fact, Professors Lupu and Tuttle argue, if the government could not "recognize and respond to the deeply held and widely varying religious commitments of its people … but remained free to respond to other needs of its citizens – say, for recreation or art – it might fairly be accused of unjustifiable hostility to religious experience."[45]

That the government *can* treat religion differently does not mean that it *should*, though, or, at least, does not mean that it should under every circumstance. And, in fact, the courts have developed a way to think about religious accommodation when somebody claims that laws infringe on their Free Exercise rights. Essentially, such requests for special treatment fall into one of three categories: mandatory, permissible, or impermissible accommodations.

The meaning of the first and the third categories are self-evident. Although the Supreme Court's current First Amendment jurisprudence may have eliminated the constitutional category of mandatory accommodation, RFRA mandates that sometimes an individual's interest in engaging in a religious practice is so essential that the government must allow it, even if the practice would otherwise violate an applicable law. At the same time, if the Establishment Clause has any purchase, it must prevent the government from favoring religious practice in some contexts.

The middle category – permissible accommodations – is not as intuitive. Someone who believes that the Free Exercise Clause should be read as narrowly as possible could reasonably argue that any accommodation that is not mandatory must be impermissible. Alternatively, to the extent that an individual believes that the Establishment Clause should be read narrowly, she could argue that any accommodation that is not impermissible must be mandatory.

In 1985, Professor McConnell proposed the third category. This category (my "permissible accommodations") existed "between the categories compelled by the Free Exercise Clause and the benefits to religion prohibited by the Establishment Clause"[46] These permissible accommodations, not proscribed by the Constitution, both intend to and do facilitate religious liberty.

Of course, with or without the third category, a taxonomy of accommodation potentially faces a significant line-drawing problem. The question of where a proposed accommodation shifts from mandatory to permissible, or from permissible to impermissible, necessarily does a lot of work. Government must accommodate religious practice where the Constitution requires that accommodation; as a result, proponents of accommodation will try to categorize their preferred accommodations as mandatory. At the same time, opponents of accommodation will invariably try to present an accommodation as impermissible, preventing the government from providing that accommodation.

And, given the fuzziness of Religion Clauses jurisprudence, that line-drawing problem is significant, and is also in a constant state of flux. In fact, the Supreme Court's 1990 *Smith* decision entirely upset whatever equilibrium at which the question of accommodation had previously arrived. In its *Smith* decision, the Supreme Court "sharply reduc[ed] the scope of the category of mandatory accommodations," and brought "the particular problems associated with permissible accommodations to the fore."[47]

The question of line-drawing faces one additional, and significant, constraint. To the extent that an accommodation is permissible, whether the government grants it is a legislative and political question. There is no legal reason that the government *must* provide permissible accommodations, but, at the same time, there is no legal reason it cannot do so. The legislature ultimately determines whether it should grant the accommodation, and presumably listens to arguments from both proponents and opponents. Without any framework, however, its decision ultimately comes down to whim and political calculation, and risks at least the appearance of corruption.

But determining into which category a proposed accommodation fits is a judicial question. The legislature can, of course, use its reasoned opinion to determine whether it has the constitutional authority to grant an accommodation, but courts ultimately determine whether the legislature was correct.[48]

Even though it has the final word, the judiciary faces a significant impediment in its ability to categorize accommodations: standing. In general, the

Constitution requires that an individual have suffered a concrete injury that she can trace back to the defendant's actions before she can bring a lawsuit. Without a concrete injury, an opponent of a particular accommodation lacks the standing to bring a judicial challenge to it and, if she does challenge it in court, the court must dismiss the suit.[49]

On its face, the standing requirement would make it virtually impossible for an individual to challenge a legislature's decision to accommodate religious practice. Those directly affected by the accommodation receive its benefits, and are unlikely to challenge its constitutionality. By contrast, those who object to accommodation have generally not suffered the kind of particularized harm that meets the constitutional standing requirements. In fact, courts have recognized that the type of injury that would grant standing to potential plaintiffs is "particularly elusive" in the context of the Establishment Clause.[50]

To deal with the elusive nature of Establishment Clause harms, courts have tailored the standing requirement to the harms violations of the Establishment Clause are likely to impose. Those harms tend not to include economic or physical injury. Rather, those opposed to accommodation are motivated by spiritual and other intrinsic values.[51] So in evaluating standing to challenge accommodations of religion and other potential violations of the Establishment Clause, courts focus on those noneconomic, nonphysical harms.

This tailored approach to standing in questions of the Establishment Clause allows the courts to fulfill their role in categorizing questions of accommodation, but, at the same time, imposes costs on those who would challenge it. Ultimately, this means that legislatures are not free to accommodate any religious practice they want, but it does mean, as a practical matter, they can exercise a reasonable amount of discretion at the margins of each category.

RELIGIOUS TAX ACCOMMODATION

Ultimately, this book does not deal with accommodation writ large. Instead, I look at what happens in the space where taxes and religious practice intersect. And questions of tax accommodation raise questions distinct from those questions of accommodation more broadly. Beginning in Chapter 3, I show that Congress has significantly more discretion in accommodating religious practice in the tax law than it does in many other areas of law. Perhaps as a result, Congress appears not to have thought through questions of religious tax accommodation in any kind of systematic way. At the same time, the disconnectedness of the various tax accommodations Congress has provided suggests that it has not thought through them from a tax policy perspective, either.

As a result, the rest of this book looks specifically at the question of what to do when tax and religious practice collide. I analyze these collisions from both a tax and a Religion Clauses perspective, and, ultimately, recommend a framework for analyzing questions of religious accommodation in the tax law.

2

On Making the Tax Law

I'm just a bill
Yes, I'm only a bill
And if they vote for me on Capitol Hill
Well, then I'm off to the White House
Where I'll wait in a line
With a lot of other bills
For the president to sign
And if he signs me, then I'll be a law.
How I hope and pray that he will,
But today I am still just a bill.[1]

Before we can address the question of how the tax law should interact with religious practice, we need to figure out how federal tax law is created in the first place. At least one generation grew up understanding the legislative process through the prism of *Schoolhouse Rock*. In theory, of course, *Schoolhouse Rock* laid out the way the legislative process should work: Congress drafts and passes a bill, which then lands on the president's desk for his or her signature. Once signed, the law is what it is.

In practice, though, the process is more complicated than the cartoon version. All three branches of the federal government have input into the shape of the federal tax law. And, in fact, all three can actually *create* tax law, albeit by different means. Each branch of government has a history with the federal tax law, and each has a contemporary role derived, at least in part, from that history. As a result, before digging in to look at the intersection of religious practice and the tax law, we must first look at how the branches of government make the tax law.

THE DEVELOPMENT OF THE TAX LAW

Congress

In its early years, the United States was skeptical of taxation. In spite of a clear need for money, the Continental Congress refused to enact any kind of national system to raise revenue. And even after emerging victorious as its own nation, the Articles of Confederation prevented the federal government from effectively collecting revenue. The federal government was, instead, dependent on the states, which themselves were unable to collect sufficient revenue from their citizens. As a result, the federal government found itself starved for money, receiving just $663 from the states between October 1786 and March 1787.

Without revenue, the federal government could not even maintain a military force to protect its borders and strengthen its diplomatic position. When political leaders met in Philadelphia in 1787 to create a new constitution for the fledgling country, they provided the federal government with a robust – if circumscribed – ability to lay and collect taxes. Although the Federalists promised that the federal government would rely primarily upon tariffs, the new Constitution also permitted the federal government to levy internal taxes, provided that any direct taxes were apportioned by state.[2]

For the first half of the nineteenth century, even with a more robust ability to impose and collect taxes, the federal government primarily funded itself through tariffs on imported goods. Occasionally, it would supplement its tariffs with internal excise taxes, but the internal taxes generally went away once the government had met its financial obligations.[3]

Tariffs proved unequal to the task of funding the Civil War though, and in 1862 President Abraham Lincoln signed a mildly progressive federal income tax into law. The Civil War-era income tax exempted a taxpayer's first $600. Taxpayers would pay taxes of 3 percent of their income between $600 and $10,000, and 5 percent on income in excess of $10,000.[4]

This income tax proved wildly successful – over the ten years it existed, it raised $376 million, or about one-fifth of the country's total internal revenue.[5] Despite – or perhaps because of – its success, however, the income tax faced significant opposition. Though Republicans had united in favor of the tax during wartime, after the war ended, the Republicans split, with members of Congress who represented the South and the Midwest supporting it, and those who represented the Northeast and West opposing it.

The members of Congress who opposed the income tax were not alone. Many groups throughout the country lobbied for its repeal. Virtually every newspaper in the United States also argued for the repeal of the income tax, and their anti-income tax views reflected the views of many of their readers. Still, the opponents of the income tax were unable to marshal enough support for its repeal, and it lived on until 1872, when Congress simply failed to renew it, allowing it to lapse under its own terms.[6]

At that point, income taxation in the United States lay dormant until the 1890s, when Congress drafted a new tariff bill. As part of the tariff bill, Congress introduced a small income tax, one that would affect perhaps 80,000 taxpayers. The income tax portion of the bill proved controversial, and in 1894 the Wilson-Gorman Tariff Act became law without President Grover Cleveland's signature.

Without a concurrent war or other fiscal emergency, though, the new tax law faced immediate opposition. Opponents laid plans to challenge the constitutionality of the income tax portions of the new law, and, within months of its enactment, the Supreme Court heard these challenges in *Pollock* v. *Farmers' Loan & Trust Co.* And less than a year after its enactment, the Supreme Court had found that those parts of the law that taxed income from property were direct taxes.[7] Under the Constitution, direct taxes had to be apportioned among the states in accordance with each state's population.[8]

If the definition of *direct tax* included taxes on income, income taxes would be impracticable. A state with 5 percent of the population, for example, would be required to provide 5 percent of the total revenue from the income tax to the government. If residents of that state were poorer than average, each would pay a higher proportion of their income in taxes, while if residents were richer than average, each would pay a lower proportion.[9] Such an income tax would be manifestly unfair, and maintaining it would be politically impossible. Even though the Court only decided that those provisions of the law that taxed income from real and personal property were direct taxes, the Court decided that these parts of the income tax were so central to the overall law that the whole law had to be struck down.[10]

The income tax disappeared from federal tax policy for nearly a decade and a half, and instead the federal government relied on its traditional arsenal of tariffs and excise taxes for revenue. These constitutionally permissible indirect taxes fell inordinately on working-class Americans, who broadly saw them as unfair.[11]

Still, it was not until the aftermath of the Panic of 1907 that progressives were able to make substantive moves toward a post-*Pollock* federal income tax. Today there is growing agreement that the Supreme Court's *Pollock* decision was wrong in holding that taxes on income from property are direct taxes.[12] Still, even wrong, the Supreme Court is famously "not final because [it is] infallible, but [it is] infallible only because [it is] final."[13] To avoid the finality of the Supreme Court's determination, then, Congress enacted a corporate income tax in 1909 and, at the same time, passed a resolution recommending that the states adopt an amendment to the Constitution that would expressly permit federal income taxation.[14]

The Sixteenth Amendment was adopted in 1913 and, in that same year, Congress enacted the first modern federal income tax. In the intervening century, the federal income tax's place in funding government has only grown: in 1880, when there was no income tax, excise taxes and tariffs on alcohol and tobacco accounted for nearly 90 percent of federal revenue. By 1930 – seventeen years into the modern income tax – their share of federal revenue had dropped to 25 percent, while the income tax provided about 60 percent of federal revenue.[15] Today, roughly 80 percent of federal revenue comes from the individual income tax and payroll taxes, while another 11 percent comes from the corporate income tax. Only about 9 percent of federal revenue comes from excise, estate, and other taxes.[16] Although Congress tinkers with the tax law constantly, and has fundamentally reformed it a handful of times, today's federal income tax is a direct descendant of the original 1913 iteration.

The vast majority of Senators and Representatives have no particular expertise in tax policy or practice. Ultimately, the majority of Congress is not involved with the actual creation of tax law. Instead, like other legislation, tax law starts in committee. The House Committee on Ways and Means is the first to consider a proposed tax bill, though it does not actually consider or draft the statutory language. Instead, staff presents members of the committee with summary proposals and, sometimes, the projected revenue from or cost of the legislation. After the Committee on Ways and Means decides the framework for the proposed tax legislation, the bill moves to the House Office of Legislative Counsel, which transforms the proposals into actual statutory language. The draft bill is then presented on the floor of the House of Representatives. At this point, Representatives can amend the language, but, after they finish their amendment process, they ultimately vote on the legislation.

Assuming it passes the House, the bill moves to the Senate. The Senate Committee on Finance plays the same role in the Senate's consideration of tax legislation as the Committee on Ways and Means plays in the House's. The Committee on Finance can consider the same or similar legislation as that originating in the House, or (more often) the Committee on Finance reports a different bill, which the Senate considers as a replacement of or amendment to the House bill. As in the House, the Committee on Finance does not draft actual language, instead leaving that to the Senate Office of Legislative Counsel.

Of course, this legislative procedure all but guarantees the bills will differ. In an attempt to smooth the reconciliation process, in 1926, the House of Representatives proposed a Joint Commission on Taxation. In its original conception, the House intended to create a temporary commission that would help the House and the Senate simplify the statutory language governing the tax law and improving the law's administration. The Senate shifted the nascent committee's commission, renaming it the "Joint Committee on Internal Revenue Taxation" and expanding its mandate to include interacting with taxpayers to improve future tax laws, preventing IRS corruption, and gathering data on revenue-raising legislation.[17]

The Joint Committee on Taxation's role has evolved over the years. Today, the Joint Committee is made up of ten members of the Senate and House tax-writing committees, and has a large staff of attorneys, economists, and accountants. The Joint Committee is nonpartisan, and, unlike many other congressional committees, rarely convenes hearings. Rather, it helps mediate the two chambers' creation of the tax law, highlighting common ground between the bills and helping each committee understand the other committee's intent. The Joint Committee also assists both tax-writing committees in conceiving, analyzing, and evaluating tax proposals, as well as providing revenue estimates. (In addition to its policy duties, it continues to monitor large refunds and otherwise oversee the IRS's administration of the tax law.)[18]

When the tax bills passed by the House and the Senate differ, they move to a conference committee, made up of senior members of both the Ways and Means and the Finance committees, who attempt to reconcile the two versions of the bill, which then gets sent again to the House and Senate for a vote.[19] As with any other legislation, once the House and the Senate have passed the same bill, it moves to the president for signature and, as *Schoolhouse Rock* taught us when we were children, once the president signs it, the tax bill becomes law.

The Executive

The president's role in the promulgation of the tax law is not limited to signing congressional bills, however. Rather, the president often participates from the beginning of the process, with a significant portion of ideas for new tax laws coming from the president.[20] Since 1921, the law has required presidents to submit an annual proposed budget. Presidents use their proposed budgets, at least in part, to stake out their tax priorities.[21]

Presidents' success in having their tax proposals enacted varies, of course. President Reagan, for example, insisted that tax reform be simple and fair, and that it lower rates while remaining revenue neutral. Within those broad strokes, though, he allowed the Treasury Department plenty of leeway to design the actual tax proposal. While President Reagan remained relatively divorced from the actual details, his support of tax reform eventually led to the Tax Reform Act of 1986, one of only a handful of fundamental tax reforms in the history of the federal income tax.[22]

Under President Reagan, the 1980s saw continual tax legislation. By the 1990s, though, the pace began to slow. This slowdown reflected, at least in part, President George H.W. Bush's lack of interest and conviction in the tax policy arena. Outside of a general commitment to not raising taxes (a commitment he ultimately violated, in part leading to his single term in office), President Bush had no strong tax policy preferences. And without strong preferences, President Bush exercised little influence over the tax legislation that did emerge during his administration.

President Bill Clinton entered office with a relatively ambitious set of tax proposals. He had promised, during his 1992 campaign, that his highest priorities would include tax reform and dealing with the budget deficit. His proposals initiated a debate over tax policy that lasted the first six months of President Clinton's presidency; once he launched the debate, though, the administration largely turned it over to Congress. Without commitment by the Clinton administration or any significant groundswell of public pressure, the tax legislation ended up being shaped largely by traditional congressional politicking. While President Clinton started the process, he ultimately had limited influence over the legislation that he ultimately signed.[23]

After his election, President George W. Bush gave tax policy a central role in his administration. During his campaign, President Bush promised the electorate significant tax and wide-ranging tax cuts.[24] In his first three years in office he delivered, shepherding through Congress three separate pieces of legislation that collectively cut taxes significantly, albeit temporarily.[25] President Obama similarly proposed significant changes to the tax law in his proposed budgets, albeit with significantly less success than Presidents Bush and Reagan.[26]

Someone must collect the taxes, of course, and when Congress created the Civil War-era income tax, it also created the Bureau of Internal Revenue, an executive agency and the direct predecessor of today's IRS. The Bureau of Internal Revenue outlived the Civil War income tax. While its operations scaled back upon the disappearance of the income tax in 1872, its institutional infrastructure remained intact. The Bureau scaled its operations back up with the reintroduction of the income tax, and especially with its World War I-era expansion. In 1953, in the wake of scandals and reform efforts, the Bureau was renamed the Internal Revenue Service.[27]

One of the IRS's principal roles is to collect taxes.[28] The IRS uses the various enforcement tools the law grants it to ensure that individuals and entities both calculate their taxes correctly and pay the amount that they owe. Where taxpayers fail to pay their taxes due, the IRS enjoys an array of enforcement mechanisms, ranging from interest and penalties to liens to summonses to, in some situations, criminal charges. But even though the IRS's principal role is to enforce the tax law, its responsibilites go beyond merely enforcing the tax law. It plays a significant part in developing tax policy, and it even creates tax law.

On the policy front, for example, the IRS's Office of Chief Counsel works with the Treasury Department's Office of Tax Policy in drafting regulations. While in theory the regulations only implement the laws passed by Congress, in practice, the complexity of the tax law leaves the IRS with significant interpretive room.[29] The IRS also drafts less formal administrative guidance, interpreting the tax law and, at times, creating new tax rules.[30]

Still, the IRS's ability to affirmatively make tax law is circumscribed by the text of the Internal Revenue Code. Ultimately, the rules and regulations it promulgates must derive from the statutory language enacted by Congress. If the IRS tries to go too far afield of the statute, courts can rein it in.

And the courts do rein the IRS in when its rules and regulations go beyond the bounds of the law as drafted. For example, during the Spanish-American War, Congress enacted a telephone excise tax on "toll telephone service." The tax law defined taxable toll telephone service as calls where the "toll charge which varies in amount with the distance and elapsed transmission time of each individual communication."[31]

In 1979, in the face of changing technology, the IRS issued a ruling that the excise tax applied to long-distance calls where the telephone company charged by the elapsed time of the call, even when the charge did not vary by distance. Effectively, it read the *and* of the Internal Revenue Code as an *or*.

By the 1990s, most long-distance service was priced by the minute, without taking into account distance. The IRS continued, based on its 1979 ruling, to impose the excise tax, a decision several corporate taxpayers challenged in the 2000s. A number of appeals courts ultimately heard the challenges, and each one held that the IRS had overstepped the tax law by treating the excise tax as disjunctive rather than conjunctive. The courts all held that the plain language of the excise tax required charges to be imposed based on *both* the length and the distance of the call. Even if current practice had effectively mooted the tax, it was Congress's job, not the IRS's, to fix the law.[32]

But while there are limits to the IRS's ability to make positive law, the IRS has the largely unconstrained ability to reject provisions of the tax law with which it disagrees. The Supreme Court has recognized that executive agencies, including the IRS, enjoy a class of prosecutorial discretion it refers to as "administrative discretion." As a practical matter, administrative discretion means that the IRS can pick and choose what provisions of the tax law it will enforce and, importantly, what provisions it will *not* enforce. And generally, courts will not second guess the IRS's nonenforcement decisions.[33]

Granting the IRS discretion to set its own enforcement priorities is probably a necessary concession. Congress has been reducing the IRS's budget for more than a decade, while, at the same time, increasing its responsibilities.[34] As it has to administer more programs with fewer people and resources, the IRS must necessarily assign a lower priority to some parts of the tax law than others. And the IRS understands its resources and institutional capabilities better than taxpayers, or even courts, do.

That is not to say, though, that the IRS faces no constraints in deciding what portions of the tax law to enforce. Where legislation explicitly requires an administrative agency to enforce some portion of the law, the agency has no administrative discretion. And even without that explicit requirement, the Supreme Court acknowledged that *some* agency nonenforcement could potentially be so egregious that courts could ignore administrative discretion and order the agency to enforce a law. In the three decades since the Supreme Court recognized the viability of administrative discretion, though, no court has found agency inaction sufficiently egregious to warrant such an order.[35]

The Courts

The Constitution gives federal courts the responsibility to adjudicate certain classes of disputes, including, for our purposes, "[c]ontroversies to which the United States shall be a Party."[36] And courts have been resolving income tax controversies between taxpayers and the federal government since the implementation of the Civil War income tax.

A number of early cases dealt with the permissibility and constitutionality of the federal government's taxing power and the scope of the tax law. In an 1864 case, for example, courts resolved the question of whether the tax law reached dividends paid by US corporations to foreigners.[37] And in 1870, the Supreme Court weighed in on the question of whether Congress had the authority to tax state judges on the salaries they received from the state. (At the time, the Supreme Court held that the federal government could not.)[38]

The courts even had to determine the constitutionality of the Civil War income tax. While almost a quarter of a century later the Supreme Court invalidated the 1894 federal income tax, the Civil War era judiciary was more willing to countenance income taxes. In 1871, a federal district court found the Civil War's tax on "the annual gains, profits, or income of every person residing in the United States, or of any citizen of the United States residing abroad" was neither a direct nor a capitation tax and, as a result, its unapportioned enactment was entirely with the constitutional powers of Congress.[39]

More often than the basic constitutionality of the tax law, though, courts must resolve questions that arise where the tax law is unclear, or where its application to a particular individual or set of facts is ambiguous. As early as 1864, a court was called on to determine whether the tax law required the shareholder of a corporation to declare and pay taxes on corporate income, even if that income was not distributed to the shareholder.[40] In yet another controversy in the subsequent year, a savings bank argued to the Supreme Court that it was not a bank in either the popular or legal sense, and was thus not subject to the taxes imposed on banks by the 1864 tax law.[41]

Taxpayers have been able to sue the federal government demanding the refund of allegedly overpaid taxes since the creation of the Court of Claims in 1855. When the government enacted the Tucker Act in 1887, taxpayers could also bring refund suits in federal district courts.[42] Even today, district courts and the Court of Federal Claims (the successor to the Court of Claims) have jurisdiction to hear taxpayer refund suits.

Taxpayers who want to sue for refunds face one significant hurdle, though: for a district court or the Court of Federal Claims to have jurisdiction to hear their complaints, the taxpayer must first pay the challenged tax assessment in full.[43] A taxpayer who lacks the resources to pay the assessed tax cannot get their case in front of these courts.

In 1924, though, Congress provided taxpayers with a workaround, creating the Board of Tax Appeals as an independent agency in the executive branch. Though controversial when initially proposed, the Board of Tax Appeals was created as a judicial body, independent of the Bureau of Internal Revenue, which would provide an alternative venue in which to challenge assessed taxes. Unlike courts, though, taxpayers would not have to pay the full tax to challenge; rather, it allowed them to challenge the *assessment* of tax.[44]

In 1942, the Board of Tax Appeals had its name changed to the "Tax Court of the United States." In spite of the name change, it was still effectively an executive agency until 1969, when it became an Article I court, and its name changed one last time to the "United States Tax Court."[45] Throughout these name and status changes, though, it maintained its position as an alternative to district courts and the Court of Federal Claims, where taxpayers could challenge IRS tax assessments without paying the tax first.

Like the IRS, courts rarely make positive tax law. They have injected a handful of common law doctrines into the federal income tax, though. Perhaps the most important judicial addition to the positive law of income tax was the Supreme Court's decision that unrealized gain fell outside the ambit of constitutionally taxable income.[46] Courts have also introduced several common law anti-abuse doctrines into the tax law.[47]

For the most part, courts' creation of common law tax rules has disappeared as time has progressed. Today, they rarely exercise that power. At the same time, because of the standing requirements, they will rarely (if ever) be called upon to evaluate the permissibility of accommodations provided by Congress or the IRS.

Still, courts have the occasional opportunity to rule on how an accommodation – or lack of accommodation – functions as a practical matter, both when the existing tax law is challenged on religious grounds and when taxpayers attempt to challenge the limited scope of an existing accommodation. As a result, while courts must evaluate cases in light of precedential law, an accommodation framework could help them evaluate what Congress or the IRS meant when they carved out a religious accommodation, but left ambiguity in that accommodation.

CONCLUSION

The next chapter will discuss what happens when a person's religious obligations conflict with the tax law created by Congress or the Executive. Where the previous chapter discussed accommodation broadly, the next looks at the idiosyncrasies of the tax law. Because of the unique importance the government places on raising revenue, questions of tax accommodation differ from more general questions of accommodation.

Most tax accommodation will come from Congress, which can (and does) pass special legislation that treats religious taxpayers differently from nonreligious taxpayers. To be effective, then, any attempt to create a framework to undergird tax accommodations must necessarily be aimed at Congress.

But tax accommodation does not come solely from the pen of Congress. As we have seen, the IRS's ability to create positive tax law must derive from statutory law, and is thus significantly constrained. But its ability to decline to enforce the law is virtually unconstrained. The IRS can use its Supreme

Court sanctioned administrative discretion to carve out accommodations for religious taxpayers. Thus, an accommodation framework must be equally able to speak to the IRS as it establishes its enforcement priorities.

Even courts – which have no affirmative accommodation creating authority – benefit from a robust tax accommodation framework. Where a tax accommodation makes its way to court, whether because of ambiguity or other considerations, understanding what underlay Congress's decisionmaking process can assist the court in determining the content and the scope of the accommodation.

3

Accommodation in the Intersection of Religious Practice and the Tax Law

The first two chapters dealt separately with the law of religion and the federal income tax. Inevitably, however, the two will intersect, and their intersection can raise significant questions. When religious actors are taxed, their religious practice sometimes becomes subject to the intrusive oversight of the IRS. If, however, the legislature chooses to exempt religious actors from taxation, the IRS must police the borders of that exemption. Either way, religion becomes entangled with the state.[1] Not all of these entanglements implicate the Religion Clauses of the First Amendment, of course; a religious taxpayer who claims no religious objection to taxation is subject to intrusive oversight, but it is the same intrusive oversight as nonreligious taxpayers. The oversight has no religious significance. Still, some entanglements between tax and religious belief or practice *do* represent a burden on individuals' religious beliefs or practices. And when the tax law impinges on an individual's religious beliefs or practices, the government must decide how to resolve the conflict.

While the Constitution, federal statutes, and current Supreme Court jurisprudence define the (fuzzy) contours of mandatory, permissible, and impermissible religious accommodations, those categories are ultimately unimportant in designing the tax law. The Constitution never requires Congress to exempt religious actions from generally applicable tax law; because of the importance of funding government, the Supreme Court has held that "religious belief in conflict with the payment of taxes affords no basis for resisting the tax." While the government *can* accommodate religious belief and practice in designing the tax law, it is under no constitutional mandate to do so.[2]

At the same time, there are no constitutionally impermissible accommodations in the tax law, either. Or, rather, while some accommodations may violate the Establishment Clause, as a practical matter, those accommodations are shielded from judicial review. Federal courts cannot review the constitutionality of laws on their own; they can only adjudicate *cases* and *controversies*.[3] To get a case or controversy in front of a court, a potential litigant must have standing, meaning she suffered an "injury in fact."[4] And, it turns out, seeing somebody else receive an unconstitutional benefit from the government does not constitute a cognizable injury for standing purposes.

There are two exceptions to the injury-in-fact requirement: declaratory judgments and Establishment Clause standing. Neither, though, is available to challenge religious accommodations in the tax context. The Declaratory Judgments Act, which authorizes courts to adjudicate some legal questions even without an injury-in-fact,[5] explicitly excludes taxes from the issues for which federal courts can provide declaratory judgments. And, while Establishment Clause standing allows uninjured taxpayers to challenge government actions that violate the Establishment Clause of the First Amendment, current Supreme Court jurisprudence has narrowed the scope of Establishment Clause standing. To invoke Establishment Clause standing, an uninjured taxpayer must show that the government exercised its taxing *and* spending powers. And the Court takes "spending" literally here. Tax expenditures (that is, reductions to the amount of taxes the government collects from a taxpayer) do not count, for Establishment Clause standing purposes, as spending.[6] In the tax context, then, the question of whether to accommodate religion is always within the discretion of the government.

INDIVIDUALIZED TAX LAW

To the extent practicable, the federal income tax tries to address each taxpayer's unique economic situation. It applies to a vast and disparate collection of individuals, individuals whose personal financial circumstances differ radically. Many individuals earn wage income; others, though, live off of inheritances or trust funds, or, through the magic of carried interest, have transformed their high-taxed wage income into low-taxed long-term capital gain.

While the type of income individuals earn is one significant difference between taxpayers, it is not the only difference. Homeowners can take deductions unavailable to renters. Married couples use a different set of tax brackets from single taxpayers or unmarried domestic partners. Self-employment can result in different tax treatment than full-time employment, which, in turn, can result in different tax treatment than independent contracting.

Congress had to decide how to deal with the substantive differences between taxpayers. On one extreme, it could ignore the differences, providing a single set of rules that applied to all taxpayers, irrespective of their situations.

This approach has the benefit of being simple and (relatively) easy to administer, which makes it an appealing idea. In 2015, for example, presidential candidate Carly Fiorina called for a three-page tax law.[7] While Fiorina was extreme in her view of how short the tax law could be, Republicans often claim that the Internal Revenue Code should be shorter and simpler.

At the opposite extreme sits a bespoke tax law, one tailored to take into account the economic peculiarities of each taxpayer. Such a tax law would theoretically be fair, but would be infinitely complex, and virtually impossible to administer.[8]

Congress has, sensibly, chosen to take a middle path. The tax law accounts for much taxpayer variation, but it ignores some differences. The result is a tax law that is long and complex: Congress has enacted approximately 700 tax provisions that deal with individuals, and another 1,500 that affect business. In all, these provisions comprise approximately 4 million words. The Treasury Department has further expanded the level of detail with another 20,000 pages – 8 million words – of regulations. And the IRS adds even more detail to the tax law, issuing thousands of private and public rulings and other tax guidance every year.[9] Furthermore, when taxpayers and the IRS cannot resolve their disagreements about what the law, regulations, and administrative guidance actually mean, the courts resolve their concerns, sometimes themselves establishing what the tax law is.

Still, in spite of this complexity, Congress has shown itself willing to add additional words to the tax law if that means treating a subset – even a miniscule subset – of taxpayers more fairly. On December 18, 2015, for example, Congress passed the Consolidated Appropriations Act, 2016, and President Obama signed the Act into law. The Consolidated Appropriations Act was an omnibus law, comprising more than 2,000 pages. While not primarily a tax bill, it included a number of tax provisions, including one targeted specifically at individuals who had been wrongfully incarcerated.[10] Under the newly enacted tax provision, exonerated convicts do not have to pay taxes on any recovery they receive as a result of their wrongful incarceration.[11]

This exemption is very tightly targeted – between 1989 and January 20, 2015, only 1,535 people were exonerated. While the annual number of exonerees is growing, in 2014, the National Registry of Exonerations only recorded 125 exonerations.[12] The prior year, Americans filed 147.4 *million* individual income tax returns.[13] Exonerees, then, make up about 0.00008 percent of taxpayers, and yet Congress is willing to face the additional complexity and cost to provide what Congress believes to be a fairer tax burden to exonerees.

By contrast, roughly 75 percent of Americans claim some religious affiliation.[14] Provisions of the tax law that address religious belief and practice, then, will apply to many more American taxpayers than the provision that affects exonerees, and there is nothing untoward or unusual about Congress demonstrating a willingness to look at religious taxpayers' specific financial circumstances. While the tax law seems a mundane and perhaps inapposite lens through which to view religion, the two are necessarily connected.[15] For many, religion is not merely a once-a-week practice; rather, it permeates their lives and plays a significant part in the decisions they make. Marilynne Robinson captures this idea in her novel *Gilead*: "It was Coleridge who said Christianity is a life, not a doctrine, words to that effect."[16]

Religious individuals' beliefs and practices impact how they act in the secular world. And even though the Establishment Clause prevents the government from entangling itself with religion, in the tax context, entanglement is unavoidable. "Extensive contact between modern tax systems and religious institutions is unavoidable. Whether religious entities and actors are taxed or exempted, there are no disentangling alternatives, just imperfect trade-offs between different forms of entanglement."[17] The government can ultimately decide whether to acknowledge religious economic behavior or not in designing its tax system, but it ultimately cannot avoid the intersection of tax and religion.

The impact religiosity can have on tax burden raises two questions. First, we must ask whether the tax law should take account of the different economic choices religious individuals make. And the answer is not immediately obvious. Certainly, traditional formulations of tax fairness require that similarly situated taxpayers bear similar tax burdens. (In tax policy discussions, this is called "horizontal equity.") The ideas underlying horizontal equity make intuitive sense: the idea that one person earning $50,000 should pay $5,000 in taxes, while someone else who earns $50,000 should owe $10,000 feels inequitable. Even if they earn that money in radically different ways – for example, the first person makes money trading stocks while the second teaches in an elementary school – they ultimately had the same amount of money before taxes, so it would seem fair that they have roughly the same amount left after taxes.

Even though this formulation of horizontal equity feels right, it has come under increasing attack. Louis Kaplow, an economist and Harvard Law School professor, argues that horizontal equity is ultimately a meaningless measure in creating and evaluating tax regimes. Because no two taxpayers are identical, tax policymakers must decide – to some degree, arbitrarily – how to classify individuals to evaluate whether they are similarly situated. Moreover, these arbitrary distinctions may lead to inefficient and nonutilitarian policy decisions.[18]

Liam Murphy and Thomas Nagel, professors of philosophy and law at New York University, agree with Kaplow that horizontal equity is meaningless in formulating tax policy, albeit for radically different reasons. Murphy and Nagel believe that horizontal equity is based on the mistaken idea that pretax income is meaningful, or even possible; pretax income, though, is illusory. Without a government and legal system to shape and protect the market, a government and legal system funded by taxes, we would have a radically different distribution of assets. Thus, evaluating the fairness of a tax system by looking at whether people would be similarly situated in an imaginary pretax world has no moral or policy valence.[19]

It is not important for our purposes to go too deeply into the weeds of the debates about horizontal equity. It will ultimately be sufficient to say that it has its defenders, too: even acknowledging the validity of the criticisms that have been leveled against horizontal equity, it may provide "cooperation between people with partially overlapping interests and differing views about distributive justice."[20] Horizontal equity may have its uses, then, even if it is arbitrary or illusory.

Moreover, discrimination between similarly situated taxpayers is wrong in at least some circumstances, even if discrimination between similarly situated taxpayers broadly has no moral or policy relevance. Horizontal equity may, for example, serve as a backstop against racial discrimination in the tax law.[21] In fact, the tax law should not discriminate on the basis of certain protected classes, including gender, race, sexual orientation, religion, and perhaps other discrete groups.[22]

Still, even if we agree that, at the very least, the tax law should not discriminate against certain classes of people, we are left with Kaplow's definitional problem: what do we use as a baseline for similarity? That is, in our case, should religious individuals be treated the same as nonreligious individuals, even where they act differently? Or should the baseline for determining a religious person's appropriate tax burden be other religious individuals, ignoring comparisons between the religious and nonreligious? And what are the constitutional implications of either treating religious individuals the same as or different from other taxpayers?

At the end of the book, I will return to these questions. Ultimately, though, the question of whether to treat religious taxpayers differently from other taxpayers is, if not irrelevant, at least not tremendously important. Because the tax law *does* treat religious individuals differently, at least in certain cases, and it has since colonial days.

Seventeenth-century American colonists believed that religious uniformity was foundational to political stability and, as a result, the colonies attempted to import the European political model that included an established church.[23] Ultimately, the colonies were unable to establish a single established church, and, by the early eighteenth century, nine of the colonies had their own established churches. The New England colonies favored Congregationalism, while Southern colonies established Anglicanism. Even churches that were powerful, but not established, did not reject the idea of religious establishment.[24]

In most colonies, the established churches enjoyed state support, in the form of church taxes. Although each colony's establishment functioned slightly differently, most church taxes were either head taxes (that is, a set amount of tax per person, unrelated to the person's income or wealth) meant to support the established church, or special levies, meant to fund particular church projects. Maryland, for example, imposed an annual head tax of forty pounds of tobacco per taxable person to support the established Church of England. In addition, in 1765, the legislature approved a levy requiring the Saint Mary's County Court to collect 200,000 pounds of tobacco from taxable inhabitants of Saint Andrews Parish; the levy would be used to fund a new parish church.[25]

Originally, these church taxes did not differentiate between taxpayers based on their religions. That is, both members and nonmembers of the colony's established church had to pay the church tax. Members of competing churches, then, faced a steeper financial burden than members of the established church – not only did they fund the established church through their taxes, but they also had to provide financial support to the church with which they affiliated.

In the early eighteenth century, Anglicans in Massachusetts and Connecticut began to rebel against their obligation pay church taxes to support the established Congregational churches. At the same time, Anglican clergy were writing to England to complain about "their parishioners' having to support Congregationalist ministers."[26] Ultimately, facing pressure from England, Massachusetts and Connecticut introduced an early version of religious accommodation into their tax laws.

Under their revised church tax, religious dissenters "who actively attended and financially supported private neighborhood churches" were exempted from the church tax. Their exemption, however, was based entirely on their religious status. Individuals who wanted nothing to do with religion at all – and even religious dissenters who lived too far from their private church of choice to attend – still had to pay the church tax.[27] The exemption from the church tax was only for religious individuals who supported their nonestablished church with both their time and their money.

Of course, established churches by and large did not maintain their privileged position into the post-Revolution period. By the mid-eighteenth century, all of the colonies practiced some sort of religious toleration, in spite of the officially established churches.[28] And by the end of the eighteenth century, the colonies, then states, began the process of disestablishment. Delaware and New Jersey led the disestablishment movement, severing their official ties with their established churches in 1776. Disestablishment continued on a state-by-state basis and, in 1833, Massachusetts became the last state to officially end its relationship with an established church.[29] Disestablishment mooted entirely the question of accommodation within the church tax. Without a state-supported church, there was no need for church taxes, and therefore no need to accommodate dissent.

Without an established church, the question of religious accommodation for taxes (at least at the federal level) remained moot until the Civil War. During most of the eighteenth century, the federal government funded itself through a combination of tariffs, excise taxes, and the sale of land. But in 1861, the Union discovered that the cost of waging war was quickly outpacing the revenue it could raise from traditional sources. It could borrow money, of course, but had to supplement that borrowing with new streams of revenue. Ultimately, the government enacted an income tax.[30]

This first federal income tax lasted until 1871, and went through several iterations. The Revenue Act of 1870, one of the final iterations of the Civil War-era income tax, provided for a $2,000 exemption from the "gains, profits, and income of any person."[31] That deduction likely exempted the vast majority of Americans from paying income tax.

The same provision of the Revenue Act of 1870 included a special rule for some religious individuals:

> For the purpose of allowing said deduction from the income of any religious or social community holding all their property and the income therefrom jointly and in common, each five of the persons composing such society ... shall be held to constitute a family, and a deduction of two thousand dollars shall be allowed for each of said families.[32]

Why would there be a special provision for communitarian religious groups? Though the origins and purpose of the provision may not be immediately obvious to contemporary Americans, the legislative history sheds some light onto what Congress was thinking. Senator John Sherman explained that the provision referenced Shakers and other such religious societies.[33]

And what about Shakers would trigger a special tax accommodation? The legislative history does not explain Congress's reasoning, but it likely reacted to two distinct features of Shakerism: its rules governing sex and marriage and its economic organization.

Shaker doctrine requires celibacy. It prohibits both sex and marriage; without those distractions, Shakers could devote themselves to establishing the Kingdom of Heaven. Without marriage, Shaker settlements were divided into community groups called "families." Although they did not marry, Shaker communities raised children – both those converts brought with them from their former lives and orphans they adopted – communally.[34]

This communal spirit also pervaded the economic life of Shakers. Although not originally communitarian, by the early nineteenth century, Shakers no longer owned their own property. Instead, deacons and deaconesses held the property of Shakers who came to their village. In fact, many Shaker communities were established on holdings donated to the group by wealthy farmers who converted to the religion.[35]

For purposes of the Civil War-era income tax, this combination of economic communalism and non-existent legal families could effectively exempt even relatively prosperous Shakers from paying any taxes at all. Although the Revenue Act of 1870 provided a $2,000 exemption to any person, that language was not the end of the story: the $2,000 exemption had to be shared among family members, with *family* defined as "one or both parents and one or more minor children, or ... husband and wife."[36]

In Shaker practice, though, there were no groups of one or both parents, or husbands and wives. As such, presumably each individual Shaker would be able to exempt his or her first $2,000 of income. And yet subgroups of Shakers called themselves families, they lived together like a family, and they shared their property and income in a manner associated with families.

In light of the unique marital and economic situation of Shakers, then, Congress limited their access to the exemption by requiring every five Shakers to be treated as a family. As a family for tax purposes, the group of five Shakers had to share the $2,000 exemption; now, if it was divided evenly, any given Shaker could only earn $400 without owing taxes. And, although they held their property in common, Shakers emphasized both work and economic success.[37]

Both the colonial exemption from the church tax for religious dissenters and the Civil War-era shared exemption for Shakers and other communitarian religious groups treated religious people differently from nonreligious people. The two provisions' purposes differed significantly, though. The church tax exemptions were enacted to prevent religious dissenters from paying for both the established church *and* the churches they attended. These exemptions functioned as tax relief. The Revenue Act of 1870, on the other hand, functioned to *increase* the taxes of (certain) religious individuals. It prevented certain religious taxpayers from evading their tax liability because their religion forbade formal family structures, while at the same time they functioned as a family economically. While Congress recognized Shaker religious practices, it was not interested in making those practices less expensive.

SHOULD THE TAX LAW ACCOMMODATE RELIGIOUS PRACTICE?

This history of the tax law accommodation of religion provides two answers to the question of whether the tax law should accommodate religion. The first is, the question is mostly irrelevant. The tax law has a long history of accommodating religion, a history that we will see extends right through the present. So whether or not it *should* accommodate religion, it will.

While pragmatic, though, that answer elides the actual normative question. The other answer is that, whether or not the tax law *will* accommodate religion, it should. Or, rather, the tax law should accommodate at least some religious practice. For many people, their religion actually and tangibly impacts their economic lives. As we have seen, sometimes their religiously motivated economic lives are tax-inefficient (meaning that they will necessarily pay more taxes than they would if they were not religious). In other cases, their religious practices will cause them to pay less, evading taxes because their lives follow forms different than those anticipated by the tax law. In both cases, as long as there is underlying economic difference, it makes sense for the tax law to understand and capture the economics of religiosity.

DESIGNING ACCOMMODATION

To the extent that the tax law both will and should accommodate religious practice, we must address a second set of questions: how should tax policymakers decide what religious practices to accommodate, and how should those accommodations look?

Although the current tax law does accommodate religion in certain instances, it does not currently address this second set of questions. Rather, those accommodations that exist today result from ad hoc, reactive lawmaking. The small handful of unrelated sections of the Internal Revenue Code that take religious practice into account were enacted at different times, in response to different questions, without any connection to or acknowledgment of other circumstances in which the tax law explicitly dealt with religion. And, in addition to these statutory treatments of religious practice, the IRS and the courts have accommodated – or ignored – religious practice in other judicial and administrative decisions. Like the Congressional enactments, individual IRS and court treatments of the taxation of religious practice have at most tenuous connections to other such treatments.

Ultimately, there is no pattern or underlying sense to the way the tax law addresses religion. And this randomness makes it harder for both religious individuals and the IRS to figure out what to do when a new religious practice implicates the tax law. Because there has been no consistency up until now, it is anybody's guess what Congress, the courts, or even the IRS will do next.

Ad hoc lawmaking is not unique to the tax law, of course. It is easier for legislators and regulators to "react to past ... mistakes than to prevent future mistakes,"[38] especially where the past to which they react is salient and memorable. Perhaps this is why Professor Nathan Oman sees danger where we "creat[e] the law of church and market by accident," which courts, legislators, and regulators do "when they resolve questions religious commerce poses by applying legal theories developed without any thought for the proper relationship between church and market."[39] That danger applies equally to the tax and religion. And that danger has been fully realized. The government approaches its tax accommodations of religious practice on an entirely ad hoc basis. Even if we arbitrarily limit our definition of the government to Congress, we see it acting in an inconsistent, mildly reactionary way.

For example, in 1921, Congress enacted the predecessor to today's parsonage allowance. I discuss the parsonage allowance in significant detail in Chapter 5, but it is enough here to say that the parsonage allowance permits religions to provide housing for their ministers without requiring the ministers to include the value of the housing in their income. Congress's precise motivation in enacting the parsonage allowance is shrouded in mystery. It was introduced to the Senate on November 2, 1921 and, after being read into the record, Senator Boies Penrose accepted the amendment. Without any discussion, the Senate agreed to it.[40] The provision was likely introduced to reverse the Treasury Department's determination that employer-provided housing *was* income to ministers, but even if that is true, Congress did not explain *why* it believed that such housing should not be included in a minister's income.

Thirty-three years later, Congress amended the allowance to provide that ministers could exclude from income not only church-provided housing, but also cash housing allowances from their employers. While the legislative history remained sparse for this change, Representative Peter Mack Jr., the provision's sponsor, explained his policy reasons for providing for ministers to receive a tax-free housing stipend. For him, it came down to equity. As the representative of a Baptist organization pointed out to him, it was unfair to clergy that those who worked for religions that owned housing could get a

tax-free benefit, while those who worked for religions that did not own housing got no such benefit.

Allowing clergy to get housing *or* a housing allowance tax-free, he argued,
would "remove this inequity and permit all clergymen to exclude from gross
income that part of a specific rental allowance up to the rental value of the
of the dwelling house actually occupied." While the Baptists inspired Rep.
Mack's proposal, it received universally positive responses. Many wrote to him
to emphasize that allowing a nontaxable housing allowance would resolve
inequities and eliminate discrimination. In fact, Rep. Mack said, while his
plan received a surprising amount of attention, all of that attention was positive. Eliminating discrimination, it turned out, was a popular move.[41]

And it makes sense that the move was popular: it reduced clergy's tax burden without (explicitly) raising anybody's taxes. True, the government would
have to make up the lost revenue by raising more money from everybody else,
but for any given taxpayer the additional tax burden would be marginal, and
virtually unnoticeable. In 1940, there were 133,449 clergy in the United States,
some of whom, presumably, would not benefit from the change (because they
already received in-kind housing without paying taxes on it). That same year,
taxpayers filed 14.8 million tax returns. About half of those taxpayers owed
taxes – on average, $199 – while the other half had credits and exemptions in
excess of their taxable income.[42]

We do not know the precise cost of Rep. Mack's proposal, but we can be
sure that it was miniscule compared to total federal revenue. Assuming that
clergy paid, on average, the same amount of taxes as the average taxpayer –
an unlikely assumption, given that the median salary for clergy was below the
median salary for all Americans – eliminating their taxes entirely would have
reduced federal revenue by $26.6 million, or less than 2 percent of individual
income tax revenue for 1940. Put another way, for the government to raise the
same amount of revenue without taxing clergy *at all*, it would have needed to
increase the average tax bill in 1940 by about $3.55.

And in truth, the increase in taxes would have been substantially lower.
The change would not have affected all clergy, and it would not have totally
eliminated their tax burden. Still, it represented a real savings to some subset
of clergy, a subset who thus had incentive to lobby for the change. At the same
time, because it imposed a very small additional burden on a diffuse group –
that is, all taxpayers – there was no equivalent body with an incentive to lobby
against the proposal.

And the discrimination it allegedly resolved? It is true that the law, as written, treated some clergy differently from other clergy. But it is hard to find
a coherent tax policy justification for the change, because it is not clear that

the proper baseline should be clergy whose employer provides housing. The very existence of the parsonage allowance discriminates between clergy and nonclergy. Instead of addressing religion in a consistent way, grounded in tax policy, the development of the parsonage allowance and its subsequent expansion demonstrate the ad hoc and reactionary nature of the legislative processes surrounding religious taxation. And where it is ad hoc, the procedure allows for bad policy-making. Arguably, Rep. Mack's proposal did not, in fact, arise out of concern for discrimination. Rather, it represented classic rent-seeking by Baptists and other religious denominations: the change they advocated presented their clergy with concentrated benefits and imposed dispersed costs.[43]

Other legislative provisions that benefit religious individuals arise in a similarly ad hoc manner, and demonstrate similar theoretical and tax policy problems. Congress created a special tax regime for communitarian religious groups that allowed members, rather than the religious community, to pay taxes. Chapter 10 deals with this provision at length. Here it is worth noting that Congress spent very little time explaining why it found such a special regime necessary, or what it intended to accomplish with the special regime. The legislative history merely states that Congress passed the special provision to give the organizations "relief" and to subject their members to a "fair tax."[44] Though the relief it offered – lower collective taxes – was self-evident, Congress did not explain how this regime was fairer than the tax regime broadly, or why Congress found it necessary (or even beneficial) to provide a special taxing regime.

If Congress's religious accommodations remain ad hoc and unexplained, those accommodations created or denied by the courts and the IRS add even more chaos into the system. Many accommodations, ranging from the tax treatment of missionaries and of ministers to the deductibility of Scientologists' payments for auditing (a religious practice), come from the IRS. These administrative accommodations generally derive from the IRS's best interpretation of the tax law, but some result from its decision not to enforce certain provisions of the law. Whether or not it *should* create accommodations, then, the IRS necessarily does in the course of determining its enforcement priorities. The reverse side of creating accommodations, of course, is denying them, something that the IRS also appears to do. Neither Congress nor the IRS, for example, has done anything to allow Muslim homeowners, whose religion forbids them from paying interest, to deduct the interest-equivalent amounts of *shari'a*-compliant mortgages.

Courts have a less-explicit role to play in the creation of the tax law, but, at least when a religious taxpayer challenges the lack of a tax accommodation, courts will have the ultimate say. And because federal judicial decisions come with written explanations of how the court came to its conclusion, it is possible to determine why a court chose to accommodate religious practice or not. But while courts often explain why they came to the conclusion they came to, their analysis has no consistent underlying framework. Rather, they evaluate each question of accommodation in isolation, deciding what the tax law and the Constitution demand, but not whether that particular decision is consistent with the way other religious taxpayers are treated.

Ultimately, this disregard of consistent policy is not the result of laziness; rather, it appears to be because tax policymakers have not even considered whether there is an appropriate way to account for religion in the tax law. Rarely do academic and judicial treatments of religion focus on policy; generally they evaluate the contours and limits of the Constitution. In those rare occasions where questions of religion and tax bubble up to the public consciousness, the questions tend to be related to the constitutional permissibility of a proposed or existing accommodation. And where the questions do not face the light of public scrutiny, they tend to result from requests by sympathetic – or connected – religious individuals. In the end, tax accommodation for religious individuals is not only ad hoc, but is also accidental, a dangerous combination.

In the following chapters, I will detail several of these ad hoc and accidental tax treatment of various religious individuals. Some of the accommodations, I will argue, are appropriate, while others have no compelling reason for existing. In the final chapter, I will lay out a robust tax policy framework that legislators, the IRS, and the courts can use to evaluate whether a given religious practice merits tax accommodation, or whether the practice should be subject to the same tax regime as nonreligious individuals' economic practices.

In approaching the various instances of tax accommodation, two considerations ultimately should guide the accommodation framework. First, the government should be extremely careful with its power to force religious change through legal pressure. The metaphorical wall of separation is, in part, meant to ensure religious autonomy to the extent possible. In general, we want to construct the tax law in a way that distorts taxpayers' economic decision-making as little as possible. Similarly, tax policymakers' choice whether to accommodate a religious practice should avoid placing distortionary pressure on religious practice.

At the same time, policymakers need to understand that they must not overdo accommodation. Overly broad accommodation imposes real costs on nonreligious taxpayers. Not only might they view the system as unfair, but every dollar of taxes that religious individuals do not have to pay is an additional dollar of taxes owed by nonreligious taxpayers.

A CAVEAT

It is important to note that the issues and framework I address in this book are specific to the intersection of religion and the tax law. They should not be read more broadly to apply to questions of accommodation in other areas where the state interacts with religion.

That caveat smacks of a flavor of tax exceptionalism. "Tax exceptionalism" is the idea that there is something so unique about the tax law that the general administrative law doctrines and rules do not apply to it. That belief has come under significant scrutiny in recent years, and is not withstanding that scrutiny terribly well.[45]

Tax exceptionalism, though, concerns specifically the manner in which the Treasury Department and the IRS create regulations; that courts and scholars are coming to the conclusion that there is nothing special about the tax law *for administrative law purposes* does not mean that there is nothing unique about the tax law. In fact, the Supreme Court's holding on the one hand that raising revenue is always a compelling government purpose (meaning that there is no mandatory accommodation), combined with the existence of the Tax Anti-Injunction Act (that effectively prevents courts from ruling on the constitutionality of tax accommodations) on the other hand, means that questions of tax and religion exist in a unique, even exceptional, legal framework.

Segregating tax from nontax accommodations does not seem like a terribly difficult task and, in most cases, it will not be. On the margin, though, the question can be hard. In fact, the 2010 Patient Protection and Affordable Care Act illustrates the potential classification problems perfectly.

The Patient Protection and Affordable Care Act required Americans to carry a certain minimum level of health insurance. To ensure that people comply with the so-called "individual mandate," the Act also imposed a penalty on those who fail to obtain the minimum level of insurance.

And that penalty ended up codified in the Internal Revenue Code.[46] While being codified in the Internal Revenue Code does not automatically mean a law is a tax law, it is a strong indicator. Moreover, although the penalty is designated a "shared responsibility payment," the Supreme Court held that it was a tax for constitutional purposes (though, interestingly enough, that it was not a tax for Tax Anti-Injunction Act purposes).[47]

And the individual mandate contains two religious accommodations. The first, a religious conscience exemption, provides that certain individuals who object to insurance as a religious matter (and whose religion is old enough – basically, it refers to the Amish) will not have to pay the penalty if they do not have sufficient insurance.[48]

A second exemption applies even to non-Amish individuals who have religious (or, interestingly enough, ethical) objections to insurance. Instead of purchasing insurance, these religious and ethical objectors can join a health care sharing ministry. Health care sharing ministries are not insurance (though they resemble it). Instead, members pay a monthly fee and, when they incur medical costs, submit those costs. Collectively, the members of the health care sharing ministry then attempt to pay the medical costs, though, unlike insurance, there is no guarantee that they will do so.[49] These health care sharing ministries attempt to meet the Christian mandate to bear one another's burdens, explicitly tying their existence to biblical principles.[50] By joining a health care sharing ministry, a religious objector to insurance will not have to pay the shared responsibility payment.[51]

Even though Congress enacted the individual mandate as part of the Internal Revenue Code, and even though the Supreme Court held that it qualified as a tax for constitutional purposes, it functions differently from most tax provisions. Its primary purpose is not to raise revenue; rather, its purpose is to provide an incentive for healthy individuals to comply with the Patient Protection and Affordable Care Act by buying insurance.

A large part of the special Religion Clauses treatment of taxes comes as a result of the essential role tax plays in making governmental action possible by funding government. It is hard to say that the individual mandate, with its different goals, implicates the same considerations.

That is not to say that the religious accommodations built into the individual mandate are either good or bad. It says, rather, that my proposed framework has a relatively narrow scope. Just because the individual mandate qualifies as a tax for constitutional purposes does not mean that it fits within the contours of this religious accommodation framework. It is a tax in a fundamentally different way from the revenue-oriented parts of the Internal Revenue Code. As a result, its intersection with religious practice should be evaluated under a nontax-specific framework.

The rest of the book will consider various instances of accommodations to revenue-raising tax laws. The majority will be federal tax laws, but one instance will address state tax laws. In both cases, though, the examples will build toward an overarching framework for determining whether the tax law should carve accommodations from particular tax law provisions for religious taxpayers.

4

Taxing Citizens of the Kingdom of God

Most Americans' religious beliefs and practices have virtually no impact on their taxes. A Catholic, a Muslim, and an atheist with the same income will pay approximately the same amount in taxes. The United States does not have a special tax regime for the religious.

Though this makes intuitive sense, it is not inevitable. A number of European countries have "church taxes." Germany, for example, guarantees its citizens freedom of religion, and has no state church. At the same time, qualifying religious organizations can levy taxes against their members. Although the churches are responsible for administering the church taxes, they can – and do – enlist the state's assistance in collecting them.

German church taxes are separate from and in addition to its ordinary taxes that fund the government. And they truly are a special tax on the religious – anybody who does not want to pay the church tax can avoid it by simply disaffiliating from their church.[1]

That the United States has no special tax applicable solely to religious individuals does not mean that the general tax law does not have any specific provisions that treat religious individuals differently than their nonreligious counterparts, of course. To understand these religion-linked departures from the standard tax law, then, we must first have an idea of how the tax law functions when it does not consider religion.

The tax law is notoriously complex: Albert Einstein apocryphally declared that the "hardest thing in the world to understand is income taxes."[2] The Internal Revenue Code itself runs nearly 4 million words.[3] On top of those millions of words are millions more in the Treasury regulations, in various administrative releases and rulings issued by the I.R.S., and in the court cases interpreting and applying the Code.

Explaining the tax law in detail, then, would go far beyond both the scope and the length of this book. Rather, in broad strokes, I will lay out a handful of foundational assumptions and rules that underlie the tax law at its most basic. Even these rules are not set in stone; Congress has enacted certain exceptions to each of them, including some that apply solely to religious individuals. Still, the following discussion of the tax law lays out the law's general contours.

Most fundamentally, the federal income tax taxes individuals on their income. Although this sounds tautological, it is neither self-evident nor obvious. Many taxes do not consider income at all. A property tax, for example, is calculated as a percentage of the value of the property to which it applies, while a sales tax is determined by the amount of money a good or service costs. Neither the value of a person's property nor the amount she spends necessarily bears any relationship to the amount of income she earns.

And *income* is a broader category than just cash wages. The Supreme Court has defined income as including any "undeniable accessions to wealth, clearly realized, and over which the taxpayers have complete dominion."[4] Income, then, includes both earned income and passive income, both compensation for services and returns on capital. It includes cash, but also includes property other than cash. Receipt of property can constitute an accession to wealth and, when it does, a taxpayer must include the property's fair market value in their income. In fact, in some circumstances, even the receipt of services constitutes income, taxable to the recipient.

As a practical matter, we do not pay taxes on *everything* of value we receive. For the most part, though, that is not because of something inherent to the tax law. Instead, it is because Congress created an exemption, for administrative or policy or other reasons. So, for instance, taxpayers do not need to include gifts and inheritances in their income,[5] not because they are somehow intrinsically untaxable, but because Congress decided they were not the kind of thing that it intended to tax. That decision was not inevitable: the federal income tax of 1894 treated gifts and inheritances as taxable income to the recipients.[6] When the income tax was reintroduced in 1913, Congress explicitly excluded gifts and inheritances from the definition of income, and they have remained outside its scope since then.[7] Without an explicit exception, though, any accession to wealth – including finding money on the street[8] – is income for tax purposes.

Moreover, for US income tax purposes, it does not matter whether a taxpayer finds money on the street in New York or in New Delhi. The US individual federal income tax is a worldwide tax. No matter where a taxpayer's money comes from, unless it is a type explicitly excluded from income, they must include it in their gross income and, ultimately, pay taxes on it.

For US purposes, then, the obligation to pay taxes is fairly broad. Every citizen and resident of the United States must include as income any accession to wealth (unless explicitly exempted), no matter where the accession occurs, and no matter where the US taxpayer is when it occurs.

If this were the whole world of income taxation, the tax law would be far simpler than it is, of course. And, when originally enacted in 1913, the tax law *was* far simpler. In 1913, the income tax comprised about twenty-seven pages, making it far shorter than today's federal income tax.[9]

Of course, the 1913 income tax did not carry the same burden today's tax does. In 1913, taxpayers were a far smaller and more homogenous group. The way Congress drafted this first modern income tax, it exempted a taxpayer's first $3,000 of income.[10] That $3,000 floor meant that only about 2 percent of households had to pay the income tax.[11]

By contrast, in 2013, 57 percent of households paid federal income taxes.[12] Where the income tax applies broadly to most Americans, though, it tries to take into account (some) variations in their economic lives. These variations add complexity to the tax law, but they also make it fairer, recognizing that there is not a single economic profile of an American taxpayer.

A simple example is the tax treatment of marriage. A married couple can elect to be treated as a single taxpayer. As such, a marriage can cause a marriage penalty (that is, the couple collectively pays more in taxes than two unmarried individuals who earn the same amount of income) or a marriage bonus (where the married couple pays less than the unmarried individuals). But there are other, less obvious, tax consequences to marriage: among other things, transferring property between spouses does not trigger gift or estate taxes and also does not transfer the recognition and taxation of unrealized gains.[13]

FAIRNESS AND EXCUSE

Of course, this book is about the taxation of religious individuals, not taxation broadly. So why spend so much time on the default rules of taxation? Because religious individuals are subject to the same broad regime of taxation as all other Americans. Though there are certain ways in which religious individuals are taxed differently than the nonreligious – and other ways in which they *should* be treated differently, even though they currently are taxed identically – in the vast majority of situations, the tax treatment of an American will be identical, whether they are religious or not.

If the tax law reaches that broadly, it should require something remark-able for a person to escape the reaches of the tax law. And generally it does: throughout the history of the modern income tax, the only sure way to avoid the federal income tax entirely has been by earning too little to be subject to the tax. The amount that constitutes too little has shifted over time; in 1913, the exemption was $3,000 (which translated to more than $71,000 in 2014[14]). By 2014, on the other hand, a family of four could only exempt their first $28,200 from taxation.[15] The current exemption makes some policy sense: the 2014 Health and Human Services poverty guidelines set the poverty level at $23,850 for a family of four.[16] The exemption amount, then, relieves a family in poverty of the obligation to pay income taxes.

Though poverty can relieve a taxpayer from their tax-paying obligations, religion offers no such relief. Poverty affects an individual's ability to pay their taxes; fairness dictates that the tax law should take their ability to pay into account in determining how much they must pay in taxes.[17] Religious belief, on the other hand, does not impact a taxpayer's financial ability to pay, even where it affects their willingness.

That is not to say that the economic lives of the religious are identical to the economic lives of the nonreligious. They can differ in a number of ways. Still, neither religious belief nor practice excuse an individual from their tax liabilities. Nonetheless, some people have tried.

The justifications proffered by those who have tried to escape some or all of their taxpaying obligations by virtue of their religious belief generally fall into one of two broad categories. The first category includes variations on the argument that earthly laws do not apply to them, and thus they have no legal obligation to pay taxes. The second category encompasses arguments that certain governmental expenditures support programs that run contrary to their religious beliefs, programs that they cannot in good conscience support. As a result, they argue, they cannot be expected to pay taxes to support that spending.

Irrespective of the sincerity of a religious individual's beliefs, though, nei-ther category of argument puts an individual outside of the broad scope of the tax law. In addition, making either type of argument can subject religious taxpayers to penalties in addition to the back taxes and interest they owe.

CLERGY AND TAXES

If any constitutional obligation to tax the religious differently than the non-religious existed, the most likely beneficiaries of such a difference would be clergy. While lay religious Americans may see and understand the world differently than nonreligious Americans,[18] they still generally live their professional lives in the secular world. For clergy, on the other hand, the professional and the religious are inextricably intertwined.

Vows of Poverty, Sincere or Otherwise

The IRS's treatment of clergy has shifted over time. In 1919, it issued a ruling holding that a "clergyman" was not taxable on the money he received from his parish, provided he had taken a vow of poverty and that he turned any money in excess of his living expenses over to his religious order. Under its ruling, the IRS essentially treated the clergyman as an agent for his order. If he acted as an agent for the order, his income belonged to the order, and it made sense to tax the order rather than the clergyman (though, because the order was tax-exempt, nobody ended up paying taxes on the clergyman's income). Conversely, clergymen were taxable on money, if any, received by them in their individual capacities.[19]

Subsequent to this ruling, the courts decided a series of cases in which they held that income is taxable to the person who earns it, irrespective of whether they keep it. In 1930, the Supreme Court introduced the *fruit of the tree* metaphor; according to the Supreme Court, fruit (that is, income) must be attributed to the tree on which it grows.[20] Even if an individual contractually agrees to give part or all of their income to somebody else – even, in fact, if they instruct the payor to give it directly to that person, and they never actually touch the money – *they* must pay taxes on the income they earn.

In the context of clergy, though, the fruit of the tree metaphor failed to catch on for nearly half a century. Through the late 1970s, the IRS continued to treat clergy who had taken a vow of poverty as agents of their religious orders. As agents, the IRS said, they did not have to pay taxes on the money they earned.[21]

Of course, where the tax law provides an advantage to a certain class of taxpayer, somebody will enter in and try to exploit that advantage. And, in the late 1970s and early 1980s, a number of taxpayers tried to exploit the IRS's treatment of religious vows. Though a vow of poverty seems a particularly unremunerative way to reduce one's taxes, a series of "mail-order ministers" obtained ordination, for free or for a fee. These supposed ministers then declared that their homes were their churches and

wrote documents declaring a vow of poverty, thus assigning 100 percent of their salary to their churches (homes), thus avoiding the payment of any taxes. In turn, of course, in each case the church provided for all the personal needs of the "minister" and his/her family: car, shelter, food, entertainment, insurance, and so forth. Of course, the "minister had total control over the finances of the church.[22]

Clearly, many of these individuals were taking a vow of poverty merely for the tax benefits, not out of any sincere religious belief. Moreover, their vows of poverty had no economic effect, as the so-called ministers continued to exercise full control over the money and assets they had formally turned over to their churches.

As these insincere vows of poverty became more and more common, they became increasingly alarming to the IRS. During the 1960s and 1970s, the Universal Life Church ordained 10 million ministers and issued tens of thousands of church charters. In 1979 alone, the Church of Universal Harmony sold 100 ordinations each month.[23]

In attacking these putatively religious tax shelters, the IRS chose not to focus on the sincerity of the ministers' religious beliefs, or the sincerity of their vows of poverty. Instead, it attacked the tax-exempt status of their supposed churches. For a church – or any other organization – to qualify as exempt from tax, an organization cannot use its earnings for the private benefit of any insider.[24] The IRS determined that where the minister controlled the finances of the church and could effectively use their donated money post-vow in the same way they did before their vow of poverty, their church did not qualify as tax-exempt. As a result, these supposed ministers were unable to avoid taxation. Courts agreed, sustaining the IRS's revocation of these churches' tax exemptions.[25] Effectively, the IRS could avoid entangling itself with the issue of the (obvious lack of) sincerity of these ministers' religious beliefs and practices, and still prevent their exploitation of the tax law, by looking at the substance, rather than the form, of their economic actions.[26]

Around the same time it shut down insincere clerical vows of poverty, the IRS shifted its view of sincere vows of poverty. In a 1977 ruling, the IRS addressed two members of a religious order who had taken vows of poverty. One, a licensed attorney, was instructed to find work with a law firm. He did, and directed that his salary be paid to his order. The second, a secretary, was instructed to work for the local business office of the church with which the order was affiliated. He also complied, and remitted his salary to the order.

Rather than treating any employment by these men as nontaxable, though, the IRS looked at their employment, and drew a distinction between working for a third party and working for the affiliated church. In the latter instance, it decided that the secretary, as an employee of the affiliated church, was acting as an agent for the religious order and, as a result, was not taxable on his income. In the former case, though, the IRS determined that, because he worked for a third party that was unaffiliated with the church, he was not acting as an agent for his order. As such, the IRS treated him in the same way it treats both nonreligious and nonclergy individuals: he was taxable on the income he earned, even though it went directly to his order.[27] The IRS followed this change up with a series of rulings that found that members of religious orders who took positions in the secular world were taxable in the same manner as nonclergy, and even as nonreligious, workers.[28]

The courts endorsed the IRS's new approach toward religious taxpayers who took vows of poverty. For example, the courts upheld the IRS's determination that Reverend Gerald P. Fogarty, S.J., owed taxes on income he earned working for an outside employer. Rev. Fogarty was a Roman Catholic priest and a member of the Society of Jesus. As a Jesuit priest, Rev. Fogarty had taken vows of chastity, poverty, and obedience. The University of Virginia offered Rev. Fogarty an associate professorship in its Department of Religious Studies. The Society of Jesus is committed to education and, in particular, to higher education. Consistent with the Society's mission, and in accordance with his religious superior's instructions and with his vow of obedience, Rev. Fogarty accepted the position and taught courses on Catholic religious thought, development, and history. (It was always clear that his continuing employment depended on his religious superior's continued approval.)

The University of Virginia paid Rev. Fogarty for his work, writing a monthly payroll check to him. Rev. Fogarty did not deposit the checks in his own account, or an account controlled by him, however. Instead, he requested that the university deposit it directly in a checking account belonging to the Corporation of Roman Catholic Clergymen. The university complied with his request.

Consistent both with canon law and his vow of poverty, Rev. Fogarty had no right to receive, direct the use of, or dispose of the money he earned from his teaching. Instead, it belonged to his Order; his Order, in turn, provided him with resources to meet his living expenses.

The university did not withhold taxes and Rev. Fogarty, believing that the amounts paid were income to his Order, not to him, did not file tax returns. The IRS disagreed and assessed taxes, which he paid and then ultimately challenged in court.[29] The court never questioned Rev. Fogarty's sincerity. He did not have the right to the income he earned and, even if he had, he did not benefit from it in any substantive way. Certainly, payments from the University of Virginia for the work Rev. Fogarty performed meant that his Order had more money with which it could support him and its other members, but there was no suggestion that his living expenses varied depending on how much he earned.

The court felt that the question in Rev. Fogarty's position was a close call. In spite of his sincerity, though, and his lack of personal economic benefit, the court ultimately upheld the IRS's post-1977 position. Rev. Fogarty earned money working outside his Order; that fruit grew on his tree and, as such, he was taxable on his income.[30]

Shortly after the United States Claims Court decided that Rev. Fogarty owed taxes on his income from teaching at the University of Virginia, the Tax Court addressed the nearly identical question of whether wages earned by Sister Francine Schuster as a nurse-midwife were taxable to her. Sister Schuster was a member of the Order of the Adorers of the Blood of Christ. Like Rev. Fogarty, she had taken vows of poverty and obedience. While a member of her Order, Sister Schuster studied midwifery; she received a traineeship to cover the costs of her program and, in exchange for the traineeship, agreed (with her Order's approval) to practice in a "health manpower shortage area."

To fulfill her practice obligation, Sister Schuster worked as a nurse-midwife for the National Health Services Corps, where she earned $15,920 a year. Although the Order requested that her salary be paid directly to the Order, the clinic Sister Schuster worked for could not do that. Instead, it paid Sister Schuster, who endorsed her paychecks over to the Order. Like Rev. Fogarty, she had no control over the money and received no direct benefit from it. Still, the Tax Court came to the same conclusion as the Claims Court had: the money represented income to Sister Schuster, notwithstanding her vow of poverty and her lack of practical control over the money.[31]

Not Subject to Human Laws

Although some of the vows of poverty discussed in the prior section appear to have been illusory, if not outright fraudulent, all of the ministers grounded their objection to paying taxes in an economic argument: their (sometimes putative) vows of poverty meant that money they earned did not, in fact, belong to them. But not all arguments for religiously based exemption from taxation are based on economic reality. Some clergy argue that they should not have to pay taxes solely as a consequence of their status as clergy.

Kent Hovind, the impresario of creationism mentioned in the introduction, succinctly laid out the basic premise of those who argue that their religion exempts them from the obligation their fellow-citizens have to pay taxes. According to a Florida bankruptcy court, Hovind maintained that "as a minister of God everything he owns belongs to God and he is not subject to paying taxes to the United States on the money he receives for doing God's work."[32]

Hovind did not claim that he had no legal or effective control over his money. He did not argue that his income provided him with no benefit. He merely asserted that the nature of his religious belief put him outside the reach of the tax system. And he was not the only person to claim exemption from taxes as a result of doing God's work.

Sandy Good's justifications for not paying taxes parallel Hovind's in many ways, but also provides an alternate vantage point from which to look at these justifications. Like Hovind, Good lived in Florida and, like Hovind, he founded a ministry. He did not get any professional help in establishing his ministry, though he did read a book by Joseph N. Sweet about taxes.[33]

Sweet was one of the biggest sellers of tax-evasion plans in the United States.[34] He self-published and sold a book – presumably the one Good read – entitled *GOOD NEWS for FORM 1040 Filers: Your Compliance is Strictly VOLUNTARY! BAD NEWS for the IRS! Everything You Ever Needed to Know About the Income Tax That the IRS Is Afraid You'll Find Out.*[35] In his book, Sweet made a number of frivolous tax-protestor arguments including, among other things, that the federal income tax was unconstitutional, that the IRS lacked the authority to collect taxes, and that the federal income tax only applied to foreign earned income.[36]

In addition to his (poor) tax advice, Sweet sold "Unincorporated Business Trust Organizations" to individuals as a (purported) method of avoiding the obligation to pay taxes. In 2002, a district court judge enjoined him from selling either his tax protestor arguments or his UBTOs, and further enjoined him from assisting or encouraging others to evade taxes.[37] Although Sweet offered followers the promise of being free from the burden of taxpaying, his tax protestor arguments had no particular religious valence: he merely revealed to people that the tax law was unconstitutional or inapplicable to them, not because of some special characteristic of his followers, but because of the intrinsic nature of the tax law.

About five years after establishing his ministry, Good sought professional help, engaging the services of Glen Stoll to restructure his ministry to avoid paying taxes. Unlike Sweet, Stoll marketed his tax evasion plans specifically to religious individuals. Stoll held himself out as an "ecclesiastical lawyer," notwithstanding the fact that he was entirely unlicensed to practice law.[38] Unlike Sweet, though, Stoll did not argue that the tax laws themselves are defective. Instead, Stoll advised and assisted his religious clients in attempting to evade taxes. In essence, he told clients that he could form various entities – largely corporations sole and ministerial trusts – that he claimed were *per se* exempt from taxation. Stoll and his organization walked clients through a number of steps meant to "sever all ties with state and federal governments in order to become 'citizens of Heaven,'" including obtaining drivers' licenses, business licenses, and identification cards from the "Kingdom of Heaven," an organization in rural Oregon with which Stoll had ties.[39]

After establishing their citizenship in the Kingdom of Heaven and arranging the appropriate ministerial trusts, in which clients were to hold all of their assets and money, and from which they were to pay their expenses, Stoll informed them that they were no longer subject to US taxation. Instead, all of their income went to a tax-exempt trust, and Stoll's minister clients could withdraw themselves from the federal tax system.[40] It is worth noting that Good was not Stoll's only religious tax-evasion client – though Stoll refused to be forthcoming with the government, he apparently sold his religiously tinged tax evasion schemes to at least thirty individuals.[41]

As with Sweet, Stoll's arguments were both frivolous and illegal. And as with Sweet, a district court shut down Stoll's operations, issuing an injunction that prohibited Stoll from selling his plans, encouraging others to fail to pay taxes, or assisting others in preparing fraudulent tax returns.[42] Unlike Sweet, though, Stoll's version of tax evasion applied solely to religious individuals, and more specifically to religious individuals who headed their own ministries. Stoll did not assert that the federal income tax was broadly inapplicable; instead, he claimed that something about religious practice made it possible for an individual to get out of most or all of her obligation to pay taxes, irrespective of her economic situation.

In spite of the frivolous nature of Sweet's and Stoll's tax-evasion schemes, Good chose to believe (as did Hovind who, in 2002, paid Stoll to reorganize the ownership structure of his ministry[43]). As one of Stoll's thirty or more clients, Good formally reorganized his ministry as a ministerial trust. He established bank accounts for the ministerial trust (using fake employer identification numbers). At the same time, he chose not to open any personal bank accounts. Instead, he commingled his money with money from his ministry.

And Good did have personal money: in addition to his ministerial and missionary work, he earned money as a carpenter, as a landscaper, as a horse trainer, and as a landlord. He deposited all of the money he earned in his various professions into ministry bank accounts, accounts over which he had complete control. And he used his ministry bank accounts to pay for his living expenses, everything from trips to Europe (which he claimed were missionary trips) to veterinary expenses, from paying his mortgage to paying for products from Walmart and Amazon.com.[44]

Still, Good claimed not to be subject to US income tax. And his argument was not merely that the government could not tax him on income he earned as a minister (although even that would misstate the reach of the tax law). Instead, he argued that, as a religious person, he did not owe taxes. Even while acknowledging that he did nonreligious work (such as carpentry), Good asserted that

> he was a man of God engaged in the work of God . . . and that everything he received or acquired belonged to God. He further contends that he is exempt from Federal taxation because his activities during the years in issue were religious. He contends that any assets he acquired were for the purpose of his ministry and any disposition of those assets should not be taxed to him.[45]

In Good's mind, then, the fact that he was religious was itself sufficient to excuse him from any obligation to pay taxes.

Of course, it is worth questioning Hovind's and Good's sincerity in asserting their exemption from federal taxes. Even assuming they were sincere in their religious belief, they specifically sought out Stoll, who sold plans to evade taxes. Both Good and Hovind ran some version of their ministries before applying Stoll's special combination of corporations sole and ministerial trusts, and Stoll does not appear to have added any spiritual value to their ministries. Moreover, their actions provide significant evidence that they were not sincere in claiming that all they had belonged to God. The bankruptcy court pointed out that, while Hovind claimed everything he owned belonged to God, he acted as if it belonged to him. Among other things, he owned the cars and a home (on which he made regular and consistent mortgage payments), and he sent his three children to a Christian private school.[46] And Good was more than willing to spend the money that putatively belonged to his ministry for his own personal consumption.

Final Thoughts on Clerical Objections to Tax

For all of the differences between Hovind, Good, Rev. Fogary, and Sister Schuster, the application of the tax law to them raises three important issues. First, although the rule that all Americans are taxable on their income generally holds true, it turns out that the tax law *does* treat clergy who have taken a vow of poverty differently than it treats other taxpayers. Although they are not always treated as agents for their Orders, as long as they work for their Order or the church, the law will view them as agents of the Order, and, as such, not subject to tax. Furthermore, the IRS does not treat the nonmonetary support (including room and board) members of these Orders receive from their Order as taxable income. The support can be treated as wages, subject to social security taxes, but only if the Order elects to have its members covered by social security.[47]

In both respects, this treatment differs radically from the treatment of non-clergy and of the nonreligious. True, like the member of a religious order, a nonreligious employee can act as an agent for their employer and they will not be taxed on the amount they earn on its behalf. An associate at a law firm, for example, may have their time billed out at $200 an hour. If they work for 2,000 hours, their firm can bill clients $400,000. Although they have created that value they will not pay taxes on the $400,000 – instead, they will pay taxes on the amount of salary their law firm pays them.

But unlike a member of a religious order, they cannot claim to be acting as an agent with respect to money they actually receive. If they worked as a secretary for a company – even for a company owned by their family, and even if they contribute all of the money back to the company – they cannot claim that they were acting as an agent for the firm, and they cannot avoid paying taxes on their salary. On the other hand, according to the IRS, a member of a religious order could.

The difference between certain religious individuals and members of religious orders does not end there, though. Taxable compensation is not limited to payments of cash: taxpayers must pay taxes on the value of in-kind compensation, too, unless that type of compensation is specifically excluded from taxes. In general, for example, employer-provided meals and lodging represent taxable compensation to employees (unless they fit within a narrow exception).[48] But the IRS currently does not tax members of religious orders who have taken vows of poverty on the support they receive from their Orders. And this represents a significant shift from generally applicable tax principles.

Second, the question of whether Rev. Fogarty and Sister Schuster owed taxes had real economic implications for them and real revenue implications for the federal government. Had they been treated as agents of their Orders, Rev. Fogarty's income from the University of Virginia and Sister Schuster's income from the National Health Services Corp would have gone untaxed. They would not have paid taxes on their income, in accordance with the IRS's rulings, and, as tax-exempt religious organizations, neither would the Society of Jesus or the Order of the Adorers of the Blood of Christ. As a result, their being treated as an agent would have reduced the federal government's revenue.

At the same time, including their salaries in their gross income represented a real economic cost for Rev. Fogarty and Sister Schuster. Because they have to include their salaries in their gross income, they also must pay taxes on it, notwithstanding the fact that they neither controlled nor benefitted directly from the money. True, if Sister Schuster is deemed to receive her salary, she can also be deemed to donate it to her Society, and take a charitable deduction.[49] But the tax law imposes two significant limitations on taxpayers' ability to deduct charitable donations. First, the charitable deduction is an itemized deduction, meaning only individuals with sufficient deductions can benefit from it. Currently, only about one-third of taxpayers itemize. Moreover, 5 percent of taxpayers claim more than 50 percent of charitable deductions.[50] Most taxpayers – possibly including Sister Schuster – simply cannot deduct their charitable contributions.

Even if Sister Schuster can itemize, she will not be able to deduct the full amount she is deemed to contribute to the Order of the Adorers of the Blood of Christ. The tax law also limits the absolute value of the deduction a taxpayer can take: an individual taxpayer (including Sister Schuster) can only take a charitable deduction for up to half of her adjusted gross income.[51] Thus, even if she itemized, when Sister Schuster earned $15,920 from the National Health Services Corps and instructed that it be paid to the Order of the Adorers of the Blood of Christ, she could not deduct more than $7,960; she would have to pay taxes (even without having access to her earnings) on the rest.

Third, it is important to point out that, contrary to the cases of Hovind and Good, Rev. Fogarty did not argue that, by virtue of being a minister and dedicating his life to God, he was not subject to the federal income tax. His argument was far narrower and more technical: he argued that, because he was acting as an agent for the Society of Jesus, he was not taxable on the income he earned from the University of Virginia. While as a practical matter that income undoubtedly represented the bulk of what he earned, there is no indication that, had he voluntarily taken on landscaping or carpentry work, he would have denied having a tax liability. Put differently, his argument was not that he was intrinsically exempt from taxes; it was that he was not subject to taxes when he acted on behalf of and in obedience to his Order.

OBJECTIONS TO SPENDING

Those who claim their religiosity exempts them from the rolls of the taxpayers are, of course, exceptional. The vast majority of religious Americans accept that the law requires them to pay taxes on their income.[52] And, in any event, most of those claiming that they are exempt from taxation because they have taken a vow of poverty or because all they have belongs to God are (at least generally) clergy. As a rule, lay members generally do not claim the same type of exemptive relationship with the kingdom of God.

That is not to say that no lay individual objects to taxation on religious grounds. But the grounds on which these religious objectors base their objections are significantly different than the grounds we saw in the previous section. Rather than claiming that they cannot be taxed, these objectors refuse to pay part or all of their taxes because they have religious objections to certain types of government spending.

These religious objections to taxpaying based on how the government spends its money can be illustrated through three different examples of individuals who protest paying their taxes because of their religious objections to government spending. First are Catholic taxpayers, some of whom object to the government paying for contraception and abortion. Second are Amish taxpayers who oppose paying social security. Third are Quakers, some of whom object to the government's military expenditures. Although their reasons – and even their techniques – for nonpayment differ from each other and from the religious individuals who claim not to be taxpayers, courts have consistently arrived at the same conclusion: there is no religious exemption from paying generally applicable taxes. Citizenship in the kingdom of God does not excuse nonpayment, and neither does sincere religious objection to the government's use of its revenue.

Catholics and Abortion

For the Catholic Church, abortion is always wrong. "Contemporary Catholic moral theology holds that abortion, as an example of unjustifiable killing, is always an intrinsic moral evil."[53] In the 1960s and the 1970s, bishops throughout the United States decried the moves to liberalize abortion laws and, in fact, used church resources to oppose legalized abortion.[54]

While the Church's opposition to abortion does not necessarily translate to lay members' views,[55] 44 percent of American Catholics believe that abortion should be illegal in most or all cases.[56] Occasionally, a Catholic's opposition to abortion transcends the purely personal and political realms, and bleeds into the world of tax protest. When it does, the protest invariably fails. Courts have consistently rejected "[a]ttempts by taxpayers to restrict the Government's use of their tax-payments."[57] This rejection occurs whether the taxpayer objected to government expenditures on religious or nonreligious grounds.

In spite of its futility, a number of people have attempted to extricate themselves from what they perceive to be a religiously untenable position – funding a government that itself funds abortion – by refusing to pay their taxes. (Their perception of the risk of funding abortion may be overstated: since 1976, federal law has prohibited federal funding to cover the cost of abortion except in cases of rape, incest, or risk to the mother's life.[58]) Like claims that religiosity excuses taxpaying, these protests have run the gamut from sincere civil disobedience to frivolous tax protests. On the civil disobedience side, we can look at Michael Pavlic. His Catholic bona fides were tremendously clear. Pavlic earned his college degree and attended a number of Catholic seminaries. After some military service, he was ordained a priest according to the Roman Catholic Rite. While Pavlic was ordained, he never had a congregation and never held himself out as a priest. Moreover, unlike Hovind and Good, he did not claim that his ordination had any bearing on his tax obligations.[59]

Yet starting in 1975, Pavlic stopped filing federal tax returns (although he filed state and local tax returns and paid those taxes, at least between 1975 and 1979). His refusal to file did not stem from any lack of income – during the years that he refused to pay taxes, he not only received a disability pension from his military service, but he also worked for various companies servicing computers, repairing calculators, and providing security.

His refusal to pay taxes instead stemmed from an article he read in *Spotlight* magazine that recommended refusing to pay taxes as a protest against government funding of abortions. The idea resonated with his sincere, religiously based objection to abortion so, without seeking legal or accounting advice, and against his wife's wishes, he stopped paying his federal income tax as a protest against abortion.

Pavlic knew that his refusal violated the law; he had to affirmatively falsify various Forms W-4 that he gave to employers in order to claim that he was exempt from withholding. And he knew that ultimately the IRS would figure out that he was not paying taxes, though he hoped that he could arrange something with the IRS to ensure that his eventual tax payments were not used to fund abortions.

The court went out of its way to acknowledge that Pavlic was not a standard tax protestor, trying solely to obstruct the administration of the tax law. Although he failed to pay the taxes he owed, he understood and acknowledged that he owed them. He also knew that he would eventually be required to pay his tax liability, and he intended to pay it. His failure to file and pay taxes – and the attendant lies he told to avoid paying – were all part of a sincere, religiously motivated protest against abortion.[60]

In spite of his sincerity and his religious motivation, the court could not "ignore his failure to file returns or pay his tax or his inexcusable filing of false W-4 forms. Feeling as strongly as he did, Pavlic nevertheless could and should have filed tax returns, as he admitted during trial, thus communicating his otherwise silent concerns about abortion funding."[61] His protest ultimately failed: in spite of his sincerity and his willingness to eventually pay his taxes, the court not only ordered him to pay back taxes and interest, but also imposed fraud penalties on him. And he did not receive any concessions about the government's ultimate use of the taxes he paid.

Gerald and Gayle Martinez appear to have been less strategic in their refusal to pay taxes. Like Pavlic, they accepted Catholic teaching that abortion is intrinsically evil. Like Pavlic, they felt that their Catholic faith required them to oppose any government funding of abortion and abortion-related education. Like Pavlic, they stopped filing their tax returns and stopped paying their federal income taxes to ensure that they did not help fund abortions.[62]

There is no indication, however, that they believed that they were trying to get concessions out of the government as to the use of their money. They merely did not want to be complicit in funding something so antithetical to their religious beliefs. And the court did not challenge the sincerity of their belief, or the fervor with which they held it. It did, however, explain that their "religious-based objection to the manner in which certain federal funds are spent does not afford them any basis for refusing to file returns or pay their taxes." True, the Bill of Rights guarantees Americans' free exercise of religion. But, the court explained, the Free Exercise Clause is not a trump card that supersedes otherwise applicable laws. In fact, the law is clear that the federal income tax does not violate taxpayers' constitutional rights – including their religious rights – even where a taxpayer objects to the manner in which the government spends its money.

Though the courts did not condone Pavlic's or the Martinezes' refusal to pay taxes, the courts also did not question the sincerity of their religious motivations for refusing to pay. But just because some religious individuals refuse to pay their taxes in good faith as a protest against abortion does not mean that all religious individuals who refuse to pay their taxes, citing abortion as a reason, are acting in good faith, though. For example, in the early 1970s, Michael Fahy filed the first page of his tax return, accompanied by a number of exhibits in which he laid out his objections to paying taxes.[63]

Fahy had plenty of objections to paying his federal income taxes. Like Pavlic and the Martinezes, he said that he refused to pay federal income taxes "because I would be compelled thereby to participate in a program which is killing thousands of unborn children. This would be a violation of my rights under the first amendment." But he leavened his religious objection to the government's spending with a number of nonreligious objections to the income tax itself. He argued that the federal income tax was unconstitutional, that the government cannot tax income from labor, and that Federal Reserve notes are not dollars, and therefore not taxable.[64]

While all of Fahy's arguments were frivolous, the court took special note of his religious argument. It summarily dismissed all of the nonreligious arguments, then addressed his religious objections to abortion separately. It accepted – or, at least, did not challenge – the sincerity of his religious objections to abortion and explained that courts have, on many occasions, rejected objections to tax on religious grounds. Fahy, said the court, had not provided any convincing arguments for why it should change course in his case.

Even though each of Fahy's points of contention – religious and secular alike – had been clearly and repeatedly found baseless by courts in the past, the court differentiated between his religious and his nonreligious arguments for not paying his taxes. As with Pavlic and the Martinezes, it assumed the sincerity of his religious objections to abortion. He lost nonetheless, but the court was more willing to engage with him, and more willing to give him the benefit of the doubt, when he said his disagreement was religious, and not constitutional.

Amish and Social Security

Inherently immoral government spending is not the only kind of spending that can provoke religious objections, and religious objection to one kind of government spending does not always mean a religious tax objector will refuse to pay *any* taxes. The Old Order Amish are broadly willing to pay taxes, but find paying Social Security taxes – and receiving Social Security benefits – incompatible with their religious beliefs and practices.

The Amish are one of several religious branches descended from the Swiss Anabaptist movement of 1525. They arrived in North America in the early 1700s, and have been relatively successful at maintaining their distinctive religious and community practices.[65] In large part, Amish religious beliefs and social behaviors date back to the Europe that they originally left. The beliefs and practices include a strong emphasis on serving God, a simple lifestyle, voluntary separation from secular world, and an emphasis on hard work. Most famously, perhaps, is their general refusal to use modern technology.[66]

Less well known, but also significant, is the social structure of Amish communities. Amish community provides a safety net for its members, minimizing economically deleterious conditions including long-term unemployment and single parenthood. Children provide for their elderly parents. And when children are unable or unwilling to do so, the Amish can fall back on a culture of mutual aid.[67]

This culture of self-sufficiency and mutual support is rooted in their reading of the Bible, which says that "whoever does not provide for relatives, and

especially for family members, has denied the faith and is worse than an unbe-
liever."[68] But this culture of religiously motivated self-sufficiency and familial support, combined with the Amish desire to separate themselves from the
world, is antithetical to Social Security, at least from the point of view of the
Old Order Amish.[69]

Social Security was born in the wake of the socially and economically disas-
trous Great Depression. Faced with widespread unemployment and poverty,
American policymakers began to internalize the need for some kind of social
insurance. The Great Depression's effects on the elderly, particularly, helped
advocates of social insurance crystallize in the American mind the need to
provide some kind of safety net for that vulnerable population.[70]

In the summer of 1934, President Franklin Roosevelt "unveiled his ambitious legislative project on economic security."[71] With President Roosevelt's
support, Congress managed to overcome contentiousness and uncertainty
and, in 1935, passed the Social Security Act, which President Roosevelt then
signed in August 1935.[72]

Social Security payments were not funded out of the Treasury's general
funds, however. Instead, Social Security was funded solely by payroll taxes.[73]
The identity of the person who writes the check for payroll taxes differs
between employees and the self-employed, but ultimately the same amount
of tax applies to both. Currently, an employee bears a 6.2 percent tax, which is
withheld and paid to the government by their employer.[74] At the same time,
the employer must pay a matching 6.2 percent tax for each employee.[75] Self-
employed individuals, on the other hand, owe the full 12.4 percent directly to
the government.[76]

Technically, an individual's payroll taxes do not fund their own retirement;
rather, current payroll taxes fund the Social Security payments to current
retirees. Still, to workers, the payroll taxes feel like insurance premiums and
pensions feel earned, and these perceptions may be by design.[77]

The Amish view participation in Social Security as violating their religious
beliefs in a number of significant ways. Accepting state aid would puncture
the separateness they have cultivated, and that they see as being religiously
mandated. It also interferes with the familial and community support the
Bible demands of them. Furthermore, it demonstrates a lack of trust in God's
promise to provide them with those things that they need.[78]

In the 1970s, Edwin Lee, a member of the Old Order Amish, decided to fol-
low his religious convictions and avoid the Social Security system altogether.
Lee was a farmer and a carpenter and, from 1970 through 1977, several other
Amish individuals worked for him on his farm and in his carpentry shop. Dur-
ing that time, he did not pay the employer share of his employees' Social
Security taxes, nor did he withhold or pay over the employee portion. When

the IRS assessed unpaid taxes – more than $27,000 – he paid just enough to allow him to file suit.[79]

He then sued, arguing that the social security taxes violated his and his employees' Free Exercise rights under the Constitution. The district court found in his favor, observing that Congress had accommodated religious objections to the self-employment Social Security tax. According to the accommodation that Congress had enacted, an individual may receive an exemption from the self-employment tax if they provide evidence that they belong to a religious group that opposes the acceptance of Social Security benefits *and* they waive all future Social Security benefits based on their self-employment.[80]

Of course, the exemption is not automatic – the Commissioner of Social Security must find that the religion does, in fact, object to the receipt of Social Security benefits, that such objection is reasonable in light of their level of living, and that the religion has been in existence since December 31, 1950.[81] This was not the first religious exemption from self-employment Social Security taxes; Congress had previously allowed ministers, members of religious orders, and Christian Science practitioners to apply for an exemption from these taxes.[82] Congress recognized, though, that these other exemptions were solely available on the basis of religious employment, not religious belief: if a minister also did nonministerial labor, they would have to pay social security taxes on their income from that labor.

While Congress recognized that some religious individuals eschewed Social Security, it did not want to provide a blanket exemption. It believed making participation in Social Security purely optional was undesirable. It also recognized that there was not necessarily consensus, even within a religion, about the religious permissibility of Social Security. Even among the Old Order Amish, there had "been some indications of a change in attitude toward social security, particularly among the younger people; some members of the Old Order Amish who have become eligible for social security benefits have claimed the benefits."[83]

Still, Congress did not think it fair that the law protected ministers' consciences, and not those of nonclergy religious individuals, so it crafted a narrow exception to the self-employment tax.[84] Interestingly enough, though, it did nothing to protect the consciences of *employees* who had religious objections to Social Security. As a result, the IRS said, Lee violated the tax law in refusing to withhold and pay over his employees' Social Security taxes. To vindicate his position – and retrieve his money – he had to file suit.

At the trial court level, things went well for Lee. The government "concede[ed] both the worthiness and the sincerity of the Amish beliefs."[85] The trial court further stated that the free exercise of one's religion "is a

fundamental, natural, absolute right, firmly entrenched in the foundation
and the history of our legal system."[86] Recognizing the fundamental right of
free exercise, as well as the fact that the tax law explicitly permitted several
religious exemptions from the self-employment Social Security tax, the trial
court found that requiring Lee to withhold and pay Social Security taxes on
his Amish employees violated his and their constitutional rights.

The Supreme Court disagreed. The statutory exemption, it held, had no
bearing on this case, because it applied specifically to self-employed taxpayers, and Lee's employees were not, by definition, self-employed. Any exemption for employees had to be constitutionally mandated, and the religious
exemption for self-employed individuals was not required by the Constitution.[87] Thus, the inquiry had to focus entirely on the constitutional status of
the tax.

The Supreme Court conceded that there was conflict between Amish
beliefs and the payment of Social Security taxes. But, the Court explained,
"not all burdens on religion are unconstitutional." Conflict between belief
and the law, standing alone, did not establish unconstitutionality. The government can burden religion where that burden is essential to an overriding
government interest.[88]

And it found a compelling government interest in the Social Security tax
regime. Essentially, the Court said, mandatory participation is necessary to
establish a widespread, functioning social safety net. Permitting voluntary participation would undermine a comprehensive national system, and would create an enormous administrative burden on the government. As such, the government had a strong and compelling interest in requiring taxpayers to pay
into the Social Security system.[89]

That compelling interest meant that Amish employees had no constitutional right to be exempt from paying Social Security taxes. While the
Supreme Court recognized that "Congress and the courts have been sensitive
to the needs flowing from the Free Exercise Clause, . . . every person cannot
be shielded from all the burdens incident to exercising every aspect of the
right to practice religious beliefs."[90] The Supreme Court came to the same
conclusion with respect to the Amish as the courts came to with respect to
abortion: one's religious convictions do not provide a constitutional right to
avoid paying taxes.

Quakers and Pacifism

While the abortion and the Amish cases dealt with religious persons who
objected to a whole category of taxation (income and social security taxes,

respectively), there are other, narrower, ways to frame religious objections to taxes. Those narrower objections can be illustrated looking at Quakers' resistance to war taxes.

The Society of Friends has embraced pacifism as a fundamental tenet of its faith since its founding in the mid-seventeenth century. During the Quakers' first two centuries, any violation of this "Peace Testimony" could result in a member's being disowned by the community. And violations of the Peace Testimony were not limited to a Quaker's personal participation in war; even paying war taxes would constitute a violation.[91] Between 1693 and 1711, the Quakers organized the first formal resistance to war taxes in America. During that period, the Quaker-controlled Pennsylvania Assembly refused requests from the Crown to help finance the England's battles with the French and the Native Americans.[92]

Over time, some Quakers dropped their absolutist stance on the Peace Testimony. During the Civil War, for example, while some Quakers believed that even paying a fee to avoid conscription violated the Peace Testimony, others allowed themselves to be conscripted into the Union army. Still other Quakers, motivated by their emancipationist beliefs, volunteered to fight in the Union army.[93]

Quakers evinced a similar split when it came to paying war taxes. Though they initially resisted, by the mid-eighteenth century, city-dwelling Quakers began to feel guilty for not contributing to the defense of frontier dwellers. Though other Quakers believed that the Peace Testimony absolutely prohibited their paying the war taxes, during the French and Indian War, the Pennsylvania Assembly voted to levy war taxes. "Clearly, Quaker unity on the war tax issue was eroding as principle gave way to practicality."[94]

By the beginning of the twentieth century, leaders of the Peace Section of the American Friends Service Committee had come to the unsettling conclusion that "most Quakers had discarded the faith's traditional peace testimony."[95] But during the Cold War, a group of Quaker pacifists launched a renewal movement and, ultimately, revivified Quaker opposition to war.[96]

Like its older strain, modern Quaker opposition to war includes conscientious objection. And, like its older strain, it includes refusal to pay taxes that fund the military and violent conflict. In comparison with both their colonial incarnation and the other religiously based tax noncompliance we have looked at, the contemporary Quaker tax protests are targeted and nuanced.

Why the nuance compared with earlier Quaker war tax protests? In part because the federal income tax differs fundamentally from the early war taxes. There is no part of the tax that is specifically allocated to fund the military or to purchase weapons, just like there is no part of the tax that was specifically allocated to fund abortions. Still, unlike federal spending on abortion, defense spending consumes a significant portion of all federal spending – about 16 percent in 2015.[97] And, like anti-abortion tax protestors, some Quaker pacifists view those expenditures as violating their religious convictions, and do not want to be complicit.

The ways by which Quaker war tax protestors try to avoid funding violence differ in their details. All share the goal of refusing to pay at least a portion of the taxes they owe, though. Many of the Quaker protestors start in the same place: they determine what percentage of federal expenditures go to the military and other war-related sources, and refuse to pay an equivalent percentage of the taxes they owe.[98] For example, Richard and Judy Jenney, a Quaker couple, attempted to take what they called a "conscience deduction." On their tax return, they explained that

> The War Resisters League states that 44% of the 1982 federal budget went for non-military purposes. We are quite willing to pay that part of our taxes. However, as a result of our religious convictions (we are both Quakers), personal beliefs (non-violence, pacifism) and professional judgment (we are both clinical psychologists) we are unwilling to support the current insane government course of action which not only condones murder but also threatens human extinction.[99]

They thus claimed a deduction that would reduce their tax liability by more than $6,000. To demonstrate that they acted out of sincere religious objections to war, rather than out of selfishness, the Jenneys promised that, rather than spend the money themselves, they would escrow it until such time as the government guaranteed that it would be used for nonwar purposes.[100]

Other war tax protestors choose not to escrow the unpaid portion of their taxes. Instead, they may donate those taxes to a charitable organization – often one that works for peace – both to demonstrate that the protest is not a matter of personal enrichment and to contribute to the well-being of humanity.[101]

Both of the strategies – and, in fact, any other strategy of war tax protest – ultimately fail, though, for the same reasons that religiously grounded tax protests against abortion and Social Security fail. That is, even though their objections to how the government spends their tax dollars is real, Quakers – and others who object to government expenditures on religious grounds – "are required to comply with the tax laws despite religious-based disagreement with the allocation of certain funds."[102]

Given the unbroken history of courts finding no First Amendment right not to pay taxes, Quaker war-tax protestors must have known in advance that their constitutional arguments would fail. In the late 1990s, though, a number of

Quakers found a new legal justification for their refusal to pay their full tax liability: RFRA.[103]

RFRA prohibits the federal government from passing legislation that burdens people's exercise of religion unless the legislation both furthers a "compelling government interest" and is the "least restrictive means" of doing so.[104] Some Quaker war protestors have argued that, in addition to looking at the permissibility of the government's using their taxes to fund war, courts must also determine whether these taxes impose an undue burden on their religious practice. Like their Free Exercise claims, though, these RFRA claims have been uniformly unavailing. Courts have consistently held that the inapplicability of RFRA to their tax claims has been well-established.[105] The voluntary compliance that undergirds the US tax system "is the least restrictive means by which the IRS furthers the compelling governmental interest in uniform, mandatory participation in the federal income tax system."[106]

Be Fruitful and Replenish the Earth

David and Margaret Klaasen lived in Marquette, Kansas, and belonged to the Reformed Presbyterian Church of North America. Among other things, their church taught that having many children was a blessing and an obligation of members. While they did not object to any particular federal spending, they, too, argued that the tax law impeded their religious practice.

How did it impede their religious practice? In essence, the alternative minimum tax increased the after-tax cost of having additional children. In January 1969, as the Johnson administration was poised to be replaced by the Nixon administration, Treasury Secretary Joseph Barr testified in front of the Congressional Joint Economic Committee that, absent reform, the country was facing a "taxpayer revolt." The revolt Secretary Barr envisioned would be led by the middle class, who, he said, paid their full taxes.

And what would precipitate their revolt? Their discovery that the wealthy were not paying their fair share of taxes. In 1967, 155 individuals with more than $200,000 of income (nearly $1.3 million in 2015 dollars) paid no federal income taxes. Worse, twenty-one taxpayers with incomes of more than $1 million failed to pay a cent in taxes.[107]

These numbers caught both the public and the Congressional imaginations. Professor Michael J. Graetz reports that in 1969, Congress received more letters about the 155 wealthy nontaxpayers than it did about any other topic – even the deeply controversial war in Vietnam. Congress immediately leapt into action and, by the end of the year, had enacted a new minimum tax, intended to prevent the wealthy from avoiding income taxes altogether.[108]

Today's alternative minimum tax is a direct descendant of the 1969 minimum tax. Though its mechanics are complicated, its theory is simple: Congress created a second income tax with a high exemption amount, relatively flat rates, and very few deductions. Taxpayers with a certain level of income must calculate their ordinary tax liability and their alternative minimum tax liability, and pay whichever amount is higher.[109]

Among the deductions lost by taxpayers who end up paying the alternative minimum tax is the personal exemption. Under the pre-2018 ordinary federal income tax, every taxpayer can deduct personal exemptions for themselves, their spouse (if they file joint returns), and for dependents. The value of the personal exemption is indexed to inflation; in 2017, the personal exemption was $4,050.[110]

While there is no direct connection between the alternative minimum tax and religious practice, it turns out that the alternative minimum tax can inadvertently burden some individuals' religious exercise. Having several children, for example, increases a taxpayer's chance of paying the alternative minimum tax. The Klassens claimed to have religious objections to birth control and abortion, objections borne out by the fact that, in 1994, they had ten children (and, in fact, by the time the Tax Court decided their case in 1998, they had thirteen). Unlike the Catholic litigants discussed earlier, though, the Klaasens did not argue that their opposition to the government's funding of birth control and abortion prohibited them from paying taxes. In fact, unlike the other religious individuals discussed in this chapter, the Klaasens never alleged that the tax law required them to directly or indirectly participate in activities to which they had religious objections. Instead, they argued that the alternative minimum tax unconstitutionally prevented them from fulfilling their religious obligations.

And how did the alternative minimum tax prevent them from fulfilling their religious obligations? By disallowing personal exemptions. Under the ordinary federal income tax, taxpayers get deductions for themselves and for certain qualified dependents, including children living at home. In 1994, the Klaasens claimed twelve such deductions, one for each parent, and one for each of ten children. In total, these personal exemptions reduced their taxable income by $29,400.

Taxpayers subject to the alternative minimum tax, however, lose their ability to claim personal exemptions. As a result, the Klaasens' alternative minimum tax liability exceeded their ordinary income tax liability, which, they argued, inhibited their ability to follow their religious beliefs. Moreover, they claimed, families like theirs were not Congress's target in enacting the alternative minimum tax. Rather, their religious beliefs, which led to their large family, inadvertently caught them in a tax trap.

The court disagreed, explaining that it was generally reluctant to find that the alternative minimum tax unconstitutionally infringed on a taxpayer's religious rights. To overcome that reluctance, the Klaasens needed to show that the alternative minimum tax did more than merely make their religious practice more expensive – they needed to show that the law was based upon a "classification grounded on religion." Otherwise, because deductions are a matter of legislative grace, whatever its effects on their religious practice, the alternative minimum tax was constitutional, even as applied to the Klaasens.[111]

The Tax Court was undoubtedly correct, if unnecessarily hesitant, in its conclusion. But answering the constitutional question does not answer the question of *whether* the tax law should have granted an accommodation to the Klaasens. And it is understandable that the court did not address this normative question – it was beyond the scope of the court's duty. The question lies, instead, with Congress, or possibly with the IRS's enforcement discretion.

Penalties for Religious Conscience

Not only is religious tax protest futile, but it carries a cost. Religious tax protestors must pay the taxes they owed and failed to pay, and any accrued interest on those taxes. In addition to taxes and interest, these protestors may find themselves subject to penalties.

The tax law provides that the IRS can penalize taxpayers up to $5,000 for filing a tax return taking a frivolous position.[112] The IRS has asserted the penalty against Quakers arguing that their religion does not permit them to pay for war, and courts have upheld its determination that, while holding such religious beliefs is not frivolous, asserting that their religiously motivated pacifist beliefs justify nonpayment of tax is, and warrants the penalty.[113]

And arguing a religious right not to pay taxes in court potentially exposes religious tax protestors to further penalties. The Tax Court can fine a taxpayer who makes frivolous arguments up to $25,000, and other courts can impose a penalty of up to $10,000.[114] The penalty does not depend on whether the taxpayer's religious objections are sincere, only on whether the argument they raise is frivolous.[115] As a result, a sincerely held religious objection to paying some or all of an individual's taxes can result in their paying not only the taxes and interest they owe, but potentially thousands of dollars of penalties.

RELIGIOUS CONVICTIONS VS. THE TAX LAW

The law is clear: the Constitution does not require the tax law to treat religious individuals differently from nonreligious individuals. Even where the spending permitted by the tax – or the tax itself – conflicts directly with a taxpayer's sincerely held religious convictions, the government's interest in an administrable revenue system outweighs a taxpayer's religious objections.

And yet we have seen a number of religious exceptions from the generally applicable tax law. The Amish, for example, do not have to pay self-employment taxes, while Jesuits who have taken a vow of poverty and who work for their religious orders do not have to recognize income from that work. If these exemptions are not constitutionally mandated, where do they come from?

They are not exempt because of some inherent incompatibility between their faith and the tax law. They are exempt because of a deliberate – and perhaps reasoned – decision to exempt them. And the gulf between incompatibility and deliberate decision is vast. This gulf means that religious taxpayers cannot get their tax accommodations from the judiciary, which, absent some constitutional infirmity, is limited to applying the tax law to parties who dispute the fact or amount of their tax liability. And, as we have seen, there is no constitutional infirmity in fully applying federal taxes to religious individuals. Instead, religious accommodation comes almost exclusively from the legislature.[116]

The Amish exemption from paying self-employment taxes illustrates the reach and limitations of relying on the legislature for religious exemptions. The tax law exempts self-employed Amish individuals from the obligation to pay Social Security taxes, in spite of the fact that a nonreligious self-employed individual (or, for that matter, a self-employed religious individual who does not belong to a sufficiently old religion that objects to Social Security) must pay.

Obtaining that exemption did not come without cost, though. When social security was extended to cover self-employed farmers in 1955, many Old Order Amish protested, refusing to obtain a social security number or pay their social security taxes.[117] The IRS filed liens against some of those Amish farmers who refused to pay their taxes, sold their farm animals to pay the farmers' tax debts, and, eventually, even arrested one Amish farmer.

After the arrest, representatives of the Amish, the IRS, and congressional leaders met and arranged for a temporary moratorium. During and after the moratorium, Amish leaders engaged in an extensive lobbying campaign to have an exception added to the social security law. Over the objections of the Department of Health, Education, and Welfare, Congress enacted the limited exception we have today in 1965.[118]

Even with all of that work, the Amish legislative victory was limited. Because there is no constitutional imperative to exempt the Amish from paying Social Security taxes, courts cannot and will not expand the exemption.

In fact, in the wake of the Supreme Court's decision in Lee, courts have consistently policed the narrow scope of the exemptions. One court held, for example, that qualifying for the example required an individual not only to have a sincere objection to Social Security; because the litigant did not belong to a religious sect with established tenets or teachings opposed to social security, the exception did not apply to him.[119] Similarly, the courts held that the statutory exemption was unavailable to a former member of the Old Order Amish who had been excommunicated. Even though he continued to hold the Amish religious objections to Social Security, because he was no longer a member, he did not fit within the statutory exemption.[120]

If the Amish want to avoid paying Social Security taxes altogether, then, they will have repeat their victory from the 1960s and again convince Congress that it should add explicit exemptions to the tax law. And there is no guarantee that they will win, as pacifist Quakers have learned. In the early 1970s, Professor Joseph Sax, a member of the faculty of the University of Michigan Law School, drafted a bill – in its current incarnation called the "Religious Liberty Trust Fund Act" – on behalf of a group of Ann Arbor-based Quakers. His bill was first introduced in Congress in 1972, and introduced (sometimes with minor changes) in basically every Congress since.[121]

In its current form, the proposed bill would establish a trust fund that would hold the taxes paid by qualifying conscientious objectors. The government could use money from the trust fund to fund nonmilitary spending.[122] Because they have no constitutional right to prevent their tax dollars from going to pay for war, this bill would allow Quakers and other conscientious objectors to pay the full amount of their taxes due without violating their religious obligations. But simply lobbying for change – even when the lobbying is accompanied by drafted legislation – does not ensure success. In spite of the sincere religious motivations underlying the bill, Congress has not chosen to enact it.[123]

The failure of the Religious Liberty Trust Fund Act demonstrates the problematic (for religious objectors) nature of relying on the good graces of the legislature for religious accommodation. Where it is up to the legislature, majoritarianism remains a real concern.[124] Members of small, unpopular, or poor religions do not have the same access to legislators or resources to lobby them and, as a result, are less likely to successfully obtain the tax accommodation they seek. In fact, even though the Amish had early success, their success was limited only to self-employed individuals. Amish employees and employers – who may have an equally strong religious objection to paying social security taxes – have not received (and, in fact, appear not to have lobbied for) the same legislative dispensation as self-employed Amish.

Almost exclusively is not *exclusively*, though. In some cases, religiously based exemptions from the tax law come from the IRS's enforcement decisions. The limited exemption for Jesuits (and others who belong to religious orders and have taken vows of poverty) is a matter of IRS discretion. Nothing in the Internal Revenue Code provides that when these members of religious orders work for their order, they will not include the amount in their taxable income. Instead, it is the result of a series of IRS rulings and practices.

In spite of the fact that religious exemptions from generally applicable tax laws cannot exist without specific legislative or administrative dispensation, the taxation of religious individuals differs from standard taxation in a number of ways beyond what we have seen in this chapter. The next several chapters will explore those places where religious taxation differs, and will explore how and why those differences exist.

The development of these exemptions has, in large part, occurred in an ad hoc, accidental, and unconnected manner. Requests for exemption have been granted or denied in a vacuum, without considering other exemptions granted or denied by the tax law. Such an accidental and untheorized set of loosely related regimes is problematic and potentially dangerous.[125] To remedy the accidental nature of the tax law's approach to religious exceptionalism, after looking at the how and why, the book will take a normative look at when the taxation of religious individuals *should* differ from the taxation of nonreligious individuals. Ultimately, it will provide both a constitutional and a tax policy framework for evaluating religious requests for different tax treatment.

5

Housing Clergy

In 1924, the First Methodist Church in Chicago completed and dedicated its Chicago Temple. The Chicago Temple was the fifth of the congregation's buildings to occupy the corner of Clark and Washington in the Chicago Loop. At twenty-eight stories, it was one of the tallest buildings in the city at the time. Since it was built, the church has occupied the first three floors and the spire, and has rented the rest of the building to commercial tenants.

In 1942, the congregation hired Dr. Charles R. Goff as its minister. Prior to his ministry in Chicago, Dr. Goff preached at a church in Rockford, Illinois. While in Rockford, he and his wife lived in a parsonage near the church. In Chicago, though, that living arrangement was impossible – Dr. Goff and his wife could not find housing near the Chicago Temple.

The spire, though, was unoccupied. The church had plans to install a small chapel on the top, a chapel ultimately funded by the widow of Charles Walgreen as a memorial to her late husband. Tired of his commute, Dr. Goff realized that it would be possible to transform the rest of the spire into a living space. In the late 1940s, at a cost of about $65,000, the church transformed the three floors in the spire into a three-bedroom parsonage for Dr. Goff and his wife. Since then, the senior pastor of the First Methodist Church has lived high above downtown Chicago, commuting only the several hundred feet from the top of the building to the bottom.[1]

The Chicago Temple parsonage offers its resident benefits beyond an easy commute. Rents in Chicago are expensive; one study found that in the downtown neighborhood where the Chicago Temple is located, the median residential rent was $1,830 per bedroom in February 2015.[2] Assuming that the parsonage would command at least median rent (which, given its location and its height seems a fair assumption), the housing benefit alone is worth at least $21,960 annually.[3] But the senior pastor in all likelihood does not pay any taxes on the value of the parsonage.

In fact, the modern federal income tax has allowed ministers to avoid paying taxes on the value of housing they receive from their churches almost since its original passage. Congress enacted the predecessor to today's parsonage allowance in 1921. In its original form, the parsonage allowance permitted clergy to avoid paying taxes on the rental value of church-provided housing. Thirty-three years later, Congress expanded the exemption to include not only housing that the church provided in kind, but also housing stipends paid to clergy in cash.[4]

The parsonage allowance provides a significant tax benefit, but provides that benefit exclusively to a subset of religious taxpayers. And unlike the various religious theories of exemption from generally applicable tax laws discussed in the previous chapter, there is explicit statutory authority allowing this religious tax benefit. There is not, though, a compelling tax policy justification for the parsonage allowance. In fact, there is widespread (albeit not universal) agreement that the parsonage allowance violates the Establishment Clause of the Constitution.[5]

NONCASH COMPENSATION AND TAXES

In general, taxpayers are taxable on any compensation they receive, whether that compensation comes in the form of cash, property, or services. Where a taxpayer receives property or services as compensation, they must determine the fair market value of the property and services they received, and include those amounts on their tax return alongside their cash compensation.[6]

Though the tax law *could* require employees to include everything they receive from their employers in gross income, Congress has provided a number of exceptions to this general rule. For example, the tax law allows employees to exclude a number of types of employer-provided fringe benefits, ranging from employee discounts on products sold by the employer to the employer's reimbursement of certain moving expenses.[7] To the extent a fringe benefit falls within a category excluded by the Internal Revenue Code, an employee can receive that benefit without paying taxes on it.

Perhaps the centerpiece of tax-free employer-provided benefits is the exclusion for health insurance. Employer-provided health insurance represents real economic benefit to employees; empirical evidence indicates that to move from a job that does not provide insurance to a job that does requires an individual to take a significant cut in their cash wages.[8]

It makes sense that receiving noncash compensation would require an individual to give up some portion of their cash compensation. Without employer-provided health insurance, an employee who wanted to buy health insurance would need to use some portion of their cash compensation to purchase health insurance. Where their employer provides insurance, they no longer have to spend money to buy it themselves. As such, they can maintain the same level of consumption while spending less money.

And excluding that type of compensation from gross income makes it even more valuable to a taxpayer. To illustrate why, imagine that Jane earns $50,000 a year and pays taxes at a 20 percent rate. On her $50,000 income, she will pay $10,000 of taxes and be left with $40,000. Out of that $40,000, she will have to pay for everything she needs, including health insurance.

Assume that both she and her employer can purchase health insurance for $5,000. If Jane has to buy insurance herself, she will have $35,000 left after taxes and insurance premiums to pay for everything else she needs. If her employer provides her health insurance, though – and assuming she does not have to include the value of the health insurance in her gross income – the calculation changes significantly, even if her employer requires her to bear the full cost of the insurance by reducing her cash wages by $5,000.

In that case, Jane will receive $45,000 in compensation. At a 20 percent rate, she will pay $9,000 in taxes, leaving her with $36,000. *But she does not need to purchase health insurance*; her employer took care of that purchase for her. The exclusion of employer-provided health insurance from Jane's taxable income has increased her after-tax compensation by $1,000.[9]

In this simplified example, the employer is indifferent to whether it pays Jane using cash or health insurance – either way, Jane's compensation costs the employer $50,000. But if the employer can purchase insurance that would cost Jane $5,000 for less than $5,000, paying a portion of her salary in kind is advantageous to the employer, as well. If, for example, the employer can purchase insurance that would cost Jane $5,000 for $4,000 (because, perhaps, of the economies of scale implicit in buying insurance for many employees), her employer can provide Jane with the $36,000 of after-tax, after-insurance benefit at a cost of $49,000 (that is, $45,000 cash plus $4,000 for health insurance).

Allowing employers to pay a portion of employees' salaries with untaxed compensation can benefit both employees and employers. But the benefit comes at a cost: it reduces federal revenue, which in turn means other taxpayers must pay more to make up for the lost revenue.

THE PARSONAGE ALLOWANCE

Like the exemptions for fringe benefits and for employer-provided health insurance, the parsonage allowance permits taxpayers to ignore certain employer-provided benefits in calculating their gross income. Unlike the exemptions for fringe benefits and for health insurance, though, the parsonage allowance is only available to a certain class of taxpayers: ministers of the gospel.

Early in the life of the modern federal income tax, the Treasury Department grappled with whether taxpayers needed to include employer-provided housing in their gross income at all. In 1919, it decided that seamen did not have to report the value of board and lodging provided to them by their employer, at least as long as the board and lodging were provided for the convenience of the employer.[10] Subsequently, the Treasury Department issued regulations providing that, in certain circumstances, employer-provided housing would be exempt from taxation. Basically, the Treasury Department provided that where the housing was compensatory, it was taxable. If it was provided for the convenience of the employer, though, the tax law would assume employer-provided housing was noncompensatory and, as a result, nontaxable.[11] Treasury followed up the new regulation by clarifying that housing provided to cannery workers[12] and to hospital employees[13] could qualify for this exclusion.

Clergy, however, could not qualify for this exemption. At the same time it was creating and applying its housing exemption to certain employees, Treasury categorically denied its availability to clergy. Unlike those situations in which housing was provided for the convenience of the employer, the Treasury Department believed that where a church allowed its clergy to live in its parsonage for free, "the fair rental value of the parsonage is considered a part of his compensation for services rendered and as such should be reported as income."[14] Because the Treasury Department did not explain its reasoning, it is impossible to ascertain why it decided that a church could never provide tax-free housing to its clergy, while other types of employers could.

Congress disagreed with Treasury's conclusion. In 1921, it enacted the parsonage allowance, which provided that gross income did not include the "rental value of a dwelling house and appurtenances thereof furnished to a minister of the gospel as part of his compensation."[15] In its initial incarnation, Congress appears to have meant for the parsonage allowance to overrule the Treasury Department's limitations and equalize the tax treatment of clergy and nonclergy. Because some nonclergy taxpayers could exclude the value of employer-provided housing from their gross income, Congress believed it was only fair to allow clergy to do the same.

In its zeal to equalize the tax treatment of clergy and nonclergy, though, Congress overshot. Even if Congress intended for the parsonage allowance to "achiev[e] tax justice for clergy who were required to live in a parsonage owned by the church,"[16] by eliminating the convenience-of-the-employer test, it also benefitted clergy who were not required to live in a church-owned parsonage. That is, clergy could exclude the value of church-provided housing even if the employer-church provided that housing for purely compensatory reasons.

In 1954, Congress codified Treasury's exemption of qualified (nonclergy) employer-provided housing.[17] That same year, it liberalized the statutory parsonage allowance even further. Until 1954, the language of the parsonage allowance only exempted a church's in-kind provision of housing. Treasury held the line, ruling that "the statute applies only to cases where a parsonage is furnished to a minister and not to cases where an allowance is made to cover the cost of a parsonage."[18] Several courts disregarded the plain language of the law, though, holding that if the tax law exempted the provision of ministerial housing in kind, it must also exempt the payment of a housing stipend to ministers.[19]

Congress stepped in to resolve the disagreement between Treasury and the courts. Representative Peter F. Mack, Jr. introduced a bill that sided with these courts. A Baptist organization alerted him to the fact that a minister could receive in-kind housing tax-free, but if, instead, ministersreceived a housing stipend (either because the church did not own any housing it could provide or for other reasons), they had to pay taxes on that amount. Rep. Mack believed that this state of affairs was discriminatory, at least between different denominations. A broad range of churches agreed, and supported his bill.[20]

Ultimately, Congress adopted his proposal to "remove[] the discrimination in existing law."[21] As part of its overhaul of the Internal Revenue Code, Congress expanded the tax-exempt parsonage allowance to include *either* church-provided housing or "the rental allowance paid to [a minister] as part of his compensation, to the extent used by him to rent or provide a home."[22] In addition, the revised parsonage allowance replaced the words "dwelling house and appurtenances thereof" with the word "home."[23] This latter change appears to have been purely stylistic; the Senate Committee on Finance said that this part of the new law did not substantively change the prior parsonage allowance.[24]

Even after Congress expanded the parsonage allowance, the IRS worked to hold the line against abuse. In 1971, it addressed the question of whether a minister could exclude his full compensation from taxation by having the church designate the full amount as a housing stipend. The IRS ruled that he could not; instead, it said, the amount a minister could exclude from income was limited to the "fair rental value" of the minister's home, including furnishings and appurtenances, as well as the cost of utilities. A church could, of course, designate more of its minister's compensation as a housing allowance, but such a designation would be ineffectual for tax purposes, and the minister would have to pay taxes on the amount of the designated allowance in excess of the fair rental value of the house.[25]

More than two decades later, Richard Warren, the founder of Saddleback Valley Community Church, challenged the IRS's ruling. Between 1993 and 1995, the church designated all of Warren's compensation as a housing stipend. Warren chose not to exclude the full amount of his compensation though; instead, he excluded the amount he spent on various housing-related expenses, including his mortgage and utility payments, amounts he spent on furnishing, landscaping, repairing, and maintaining the property, and the real property taxes and homeowner's insurance premiums he paid. Warren paid taxes on the amount of his putative housing stipend left over after those expenses.

Even the amounts he spent on his housing-related expenses, though, exceeded the fair rental value of his home by about $20,000 in each of the three years. The IRS demanded that he pay taxes on those amounts, arguing that Congress had intended to limit the parsonage allowance to the lesser of the amount a minister spent on their home or the fair rental value of a minister's home.

The Tax Court disagreed, holding that the Internal Revenue Code imposed no fair rental value limitation on the amount of the parsonage allowance, and that the legislative history did not demonstrate Congressional intent to create such a limit. As such, it upheld Warren's exclusion.[26] The IRS appealed the Tax Court's ruling.[27]

Prior to deciding the case, the Court of Appeals decided, *sua sponte*, to explore the constitutionality of the housing stipend. It requested briefing on the constitutionality from both parties and, in addition, appointed Erwin Chemerinsky, at the time a professor at the USC Gould School of Law, to provide an *amicus* brief, providing the court with a nonparty argument about the constitutionality of tax-exempt housing allowances for ministers.[28]

The court's move terrified Congress. Representative James Ramstad called it "one of the most obvious cases of judicial overreach in recent memory." The Court of Appeals, he said, was "poised to inflict a devastating tax increase on America's clergy. Unless Congress acts quickly, the eighty-one year-old housing tax exclusion for members of the clergy will be struck down by judicial overreach on the part of America's most reversed and most activist circuit court."[29]

Though technically Rep. Ramstad was incorrect – the court was only considering constitutionality of the forty-eight-year-old housing stipend, not the eighty-one-year-old in-kind exemption[30] – Congress acted to prevent the "devastating tax increase of $2.3 billion" that clergy risked facing over the subsequent five years.[31] The House and the Senate quickly and unanimously passed the Clergy Housing Allowance Clarification Act of 2002. The Act codified the IRS's position that a minister's excludable rental allowance cannot exceed the fair rental value of the property (including furnishings and appurtenances) plus the cost of utilities.[32]

The newly codified fair rental value provision only applied prospectively though. The Act also provided that, irrespective of what the regulations or IRS rulings said, the fair rental value limitation did not apply to any year prior to 2002.[33] On its face, this kind of retroactive reversal of the IRS, while at the same time prospectively codifying the IRS's position, appears odd. Congress chose to implement the restrictions in this manner, though, to moot the case in front of the Ninth Circuit so that the court could not rule on the constitutionality of the housing stipend.[34]

Although the compromise legislation imposed significant limits on the amount of untaxed housing allowance clergy could receive, churches almost universally favored the new legislation. Rep. Ramstad said that it was "important to virtually every religious congregation in America, to every church, every temple, every synagogue, and every mosque."[35] Without the parsonage allowance, pastors explained, either their tax bills would go up, reducing their after-tax income, or their churches would have to make up the difference. And making up the difference, he argued, might force churches to "literally... divert dollars from constructing a Sunday school playground to send it to the IRS."[36]

Congress's plan worked. The parties agreed to dismiss the appeal and, even though Professor Chemerinsky opposed its dismissal, the Ninth Circuit denied his motion.[37] As a result, the statutory parsonage allowance today looks identical to how it looked in 2002: ministers of the gospel do not have to pay taxes on church-provided housing. If a minister's church does not provide housing, the minister can, instead, exclude a housing allowance, provided that allowance does not exceed the fair rental value of their home.[38]

Even after the 2002 restrictions on the scope of the parsonage allowance, it provides clergy with broad benefits. The tax law is clear that a minister can use their parsonage allowance to purchase a home or to pay their mortgage.[39] If a minister could also deduct the mortgage interest they paid, that would provide them with a double tax benefit: they could pay their mortgage (including interest) with untaxed dollars, and then deduct a portion of the amount they paid against their otherwise-taxable income.

In 1983, the IRS tried to prevent this double benefit. It issued a ruling that denied deductions for mortgage interest and property taxes to the extent they were allocable to the parsonage allowance a minister received from their church.[40] Again, Congress reversed the IRS's position, explicitly providing that ministers who receive in-cash parsonage allowances can deduct the mortgage interest and property taxes they pay.[41]

Ministers may also be able to receive parsonage allowances for second homes. Philip Driscoll, an ordained minister, owned a principal home in Cleveland, Tennessee, and a lake home nearby. The church that employed Driscoll paid him a parsonage allowance with respect to both homes; Driscoll did not pay taxes on any of his parsonage allowance. A closely divided Tax Court voted seven to six that the plain language of the parsonage allowance did not limit the benefit to a minister's principal residence. As such, it allowed Driscoll to exclude the full amount he received from his gross income.[42]

The Court of Appeals for the Eleventh Circuit reversed. It held that the Tax Court had misconstrued the allowance, and that the plain language of the provision, combined with Congress's intent in enacting it and the Supreme Court's admonition that income exclusions be narrowly construed, militated in favor of the government. According to the Court of Appeals, the parsonage allowance is only available for the fair rental value of a single home.[43]

In spite of the Eleventh Circuit's decision, a minister who does not live in Alabama, Florida, or Georgia may be able to receive a parsonage allowance for more than one home. Though the Tax Court was closely divided, it ultimately came to the conclusion that the parsonage allowance was broad enough to apply to multiple residences. And, even though it is bound to apply the Eleventh Circuit's decision to ministers who live within the jurisdiction of the Eleventh Circuit, it can decline to follow that decision for cases that would appeal to other circuits.[44]

"MINISTERS OF THE GOSPEL"

The parsonage allowance, both in its initial incarnation and in its current version, exempts housing provided to "ministers of the gospel."[45] Whatever Congress meant by *gospel*, the plain language of the parsonage allowance seems to apply solely to Christian clergy; "Jewish, Moslem, and Buddhist clergymen are obviously not 'ministers of the gospel.'"[46]

Such a literal reading would clearly violate the Establishment Clause of the Constitution. Although the Supreme Court's Establishment Clause jurisprudence is in many respects incoherent and contradictory,[47] it is clear that the Establishment Clause prohibits the government from preferring one religion to another.[48]

The IRS and the courts have worked to fix this apparent unconstitutionality. In 1958 (more than a quarter century after the enactment of the parsonage allowance!), the IRS explored whether an individual who performed duties generally performed by a rabbi could qualify as a "minister of the gospel."

In its ruling, the IRS never says whether the individual in question was, in fact, a rabbi. But he was employed at a Jewish community center and temple. As a prerequisite to his taking the job, he had done post-graduate religious study, and had been ordained by a theological seminary. His duties generally involved preparing and delivering sermons, conducting services for children and young teenagers, and supervising bar mitzvahs and other religious preparations of children. He was also responsible for assisting the rabbi and, occasionally, for doing administrative work.

The IRS determined that the work this individual did constitute "the conduct of religious worship or the ministration of sacerdotal functions according to the tenets and practices of the Jewish faith." Given that conduct, and the fact that he had been ordained, the IRS found that he qualified as a minister of the gospel for purposes of the parsonage allowance, and that he qualified to receive housing or a housing stipend tax free.[49]

The following year, the IRS decided that neither "ministers of music" (who were in charge of a church's choir and music program) nor "ministers of education" (who were in charge of Sunday School and youth training) qualified as ministers of the gospel for purposes of the parsonage allowance. Because neither was ordained, commissioned or licensed as a minister of the gospel, the IRS decided that they did not qualify for the parsonage allowance.[50]

Based on the criteria it had established for the ministers of music and education, the IRS subsequently decided that an unordained Jewish cantor also did not qualify as a minister of the gospel.[51] The IRS's move here is odd, though: the standard it established with regard to ministers of music and education was largely circular and inapplicable to nonChristians. In essence, the IRS said that the ministers of music and education were not ministers of the gospel, and therefore did not qualify for the parsonage allowance, because they were not ordained as ministers of the gospel. But under no circumstance would a Jewish cantor be ordained as a minister of the gospel.

The Tax Court disagreed with the IRS, holding that a cantor did qualify for the parsonage allowance.[52] The IRS refused to acquiesce to the Tax Court's decision, though, for another twelve years. (*Nonacquiescence* means that the IRS disagrees with a court's holding and will not treat it as precedential.)[53] Nearly twenty years after its original determination, the IRS finally acknowledged the uncomfortable nature of its previous decision. It determined that, although cantors were not required to get a formal degree from a higher ecclesiastical body, they did go through training and were certified. As such, the IRS revoked its earlier ruling and, instead, looked to the function of a cantor within his own religious tradition. In its new ruling, the IRS held that although the cantor was not formally ordained, he was licensed by the congregation he served. The IRS decided that, because cantors provide the worship, sacerdotal, and educational functions the Judaism requires, cantors would qualify for the parsonage allowance.[54]

While the courts and the IRS have only explicitly dealt with Christian and Jewish clergy in considering the parsonage allowance, "minister of the gospel" reaches more broadly than just these two religions. The Tax Court has recognized that even though "'minister of the gospel' is phrased in Christian terms, we are satisfied that Congress did not intend to exclude those persons who are the equivalent of 'ministers' in other religions. Nomenclature alone is not determinative."[55] Similarly, other courts have recognized that the parsonage allowance "is non-sectarian in nature as it clearly applies to clergy of all faiths."[56] To qualify for the untaxed parsonage allowance, an individual must receive the allowance in exchange for services that are ordinarily the duties of a minister of the gospel, as that phrase has been interpreted by the IRS and the courts.[57]

NOT JUST CLERGY

In fact, even taking into account the expansive sectarian scope of the parsonage allowance would cause one to underestimate its generosity. The parsonage allowance is available to a much larger set of individuals than one would intuitively expect. In 1970, the IRS ruled that an ordained minister who serves on the faculty of a church-affiliated college can take advantage of the parsonage allowance. In that case, the religious college was governed by a board of directors that was under the control of the church's elders. Every teacher at the school was a member of the church in good standing, as were a majority of the students. Moreover, all of the subjects taught at the school, from math to languages, were taught with an emphasis on religious principles. Under these circumstances, the IRS decided that the college was an integral agency of the church, and that serving on the faculty fell within the exercise of the minister's ministry.[58]

There are scores of colleges in the United States that probably qualify as integral agencies of a church, and any ordained minister who teaches at one of those schools, irrespective of the subject taught, qualifies for the parsonage allowance. Until 1986, Wake Forest was such an integral agency of the Southern Baptist Convention. Between the 1950s and the severance of the school's close relationship with the Southern Baptist Convention, Wake Forest provided ordained ministers on its faculty with a housing allowance.

Unsurprisingly, faculty in the religion department took the benefit, but members of the education and chemistry departments did, too. In the final years that Wake Forest designated parsonage allowances, about a dozen faculty members took the benefit, receiving $15,000 each year in untaxed compensation.[59]

Although the parsonage allowance seems to be available to a far broader group of people than we would intuitively believe it should apply to, the IRS has attempted (perhaps quixotically) to police the boundary between ministers' employment that qualifies for the parsonage allowance and employment that does not. It has clarified, for example, that not all service an ordained minister performed for a church-affiliated entity qualifies the minister to receive an untaxed parsonage allowance. The IRS determined that an ordained minister who worked at a retirement home affiliated with – but not controlled by – the minister's denomination could not exclude compensation that the retirement home had designated as an exempt housing allowance from his gross income. Compensation for services performed for an entity other than the church would only qualify for the parsonage allowance if the entity were an "integral agency" of the church.[60]

It should come as no surprise, though, that the IRS's clarification has not entirely succeeded at policing these boundaries. Although the IRS has clearly stated that the parsonage allowance is only available to ordained ministers (or their nonChristian equivalents) in compensation for services performed for integral agencies of the church, in fact, religious taxpayers frequently cross that line.

Biola University is a private Christian university in Southern California. Its faculty, staff, and students are all professing Christians, and it provides an education steeped in Christianity.[61] It is not, however, owned by or affiliated with a particular Christian denomination. As a result, Biola does not qualify as an integral agency of a church.

Still, some Biola faculty take advantage of the parsonage allowance. In its faculty handbook, Biola acknowledges that it does not technically qualify to pay untaxed housing stipends to its faculty. Still, it says, in practice "many [nondenominational] schools do feel that there is justification in offering the allowance." While warning its professoriate that there is no way to predict the outcome of an audit, the school implicitly recommends that qualifying faculty take the benefit, writing that to the school's knowledge "the housing allowance itself has never been disallowed to faculty assigned to the University's biblical studies and professional seminary programs."[62]

While faculty members ultimately have to decide whether to take the housing allowance, the school is complicit in their decision. A minister of the gospel cannot decide for herself that a portion of her salary represents a housing allowance. Rather, even if she performs qualifying services, the relevant portion of her salary must be designated by her employer as a parsonage allowance.[63] Biola (and perhaps other nondenominational schools) appears willing to make that designation.

<h2 style="text-align:center">TREATING CLERGY PREFERENTIALLY</h2>

Clearly, the parsonage allowance benefits churches and their clergy, in much the same way as the untaxed provision of health insurance benefits employers and employees. While health insurance is a virtual necessity in the contemporary United States, housing is an absolute necessity, something which all employees need to acquire.

As a result, it makes sense that a minister would be willing to accept a portion of their salary in the form of either a housing stipend or housing. By paying for its minister's housing, the church can reduce the amount it pays them by roughly the fair rental value of the home: because the minister does not need to pay rent, they can afford to forgo that portion of their salary.

And, in much the same way as the earlier health insurance example, the tax benefit reduces the cost even further. To illustrate this reduction of costs, imagine a minister in the 25 percent tax bracket. If rent cost them $25,000 a year, and they need $50,000 to live on after taxes and rent, the church has to pay them $100,000 a year. But if, instead, it can provide them with an untaxed housing stipend, the church can reduce the cost of employing the minister to just less than $92,000. The $25,000 housing stipend would go untaxed and a pre-tax salary of $67,000 would leave the minister with just over $50,000 after taxes. As a result of exempting a minister's housing stipend, the minister earning $92,000 can engage in the same amount of consumption as a nonminister earning $100,000.

And the cost to the church may be significantly less if it owns housing that it provides to its minister, depending on its costs in maintaining the property. In the most extreme case, where the church faces no costs in carrying and maintaining the property, the cost of employing a minister drops from $100,000 to $67,000. And, as long as the property costs the church less than $25,000 to maintain, providing housing in-kind is better for the church either than paying the full cost of the minister's salary in pre-tax dollars *or* providing a housing stipend.

Though Congress explained that its goal in providing for the tax-free treatment of housing stipends was to eliminate discrimination between churches that owned parsonages and those that did not, its inclusion does not, then, create complete parity between the two. Still, the government effectively subsidizes the labor costs of both types of churches (and of religious schools, and other employers that can claim to be integral agencies of churches).

Of course, whether or not the current parsonage allowance discriminates between denominations, it clearly treats religious and nonreligious taxpayers differently; by its terms, the parsonage allowance is available only to ministers of the gospel, however that phrase is defined.

It is worth noting that, even today, the parsonage allowance is not the only provision in the tax law permitting taxpayers to ignore employer-provided housing when calculating their income. Remember, as early as 1919, the Treasury Department determined that employer-provided housing was not taxable where it was paid for noncompensatory reasons; it went on to develop the "convenience of the employer" test. Within a decade, though, both the IRS and the courts were issuing seemingly contradictory rulings, attuned to the facts of the cases at hand without providing any significant analysis of *why* one employer's provision of housing was compensatory, while the next employer's was not.[64] In 1954, at the same time it expanded the parsonage allowance, Congress also codified Treasury's general exemption for employer-provided housing,[65] the exemption that appears to have led directly to the development of the parsonage allowance.

But, while there continue to be minor differences between the tax treatment of ministers who receive in-kind housing and those who receive a housing stipend, that difference is nothing compared to the difference between ministers who can exclude employer-provided housing from their taxes and nonministers who can. Under the codified general exemption, a nonminister employee can only exclude employer-provided housing from their gross income if their employer required them, as a condition of their employment, to accept the housing and if the housing is located on the employer's premises.[66]

The differences between the parsonage allowance and the general exemption of employer-provided housing are stark. In the first instance, qualifying for the parsonage allowance has only two prerequisites: that an individual be a minister of the gospel and that their employer church either provide them with housing or designate a portion of their salary as a housing allowance. Outside of that, though, they can live anywhere that they want, and they have the discretion to choose. For a minister, the church's provision of housing can be expressly compensatory, and they can still exclude it from their gross income.

By contrast, the impediments the tax law puts in front of qualifying for the standard housing exemption attempt to ensure that the employer-provided housing benefits the employer, and the employee's benefit is merely ancillary. Essentially, the requirements that an employee must meet to qualify ensure that the employee be available for work at all times, or otherwise be able to fulfill the employer's needs.[67]

And qualification is not the only difference between the standard and the ministerial housing allowances. For nonclergy employees, only in-kind housing qualifies for the exemption from tax. Under current tax law, a cash housing stipend to nonclergy is always treated as taxable income, even if the employer designates the stipend as a housing stipend. It is, in fact, taxable to an employee even if the employer requires them to use that stipend to pay for housing.

That clergy are treated differently for tax purposes than nonclergy does not mean, of course, that there is no underlying economic logic or justification for the different treatment. Arguably, the principal benefit being provided by the parsonage allowance is the government subsidizing churches' payroll costs. (That benefit may accrue entirely to the church, entirely to the minister, or may be split between the two, depending on how they allocate the after-tax savings.) But that is not necessarily wrong: the government subsidizes *most* employers' payroll costs. The tax law allows employers to deduct the amount they pay in salaries and other compensation, provided the salaries are not excessive.[68] The deduction effectively means that the government bears a portion of the employer's payroll costs.[69]

Churches, however, do not pay taxes.[70] As a result, they cannot deduct the compensation they pay to their ministers, so, unlike for-profit employers, they bear the full cost of paying their employees. Perhaps, then, one could argue that the parsonage allowance, with the nominal federal subsidy it provides, functions to narrow this gap.

Ultimately, though, while true on a superficial level, this argument is less than compelling. Yes, the federal government does not directly subsidize churches' payroll costs by allowing a deduction for those costs. But the only reason it does not provide a deduction is because churches have no tax liability in the first place; where for-profit businesses must pay taxes on their income, churches are almost entirely exempt from taxation.

Moreover, it cannot be that the purpose behind the parsonage allowance was to subsidize churches' labor costs. While it may do just that,[71] it only subsidizes the costs *related to ministers*. Although some employees (at least at religiously affiliated schools) appear to stretch the boundaries of who qualifies as clergy, a significant portion of church employees, including administrative and janitorial staff, among others, would not qualify for the parsonage allowance. Churches thus bear the full costs of the salaries they pay employees.

Even if the argument that the federal government does not subsidize a church's payment of wages had some relevance, that lack of subsidy is not unique to churches. In fact, no tax-exempt organization gets to deduct its labor costs, and thus the tax system does not offset the employment costs of any tax-exempt organization. For that matter, the tax subsidy available to for-profit employers can also be significantly limited – if the employer fails to earn a profit for enough years, it disappears entirely.[72]

PROBLEMS CHALLENGING ITS CONSTITUTIONALITY

Irrespective of the ambiguity surrounding the precise contours of the Establishment Clause, the parsonage allowance seems to fall on the wrong side of that line. The Supreme Court has held that when the government provides a subsidy exclusively to religious organizations, that subsidy is not required by the Free Exercise Clause, and that subsidy either markedly burdens non-recipients or, alternatively, cannot reasonably be seen as removing a significant deterrent to the free exercise of religion, that subsidy violates the Constitution.[73]

The parsonage allowance clearly provides a subsidy to churches – it reduces their cost in hiring clergy. And nothing in the Free Exercise Clause requires the government to subsidize the compensation churches pay their clergy. Even if a church's doctrine for some reason required it to provide its pastor with housing, the lack of a parsonage allowance would not prevent the church from doing so. Notwithstanding the Treasury Department's long-ago ruling that ministers did not qualify for the administratively created housing exemption, in today's post-codification world, any minister who was required to accept housing and whose housing was located on church premises would qualify for the broader exemption. At worst, without the parsonage allowance churches would have to pay higher wages.

On the other hand, it is difficult to argue that the parsonage allowance substantially burdens nonrecipients. In permitting the allowance, the federal government only forgoes a (relatively) modest amount of revenue. Although Congress estimated that, between 2003 and 2007, the parsonage allowance would reduce federal revenue by $2.3 billion,[74] during those same years, individual taxpayers paid about $4.7 *trillion* in taxes.[75] The five-year cost of the parsonage allowance made up about 0.05 percent of the federal government's total revenue over that period. While it clearly increased the tax burden on nonclergy, the increase was virtually unnoticeable. If the parsonage allowance went away, but the government raised the same amount of revenue, an individual who paid $10,000 in federal income taxes would see their taxes go down by about $5.

At the same time, though, neither a church paying higher wages nor a minister paying taxes on the value of housing provided to them impedes the church's or the minister's free exercise of religion and, in fact, churches have other avenues by which they can provide tax-free housing. As a result, the parsonage allowance appears to fail the Supreme Court's test of constitutionality.

And yet it still exists. Congress thwarted the Ninth Circuit's 2002 *sua sponte* effort to examine its constitutionality. But it has been subsequently (and, initially, successfully) challenged. In 2011, the Freedom from Religion Foundation (an organization formed to promote the separation of church and state) and three of its directors filed suit to have the parsonage allowance declared unconstitutional.[76]

The Freedom from Religion Foundation enjoyed some early success: at the trial level, the district court held that the tax-free housing stipend available to ministers of the gospel violated the Constitution. At the same time, though, the court dismissed the Freedom from Religion Foundation's claim that tax-free provision of actual housing violated the Establishment Clause. Predicate to both of these holdings was the question of standing: the court found that the plaintiffs had standing to challenge the stipend, but lacked standing to challenge the in-kind housing.[77]

Although the standing requirement is merely a procedural gate, it is a procedural gate through which all federal plaintiffs must successfully pass. The standing requirement is incident to Article III of the Constitution, which provides that the federal judiciary has power to decide *cases* and *controversies*.[78] The Supreme Court has explained that standing requires, at minimum, that a plaintiff have suffered an "injury in fact" that is concrete and particularized, not hypothetical or conjectural. That injury must have arisen from the bad actions of the defendant. Finally, it must be likely that the injury can be redressed by a favorable decision from the federal court.[79]

On appeal, the Seventh Circuit found that the plaintiffs had failed to demonstrate that they had suffered a concrete injury, one that would allow them to pass through the standing gate. Offense at the government's violation of the Establishment Clause may provide psychic injury, but such a generalized injury is not enough to confer standing on the plaintiffs.[80] The Establishment Clause protects "noneconomic interests of a spiritual, as opposed to a physical or pecuniary, nature."[81] And violating these noneconomic interests rarely causes individualized injury.

In some cases, if nobody can assert an individualized injury, the standing requirements could prevent anybody from challenging governmental action in court. That does not mean, of course, that this type of nonspecific bad action by the government cannot be challenged at all. Standing does not bar individuals from asserting their positions at the polls or in political fora.[82]

But political solutions may be insufficient to remedy violations of the Establishment Clause area, violations which may affect large groups, albeit without sufficient concrete injury. As a result, the courts have allowed a special taxpayer standing where an alleged violation of the Establishment Clause is at issue.[83] Taxpayer standing provides a narrow exception to the rule of concrete injury: a taxpayer will have standing to challenge legislation in cases where Congress acts under its constitutional taxing and spending power and where that legislation exceeds specific limitations imposed on Congress by the Constitution (here, notably, the Establishment Clause).[84]

It is important, though, to emphasize *how* narrow this exemption to the general standing rule is. While taxpayer standing grants a taxpayer *qua* taxpayer standing to challenge Congressional legislation, it does not erase the need for concrete injury to challenge Executive actions, or even Congressional actions taken under powers other than the taxing and spending power.[85] And the Supreme Court has subsequently read the *taxing and spending* requirement literally, requiring that the challenged law actually cause direct government spending in violation of the Establishment Clause before taxpayers will qualify for taxpayer standing. Even if the challenged law provides a tax credit in violation of the Establishment Clause, a challenger must show concrete injury, or the suit will be dismissed for lack of standing. The grant of a tax credit – though economically equivalent to direct spending – will not support taxpayer standing.[86]

The district court acknowledged that the plaintiffs had not suffered a concrete injury that would give rise to traditional notions of standing. Generally, claiming a tax benefit and having that benefit denied by the IRS constitutes a concrete injury and thus provides a taxpayer with standing to challenge the provision. But the directors of the Freedom from Religion Foundation had not claimed that their housing stipends qualified as tax-exempt parsonage allowances, and had thus not had their claims denied.[87]

Still, the court recognized that, given the narrowness of taxpayer standing, for the suit to go forward, the plaintiffs needed to pass through the gate of

actual standing.[88] And, the court held, the plaintiffs did not need to file a claim
and have it denied to suffer a concrete injury. Rather, the court found that
there was no conceivable interpretation of "ministers of the gospel" that would
encompass the directors of a nonreligious organization. As such, the court
held, requiring "plaintiffs to claim the exemption and wait for the inevitable
denial of the claim" would serve "no legitimate purpose."[89] Rather, the court
found that the fact of different – and inferior – treatment for the plaintiffs
represented a sufficiently cognizable injury to provide them with standing to
challenge that parsonage allowance.

Having successfully navigated the standing gate, the court then moved to
the merits of the complaint. It underlined that the housing stipend was available *solely* to religions; worse, not only did it favor religion over nonreligion,
but it discriminated between religions, preferring those with formal clergy
over those without. The government failed to identify any overarching secular purpose behind the parsonage allowance and, as such, the court found it
unconstitutional.[90]

The district court enjoined the IRS from allowing ministers to claim a tax-
free housing stipend, but stayed their injunction until after the appeal, if any.[91]
And the IRS did appeal, challenging both the district court's procedural determination that the plaintiffs had standing to challenge the law and its substantive determination that the parsonage allowance was unconstitutional.[92]

The Freedom from Religion Foundation fared far worse at the Seventh Circuit. On appeal, the court did not even address the merits; rather, it held that
the district court had been wrong on the standing question – the Freedom
from Religion Foundation plaintiffs lacked standing to challenge the constitutionality of the parsonage allowance and, as such, the court did not have
jurisdiction to hear their case.

The Seventh Circuit agreed with the district court that the special standing rules available for Establishment Clause violations would have been
unavailable to the plaintiffs, even if they had pressed the issue. The Seventh
Circuit explained that there are three ways a taxpayer can establish standing in an Establishment Clause case without demonstrating concrete harm.
The first is a type of direct harm that follows from, for example, mandatory
prayer in a public school or being exposed to religious symbols. The plaintiffs could not rely on the direct harm doctrine, though, because the parsonage allowance did not require them to do or see anything. Alternatively,
they could have used the Supreme Court-created exception from the concrete
harm requirement to demonstrate taxpayer standing. Because the government
made no actual expenditure, though, taxpayer standing was unavailable. The

parsonage allowance did not require the plaintiffs to see or do anything. It did not constitute an expenditure of federal funds.[93]

Finally, the court dealt with the issue of actual harm. Here it fundamentally disagreed with the district court. Quite simply, said the Seventh Circuit, the plaintiffs were never denied a tax benefit as a result of their lack of religious affiliation. And they were never denied that tax benefit for the simple reason that they *never asked for the benefit*. Whether or not asking would be futile, the court held, without asking, there could be no denial of the claim. And without a denial, their claim "amounts to nothing more than a generalized grievance about [the parsonage allowance's] unconstitutionality, which does not support standing."[94] Even if making the request would be a waste of time, its futility is irrelevant. The standing requirement, as much as the Establishment Clause, is a constitutional principle, one predicate to federal courts' ability to adjudicate suits.[95] Not merely a gate that must be passed, the standing requirement is "part of the basic charter promulgated by the Framers of the Constitution at Philadelphia in 1787."[96]

Moreover, the Seventh Circuit believed that it would have been relatively easy for the plaintiffs to establish standing. In fact, the court said, the plaintiffs had at least two paths through which they could have established concrete injury. The less-expensive path would have been to exclude their housing allowances on their tax returns and sued in the Tax Court had the IRS disallowed their exemption. Alternatively, they could have paid taxes on their housing allowances, claimed a refund, and then sued in the district court if the IRS rejected or failed to act on their claims for refunds.[97]

The Appeals Court clearly got the law right. The Constitution requires a plaintiff to have standing for the courts to hear and adjudicate their question. And, under current standing jurisprudence, the Freedom from Religion Foundation officers did not have standing to challenge the law – they suffered no personal, concrete harm from the existence of the parsonage allowance, and they did not fit within the current contours of taxpayer standing. And plaintiffs may be correct that nobody fits within those contours. That nobody can sue, though, does not somehow deconstitutionalize the standing requirement.

Their loss at the Seventh Circuit does not mean the parsonage allowance is secure, irrespective of its constitutionality, though. After losing in the Seventh Circuit, the Freedom from Religion Foundation took the Court of Appeals's advice: it designated a portion of the compensation it paid to three executives as a housing stipend. Those three executives filed amended returns, claiming that the stipend was not taxable as a parsonage allowance and, when the IRS did in fact decline to refund a portion of their taxes, filed suit. In that suit, the plaintiffs chose not to ask for the refund they claimed. Instead, they requested that the court declare the parsonage allowance unconstitutional and prohibit the IRS from treating housing stipends as tax-free.[98] And on October 6, 2017, the same district court again held that the exemption for ministers' housing stipends was unconstitutional.[99]

Of course, even here, the story is not over. The district court's opinion is compelling, but the Seventh Circuit did not address the merits of the case in its prior opinion. It is almost certain that the Seventh Circuit will hear the case again, and next time, will probably provide a ruling on the merits. While it seems likely that the court of appeals will uphold the district court's decision, it is not certain. In any event, while the court found the exemption of ministers' housing stipends was an unconstitutional preference for religion, the court accepted that religious tax accommodations, where warranted, could meet the requirements of the Establishment Clause.[100]

CONCLUSION

The parsonage allowance has a history nearly as long as the modern federal income tax itself. The long pedigree of the parsonage allowance does not mean, however, that it is good policy. Rather, like most religious tax accommodations, Congress created and amended it in an *ad hoc* manner. Rather than prospectively designing the allowance, Congress designed it in response to specific requests for accommodation, and amended it to preempt judicial and administrative threats to the allowance's future viability. Whether or not courts ultimately find that the Freedom from Religion Foundation plaintiffs have standing to challenge the tax-free housing stipend, and whether or not the courts ultimately find the provision unconstitutional, the parsonage allowance underlines the problems with *ad hoc* accommodation. In its original iteration, the parsonage allowance resolved Treasury's discrimination against clergy. But when Congress stepped in and provided statutory rules for excluding employer-provided housing, it mooted that discrimination.

Rather than rethinking the appropriateness of the parsonage allowance when it faced obstacles, Congress not only kept it, but doubled down on it. That, in spite of the fact that the parsonage allowance has no connection to religiously motivated behavior. It is true that ministers of the gospel, however defined, need a place to live. But they share that need with all of their neighbors, religious or not. Nothing about ministers' religious beliefs or practices causes them to act any differently with respect to housing than any other taxpayer.

To the extent a church *did* require its minister to live in church-provided housing, the tax law provides a broader exception that could apply to ministers, too. Although Congress convinced itself that the parsonage allowance was warranted – and, in fact, was important enough to protect from attack as recently as a decade and a half ago – measured against any type of tax policy considerations, it makes no sense.

6

Neither a Borrower nor a Lender Be

Javed Ahmed pays his credit card bill in full every month. When he bought a car in 2003, he, along with only about 8 percent of car purchasers in the United States,[1] saved up and paid cash rather than financing his purchase. Two years later, Ahmed, who lived in Seattle and was approaching his thirtieth birthday, wanted to buy a house. But as the housing bubble was reaching its apex, paying cash for a house was out of his reach. The median price for a single-family home in King County, which includes Seattle, had reached about $350,000.[2]

Of course, while a $350,000 house is expensive, it is not entirely out of reach. Ahmed worked at Voyager Capital, a venture capital firm, and presumably made a reasonable living there. Mortgage lending was tremendously liberal in the first half of the first decade of the 2000s. And even if Ahmed was conservative in his finances, a traditional thirty-year mortgage would only require him to pay 20 percent of the purchase price – $70,000 – as a down payment. Admittedly, $70,000 is a lot of money. But for Ahmed, who had managed to save enough to buy a car for cash and was responsible enough with his finances to pay off his credit card bills every month, it should not have been impossible.

But for Ahmed, a traditional mortgage was not an option. The *Qu'ran* forbids *riba*, the paying or receipt of interest. And Ahmed, who paid cash for his car and paid off his credit card bills monthly to avoid paying interest, was Muslim.[3]

The prohibition on interest is not unique to Islam, of course. Virtually every major religion has prohibited usury at some point in its history. Over time, though, most religions have dropped or modified their prohibitions. Jewish scripture, for example, prohibited Jews from charging interest to other Jews, but they could make loans to and receive interest from nonJews. And, while

Christians could not charge interest until around the 1620s, they could borrow money from and pay interest to nonChristians.[4]

Islam, alone in the United States, did not drop its prohibition on interest. And that prohibition puts Western Muslims in a difficult position. Some, including Ahmed's parents, feel that they have no choice but to borrow to buy a house. Others remain renters throughout their lives. All, though, are confronted with the question: will purchasing a house anger Allah?

INTEREST IN THE TAX LAW

By the twentieth century, most Americans did not even consider the possibility that paying interest might be sinful. The tax law, in fact, encourages borrowing and paying interest. Ever since its inception, the federal income tax has allowed some borrowers to deduct some interest that they paid. For corporations, which cannot deduct dividends, this means that debt financing is less expensive than equity financing, because the tax law essentially subsidizes the cost to a corporation of borrowing money.

Until 1986, all taxpayers could deduct all of the interest that they paid. In 1986, Congress limited the ability of individuals to deduct nonbusiness interest. In 1986, Congress changed the law, eliminating the deductibility of most nonbusiness-related interest paid by individuals. Even after 1986, though, Congress preserved individual borrowers' ability to deduct their mortgage interest. It preserved the deduction because it believed that encouraging Americans to purchase homes was an important policy, and that by reducing the cost of borrowing, it could encourage home ownership.[5]

There is no indication that, as Congress decided to allow a deduction for mortgage interest or as it decided to retain that deduction for homeowners, it considered the question of Islam's prohibition on interest. Muslims represent a tiny minority of Americans; although the Census does not ask about religious affiliation, the Pew Research Center found that in 2014, Muslims accounted for 0.9 percent of Americans, and that that miniscule percentage was up 0.5 percentage points over 2007.[6] It is virtually unthinkable, then, that Congress considered the *Qu'aranic* prohibition on interest, much less decided explicitly not to accommodate Islamic practice, in allowing interest to be deductible.

In many ways, the tax law's treatment of Muslim borrowing represents the exact same approach as its treatment of pastoral housing, but with the opposite result. Where the tax treatment of pastoral housing benefits ministers without looking at the underlying economics, its treatment of *riba* penalizes Muslim borrowing by refusing to look past the labels the borrowers and lenders use and instead look to the substantive economics of the transaction.

As we have seen, sometimes pleas for religious tax accommodation are, in fact, pleas for preferential treatment for some or all religious individuals, effectively requesting that taxpayers at large subsidize the religious practice of some. Not all religious tax accommodation necessarily provides preferential treatment to the religious, however. In some cases, the default treatment, while not deliberately punitive, effectively penalizes religious individuals for their religious compliance. Nowhere, perhaps, can this be better illustrated than in looking at the tax treatment of Muslim homeowners.

Along with other faiths, Islam teaches that everything in life has a spiritual dimension. Islamic jurisprudence tried to sacralize Muslim life, leaving no part as purely secular, without any religious implications at all.[7] Even the world of economics has religious and moral implications, and Muslims have religious obligations even in their economic and financial lives.[8] As with other Islamic law (or *shari'a*), Muslims derive their economic laws from the Qur'an.[9] And several passages of the Qur'an prohibit *riba*. In each of the passages in which the Qur'an mentions *riba*, it consistently condemns the practice of paying or charging interest.[10] In fact, while the Qur'an includes no financial penalties related to *riba*, the condemnation of *riba* is more severe than any other Qur'anic condemnation.[11]

That it is universally condemned, though, does not mean that the Qur'an unambiguously explains what constitutes the proscribed *riba*. In fact, since the 1960s, there have been two major views of how to define the prohibited *riba*. One view says that *riba* refers to any amount in excess of principal charged in a loan – basically, that *shari'a* prohibits interest. The other view sees the prohibition on *riba* as prohibiting the affluent from exploiting the poor, but not necessarily as condemning interest.[12] Rather, under this second view, loans during Mohammed's lifetime were substantively different than loans today, and, as such, today's loans do not invoke the Quar'an's prohibition of *riba*.

The history of the Ottoman Empire provides some support for the second definition. From 1299 until 1922, the Ottoman Empire was central to the Muslim world. To finance its expansion, the empire introduced a banking system that included interest on loans. At the same time, though, most Islamic jurists believed that this banking system violated the prohibition on *riba*.[13]

The dominant view today in the Muslim world is that the prohibition on *riba* is a prohibition on any payment in excess of principal on a loan – including interest – even if today's incarnation of interest is fundamentally different than interest at the time of Mohammed.[14] In fact, the prohibition on interest is one of the foundational pillars of the Islamic economic system.[15]

The prohibition on interest has very real consequences, though, for Muslims attempting to navigate modern economic life, at least in the West. It limits both their ability to invest (because they cannot earn interest-based returns) and their ability to consume (because they cannot pay interest as they borrow money). And yet Muslims, like other Americans, want to purchase homes.[16]

In 2014, the median price of a single-family home was almost $210,000.[17] At the same time, the median net worth of middle-income families was less than $100,000.[18] With this disparity between net worth and housing prices, it should come as no surprise that, in 2014, nearly 90 percent of homebuyers had to borrow money to purchase their homes.[19]

The inability to pay interest (and, as a result, the inability to borrow) puts potential Muslim families at a serious disadvantage in the housing market. Without the ability to finance their purchase, these families are essentially locked out of a large swath of housing.

With financial disconnects come opportunities, though. And out of *riba's* prohibition on interest came innovation in Islamic finance. Today, a Muslim family in the United States can finance its purchase of a home, and the family can do so without paying any interest. Banks provide three principal *Shari'a*-compliant mortgage-equivalent instruments: *murabaha, ijara-wal-iqtina,* and *musharakah* financing.[20]

Though each financing method ultimately has the same result – allowing an individual to finance the purchase of a home without paying interest – the technical details of each type of instrument differ slightly from the others. In the case of *murabaha* financing, a potential buyer will find a home and negotiate the price, just like a nonMuslim homeowner. At that point, though, the form of the transaction changes. Rather than the bank loaning money to the buyer so that the buyer can pay for the house, the financial institution instead purchases the house itself. It then sells the home to the final buyer at its cost plus a predetermined amount of profit. The purchaser pays the financial institution on a fixed payment schedule. Ultimately, although there are marginal differences between *murabaha* financing and traditional fixed-rate mortgages, they feel nearly identical.[21]

Ijara-wal-iqtina financing provides Muslims with an alternative method of financing their home purchases without paying interest. This type of financing is essentially a rent-to-own transaction. As with *murabaha* financing, the financial institution purchases and owns the house; over time, the Muslim purchaser will buy the house from the financial institution at cost. At the same time, the buyer pays rent to the financial institution. Title does not transfer from the financial institution to the buyer until the buyer has paid the full cost of the house.[22]

Finally, *musharakah* financing functions like a partnership. Where a financial institution provides *musharakah* financing, the financial institution and the Muslim homebuyer are co-owners of the property. The homebuyer makes regular payments to the financial institution. These payments include components of both rent and principal. With each payment, the financial institution's ownership share of the property diminishes, until ultimately the homebuyer alone owns the house.[23]

While there are subtle legal and formal differences between each of these types of Islamic finance, they each ultimately achieve a similar goal: they allow Muslims to finance the purchase of a home without requiring them to violate the Qu'ran's prohibition on *riba*. They also effectively place Muslims on a similar footing as nonMuslims. While lenders charge slightly more for *shari'a*-compliant mortgages than they do for conventional mortgages, the costs are similar,[24] and there is no reason to believe that, as *shari'a*-compliant instruments become more familiar and more common, the costs will not converge even more.

In spite of the economic similarities between *murabaha*, *ijara-wal-iqtina*, or *musharakah* financing and conventional mortgages, the tax law treats these Muslim borrowers in a significantly different – and worse – way than it treats nonMuslims, who are able to borrow using conventional mortgages.

The most obvious difference between Muslim and nonMuslim borrowers is in the tax treatment of interest. At the broadest level, US taxpayers can deduct interest they pay.[25] Only corporations can take advantage of the interest deduction at this broadest level, though. Generally, noncorporate taxpayers can only deduct interest if it is not "personal interest." Personal interest is basically any interest that is not accrued in the course of a person's business or investment endeavors.[26]

Of course, as often as not, the tax law presents an exception to an exception, and the personal interest rules are no different. While noncorporate taxpayers generally cannot deduct personal interest, they can deduct at least some of the interest they pay on home mortgages. While the permissible deduction is not unlimited, it is quite generous. An individual can deduct interest on mortgages of up to $1.1 million. That $1.1 million must be secured by an individual's principal residence and by up to one other home.[27] And for purposes of the mortgage interest deduction, the IRS interprets "home" broadly. It includes not only single-family houses and condominiums, but also mobile homes, house trailers, and even boats, provided that the mortgaged "home" has a place to sleep, to cook, and to use the bathroom.[28]

Why does it matter if an individual can deduct the interest they pay on their mortgage? The deduction reduces the cost of acquiring a home (or boat or mobile home). Essentially, a tax deduction reduces a taxpayer's taxable income, thus reducing their ultimate tax liability. With the mortgage interest deduction, the government reduces the cost of borrowing money to buy a house, in essence subsidizing homeowners.

Or, at least, subsidizing nonMuslim homeowners. Because as a formal matter, Muslim homeowners who borrow using Islamic finance instruments do not pay mortgage interest. In fact, they structure their loans specifically to avoid paying any interest. While *murabaha, ijara-wal-iqtina,* and *musharakah* financing have approximately the same pre-tax cost as conventional mortgage financing, they are potentially far more expensive after taking taxes into account.

Horizontal equity – a fundamental tax policy foundation – demands that people with similar economic situations be taxed in a similar manner.[29] But deductions – including the mortgage interest deduction – are a matter of legislative grace, and a taxpayer who wants to take a deduction must be able to point to an express authorization for the deduction.[30] Though homeowners who have used Islamic finance instruments may have some arguments for why the law should allow them to deduct some kind of interest-equivalent payment, there is no clear authorization for deduction.

Which is not to say that Muslim homeowners categorically do not take a deduction for some interest-equivalent amount. There is at least anecdotal evidence that some people believe that Islamic borrowers can deduct a portion of the amount they pay on their *shari'a*-compliant mortgages. Professor Haider Ala Hamoudi, for instance, does not take Islamic finance instruments seriously, in part because he says they effectively charge interest. Part of the reason he believes that they do not manage to avoid interest is because he believes that a Muslim borrower can still claim the mortgage interest deduction for a part of their payment under the *shari'a*-compliant instrument.[31]

But although the Treasury Department initiated an Islamic Finance Scholar-in-Residence program more than a decade ago,[32] neither Treasury nor the IRS has issued any formal or informal guidance to the tax treatment of *murabaha, ijara-wal-iqtina, mushurakah,* or any other Islamic finance instrument. As Islamic finance continues to grow, this lack of guidance will become more and more problematic.[33] Moreover, if Muslim homeowners are deducting some interest-equivalent amount on their *shari'a*-compliant mortgages, they are currently taking an aggressive position, and potentially exposing themselves to interest and penalties if the IRS or the courts disallow the deduction.[34]

A Muslim taxpayer could reduce the risk of facing penalties – though not interest – by relying on professional tax advice. Following formal tax advice does not make a taxpayer's return unassailable. Tax advisors can get the tax law wrong, and even where the advisor is not necessarily wrong, tax law provisions can be ambiguous. Relying on professional tax advice, even when that advice is wrong, provides some benefit for taxpayers, though – if a taxpayer reasonably relies on such advice, the IRS cannot impose penalties for the underpayment.[35] Tax advisers also face potential penalties unless there is sufficient authority for their advice, though, and there currently is not enough authority for treating payments on Islamic finance instruments to meet the tax law's bar.[36]

Even if a Muslim homeowner were willing to take an aggressive tax position and chose to deduct an interest-equivalent amount on their *shari'a*-compliant mortgage, their mortgage would cost more than a nonMuslim's conventional mortgage. The cost of the mortgage would not only include their payments, less a proportion of the deductible interest, would also include the expected penalty for noncompliance or the additional amount they had to pay to their tax adviser to provide them with an opinion that protected them from liability.[37] Without clear guidance permitting Muslim borrowers to deduct an interest-equivalent amount, then, the costs of borrowing using Islamic financing instruments will always be more expensive than the costs for nonMuslim borrowers who have no religious prohibition on paying interest.

And home ownership is not the only place that the tax law disadvantages Muslims who cannot pay *riba* for religious reasons. While this chapter has focused largely on Islamic alternatives to home mortgages, the same analysis applies to other borrowing. *Murabaha* financing, for example, is not limited to home mortgages; in total, it represents about three-fourths of the loans made by Islamic banks. These banks use *murabaha* financing to provide short-term loans that permit Muslim merchants to purchase goods for sale.[38] Islamic banks can also use *musharaka* financing to fund commercial projects; *musharaka* financing also funds new industrial and agricultural projects.[39]

In the commercial realm, no less than the personal realm, borrowing is important. The vast majority of small businesses rely on some level of leverage to function.[40] NonMuslim business owners, like nonMuslim homeowners, can use conventional lending sources, including banks and credit cards, when they need to borrow money for their business. But bank loans and credit card balances accrue interest. The tax law reduces the cost of interest paid, though, by allowing businesses to fully deduct their business-related interest. But, as in the context of Islamic mortgage-equivalent instruments, there is no interest on the Islamic instruments used to finance business expenditures. As such, the interest-equivalent portions of these instruments are not deductible to Muslim businesses. Not only do Muslims' religious practices increase the cost of acquiring housing, then, they also increase the cost of starting and running businesses. And the difference in cost is real: according to the Treasury Office of Tax Analysis, in 2014, corporations paid taxes at an effective marginal rate of 27 percent on equity-financed investment, and a rate of *negative* 39 percent on debt-financed investment.[41]

The inability of Muslim borrowers to deduct interest-equivalent payments, with the concomitant higher cost of borrowing they face, is clearly the largest tax disadvantage most Muslims will face as a result of their religious practice. But it is by no means the only way in which Muslim homeowners are forced to pay more in taxes than their nonMuslim counterparts. In addition to the federal income tax, they can face state property tax obstacles, depending on the state in which they live, that can radically raise the tax cost of buying a house. While I am not focusing on state tax issues in this book, Muslim property owners' experiences with state tax systems demonstrate that clashes between religious practice and tax systems are not limited to federal taxation. A systemic way to think about tax accommodation would help at all levels of government.

As with the lack of deductible interest on Islamic financing instruments, the state property tax problems come because the instruments do not fit comfortably into the ownership boxes with which state laws tend to be familiar.

These disconnects happen because of the unusual ownership and transfer aspects of transactions funded through Islamic finance instruments. Although the subject of this book is the taxation of religious adherents, not religious institutions, an institutional example can easily illustrate the property tax disconnect between using conventional and Islamic financing.

In 1995, the Islamic Center of Nashville opened a religious school. A year later, the state granted a property tax exemption to the school. Twelve years later, the Islamic Center began construction on a new school building. Because of the Quar'anic prohibition on *riba*, though, it could not fund the construction with a conventional loan.

Instead, the Islamic Center sold its property to Devon Bank, an Illinois bank that provides Islamic lending.[42] It appears that Devon Bank provided *ijara-wal-iqtina* financing: at the same time the Islamic Center sold its property to Devon Bank for $900,000, the Islamic Center agreed to repurchase the property from Devon Bank for the same $900,000, plus rent. The amount of rent the Islamic Center would pay was laid out on a twenty-year payment schedule. In the end, though, it only took five years for the Islamic Center to pay the full $900,000 to the bank, at which time it regained title to the property.

Shortly after the Islamic Center transferred its property to Devon Bank, the state revoked the property's tax exemption. Upon reacquiring the school property, the Islamic Center requested that the exemption be reinstated retroactively for three years. Under Tennessee law, a religious institution that acquires property to replace its own exempt property can receive a three-year retroactive exemption on the property.[43]

The Board of Equalization recognized the predicament that the Islamic Center found itself in; if it could pay interest, the property would have remained exempt during the full five years, because there would have been no transfer of title. Instead, the bank would have loaned the Islamic Center $900,000, secured by the property. The Islamic Center would have then repaid the loan, plus interest (which, presumably, would have been roughly the same as the amount of rent the Islamic Center paid to Devon Bank).

And yet, the administrative judge wrote, there was nothing he could do. To receive a tax exemption, the property had to not only be occupied and used by an exempt institution, it had to be *owned* by one. And the Islamic Center had expressly structured the transaction in a way that shifted ownership. Moreover, the administrative judge wrote, property owned by an exempt organization that generates substantive rent does not qualify for exemption; as such, he could not fathom how property formally owned by a for-profit bank and generating rent for that bank could possibly qualify for an exemption.[44]

Even though sincere religious conviction underlay the transaction's structure, and the economics were nearly identical to a traditional secured bank loan, under Tennessee law, the form trumped the substance of the loan. That form required the Islamic Center to pay five years of property taxes that a similarly situated religious – or otherwise exempt – institution would not have to pay, provided it could pay interest and obtain a conventional loan. Entirely aside from the question of the deductibility of interest, the proscription on *riba* imposed a real additional cost on the Islamic Center. And the Islamic Center presumably passed the costs on to its members, whose donations did not go as far, and parents, who had to pay more in tuition.

Of course, although parents and donors probably ultimately bore the Islamic Center's additional tax costs caused by the unconventional Islamic financing instruments, they bore those additional costs indirectly. Moreover, any individual parent or donor could avoid the additional tax cost altogether; even if the Islamic Center needed to raise more money, no donor was obligated to donate more than they would have otherwise donated. And if tuition rose in response to the additional tax cost, parents could move their children to another school. In the end, the additional cost of taking a *shari'a*-compliant loan fell on a religious institution, not religious individuals.

But Muslim homeowners can also directly bear the additional cost of real property-linked taxes, and bear that cost in a way that they cannot reasonably avoid. Specifically, without some kind of dispensation, Muslim homeowners who borrow using Islamic financing instruments may pay twice as much in state real estate transfer taxes as nonMuslim homeowners.

Why is that? Because they may be required to pay the transfer tax twice. About three-quarters of US states and the District of Columbia have some form of real estate transfer tax.[45] While the details of the taxes differ from state to state, in general the tax is calculated as a percentage of a house's sale price. In some versions of real estate transfer taxes, the tax nominally falls on the seller, while in others it nominally falls on the buyer. In New York, the tax can fall on both.[46]

Irrespective of the incidence of the real estate transfer tax, with conventional financing, a homeowner only faces the tax one time, when either they buy or sell the property. At that point, they will pay a percentage of the sale price to the state (and, sometimes, local) government. Remember, the major Islamic financing instruments require the bank to initially acquire the property. The bank eventually sells it at cost to the ultimate Muslim buyer. As a result, there are two nominal sales, even if, economically, one could recast the transaction as being the same as a conventional mortgage – the only substantive difference is whether the homeowner or the bank holds title to the property while the homeowner is still paying off the loan.

And yet, the Islamic Center property tax exemption demonstrates that, even where the state recognizes the religious sincerity of those who borrow using these *shari'a*-compliant instruments, it is hard to avoid the transaction's form. And if a state has no exception to the general rule that allows the taxing authority to disregard the form of the loan and look instead to the substance, Muslim borrowers will face significant extra expense.

How much? The median price of a new home in the United States in 2014 reached $300,000. Transfer tax rates vary among states, but at a 0.5 percent rate, the homebuyer or seller with a conventional mortgage would pay $1,500 in real estate transfer taxes. By contrast, if a state imposes its real estate transfer tax on the buyer, a Muslim homeowner would pay $1,500 when the bank acquired the property, then another $1,500 when they acquired the property from the bank. If the tax falls on the seller, the Muslim homeowner would pay the tax when they acquired the property from the bank, then again when they sold it to a third-party buyer. (Technically, the incidence of the tax would fall on the bank on one of the two formal sales, but the bank is merely facilitating the buyer's religious obligations and presumably has no interest in holding the property. As a result, the bank would almost certainly pass the cost of the tax on to the actual owner.)

It is possible to eliminate this double taxation, of course. The United Kingdom, for example, amended its tax law in 2003 to prevent the state from imposing its real estate transfer tax twice on Islamic mortgages.[47] In the United States, though, real estate transfer taxes are a state-level issue, and no state appears to have dealt specifically with the question of transfer taxes and Islamic mortgages.

That is not to say that every Muslim homeowner faces two levels of transfer tax. In New York City, for example, generally applicable law requires the seller of a piece of real property to pay two taxes: the state-level real estate transfer tax,[48] and a city-level real property transfer tax.[49] Neither the city nor the state law contains an exemption for Islamic financing instruments, and, if the state were to privilege form over substance, presumably the tax would be due on both the initial transfer to the bank and on the final transfer to the putative borrower.

But both the city and state of New York have released administrative guidance in which they give up their right to the second level of taxation. In a pair of advisory opinions, the state Commissioner of Taxation and Finance addressed the real estate transfer tax consequences of *ijara* financing. In its guidance, the state said that, where a bank purchased property on behalf of a Muslim buyer, leased the property to the buyer, and, ultimately, transferred it to the buyer, the real estate transfer tax would only be due upon the initial transfer. Because the bank had no intention of using or maintaining the property, the Commissioner recognized that the economics replicated a standard mortgage, and was willing to look at the substance of the transaction.[50] Similarly, when a property owner transferred their property to the bank in the process of an *ijara* refinance, the Commissioner said that he would ignore the transfer to the bank and the transfer back for real estate transfer tax purposes, instead recognizing that the transfer was the economic equivalent of giving the bank a security interest in the subject property.[51]

Similarly, New York City has issued administrative guidance ignoring the structure of Islamic financing instruments and, instead, looking at their substance. In one finance letter ruling, the city's Department of Finance held that the real property transfer tax would be imposed only on the initial sale in a *murabaha* financing.[52] In another, the Department stated that it would only impose the real property transfer tax on the initial sale of a purchase using *musharakah* financing, and would not impose it at all in a *musharakah* refinancing transaction.[53]

While it is beneficial to Muslim homeowners that New York will look past the form of Islamic finance and, instead, focus on the economic substance, it is not clear that all – or even most – states will do the same. A number of states have enacted anti-Shari'a laws, forbidding their courts from recognizing or applying *shari'a* law; these laws forbid courts from enforcing contracts that import rules from religious or foreign law.[54] Such a law would clearly not allow state taxing authorities to overlook the form of these *shari'a*-compliant mortgages, even if banks could provide Muslims in these states with such mortgages.

But even New York's solution is limited, and imposes costs on Muslim borrowers it does impose on nonMuslim homeowners. The city and state do not exempt the additional transfers in Islamic financing from transfer tax by statute or by regulation; instead, the exemptions come through finance letter rulings and administrative opinions, respectively. But neither form of administrative guidance has any precedential value – they only provide certainty to the taxpayer who requested the ruling.[55] If a Muslim buyer – or a bank that provides Islamic financing instruments – wants to be sure that a *shari'a*-compliant mortgage in New York will not be subject to multiple occurrences of the transfer tax, then, the buyer or the bank must go to the relevant taxing authority and request a ruling, a process that imposes both financial and temporal costs. Even where the state is willing to look beyond the form, then, without formal permission, the risk of taxing the same transaction multiple times raises the cost of borrowing.

FORM VERSUS SUBSTANCE GENERALLY

In the tax law, elevating the substance of a transaction over its form is not only permissible, but is quite often the rule. Nearly a century ago, during the infancy of the modern federal income tax, the Supreme Court recognized "the importance of regarding matters of substance and disregarding forms in applying" the tax laws.[56] Rather than taking at face value the form employed by taxpayers, the courts must look "to the objective economic realities of [the] transaction."[57] If there is no economic reality to the form the parties have chosen to employ, courts can disregard the parties' form for federal income tax purposes. Though the various doctrines that allow the IRS to disregard a taxpayer's form and, instead, tax the underlying substance originated in the common law, in 2010, Congress took the additional step of codifying the economic substance doctrine, one of the underlying judicial form-piercing doctrines.[58]

By and large, states also can look through the form of transactions to tax their actual substance. A number of states have enacted legislation expressly providing this authority; moreover, these laws and regulations are often more expansive than their federal counterparts, applying not only to state income taxes, but to other taxes (including, especially, property taxes) as well.[59] Even states without substance-over-form legislation may have judicial or administrative guidance incorporating these doctrines.[60]

The major tax issue Muslim borrowers face is that they do not *formally* pay interest on Islamic financing instruments, and, when they borrow using those instruments, ownership of the underlying property formally changes hands. In both cases, though, the substance of the transaction looks like the Muslim borrower is paying interest, and like the bank only retains a security interest in the property, not actual ownership of the property. If the IRS and state revenue agencies can look past the form, then, why would Muslims face worse tax consequences than nonMuslim borrowers, even without explicit administrative guidance recasting the transaction in conventional form?

Because the substance-over-form doctrines do not work both ways. While the IRS, courts, and state taxing authorities may be able to disregard the form that taxpayers chose, taxpayers are generally bound by it. The Court of Appeals for the Fifth Circuit colorfully explained that, although courts have

> never hesitated to pierce the paper armor of a taxpayer's characterization of a particular transaction in order to reach its true substance ..., [they] have done so at the request of the Commissioner to prevent a taxpayer from unjustifiably using his own forms and labels as a shield from the incidence of taxation. A taxpayer's attempt to pierce his own armor does not merit the same consideration.[61]

Taxpayers are stuck with the form they have chosen for their transaction. Even where a taxpayer is trying to comply with their religious obligations, and has not even considered the tax consequences of their transaction, the tax law does not permit them to unilaterally disregard the form they have chosen and opt, instead, for different tax treatment.

In most circumstances, preventing taxpayers from disavowing the form they have chosen makes sense. A taxpayer has the ability to structure the transaction however they want in the first instance, an ability the courts and the IRS lack. Disavowing their own form after the fact adds significant complexity and unfairness to the tax law. When a taxpayer plans and structures a transaction, they generally choose the form that will best accomplish their nontax goals.

And if they choose the form solely to reduce their taxes, the IRS and the courts can look through it.

But if they could choose their form after the transaction was complete, they would always choose the lowest-tax option. And they would not face any business risk in that choice, because the transaction would already be complete. In essence, a form chosen after the fact is "no more true to the transaction's underlying substance than the form actually used by the taxpayer."[62] Requiring taxpayers to live with the tax consequences of the form that they chose prior to the transaction does not generally result in unfair consequences because, before entering into the transaction, taxpayers had broad discretion as to the form that they would choose. It does, however, prevent taxpayers from choosing the amount of tax they want to pay with perfect knowledge of what the tax consequences are. For taxpayers, the form they choose generally represents their *ex ante* perspective on the substance of the transaction.

In the case of Islamic finance, though, the form is economically illusory. Muslim borrowers do not choose to borrow using a *shari'a*-compliant mortgage for any kind of business or tax reason. Rather, they do so because of their religious commitments. Still, because Muslim borrowers have chosen a form of borrowing that does not include interest, they cannot recast their payments to treat some portion as interest without the government explicitly permitting it.

If a Muslim borrower chooses the form of their transaction for religious reasons, the form does not represent any business or economic goals. In trying to recast payments on the mortgage as dividend-equivalents, they did not decide after the transaction was done that they could have had a lower tax bill had they taken out a conventional mortgage. They knew, prior to borrowing money, that they were choosing a disadvantageous form for tax purposes, and that it had no economic benefits that outweighed the tax cost. And, in spite of receiving no financial benefits, they chose the *shari'a*-compliant mortgage anyway, because that was what their religious convictions required them to do.

It is important to emphasize that there is no way that an Islamic financing instrument would put them in a better economic position, before or after taxes, than a conventional loan. The borrower's cost seems to be approaching the cost of a conventional loan, but Islamic financing instruments still cost more. And with the additional real property transfer taxes (or the cost of getting an individual exception) and the inability to deduct any part of the borrower's payments, after-tax, Islamic finance can cost considerably more than conventional borrowing.

Because the driving impetus behind this specialized Muslim borrowing is religious, not economic, and because Muslim borrowers are not waiting to see what form would give them the better after-tax treatment, the economic policy underlying locking taxpayers to their chosen form does not apply. At the same time, though, allowing borrowers to disregard the form of their borrowing, without creating a special regime delineating the boundaries of such disregard, could create problems for the IRS. While religiously motivated Islamic finance does not present the opportunity for tax arbitrage, there may be other forms of unconventional borrowing that would, and allowing any taxpayer to choose the form of their borrowing after the fact could create administrative burdens as the IRS attempts to enforce the tax law.

BURDENING TAX ENFORCEMENT

This question of administrative burden is essential in determining whether to create an accommodation for religious borrowers who cannot pay interest. In determining whether to accommodate religious beliefs and practices, it is not enough merely to determine whether a taxpayer's religion prevents them from enjoying a generally applicable tax benefit. At least in the context of taxes, we must also look at the burden the government faces in creating and administering the accommodation.

Here, the burden would be minimal. *Interest*, after all, is not a sacred, immutable category. And the government has already provided in other contexts that certain non-interest payments will be treated as equivalent to interest for tax purposes. In a number of contexts, the tax law already treats non-interest payments as interest for tax purposes. In some, in fact, the tax law creates interest payments where no payment even occurs.[63] Treating interest-equivalent payments on Islamic financing instruments as if they were interest, then, does not even represent a novel idea that the IRS would have to wrestle with. It would present at most marginal additional administrative obligations on the IRS.

MUST THE TAX LAW ACCOMMODATE ALL RELIGIOUS OBJECTIONS TO INTEREST?

By and large, Muslims who are religiously opposed to paying interest have access to alternative financing methods that provide for alternatives to interest. That does not mean, however, that all religious borrowers can pay interest-equivalent amounts, or even that Muslims can entirely avoid paying interest. As I will explain in the final chapter, Congress or the IRS should certainly accommodate the Qur'anic prohibition on interest, allowing Muslim borrowers to deduct the interest-equivalent amounts they pay and recognizing the substance of ownership rather than the form they use to avoid interest. A blanket accommodation, though, that recharacterizes any borrowing as including an interest component or that allows religious taxpayers to avoid paying interest under any circumstances would be both unfair and unadministrable.

Interest from Whole Cloth

Islam is not the only religion to have banned interest. Although Christians and Jews have subsequently become comfortable with interest, both Christianity and Judaism have, in the past, prohibited their adherents from charging or paying it. It is not inconceivable, then, that some religion will, in the future, revive its ban on interest.

And there is no way to know what such a ban would look like. But it could conceivably lack the workaround that Islamic finance has provided for Muslim borrowers. Islamic finance is sophisticated, and there are enough Muslim borrowers throughout the world to provide incentive for banks to create and provide *shari'a*-compliant lending instruments.[64]

But a new religious movement that lacked the number of adherents that Islam enjoys would have a much harder time getting banks to cater to their idiosyncratic religious needs; to the extent they found Islamic finance insufficient to meet their religious obligations, they would be out of luck.

It would be possible, of course, that they could create instruments similar (in purpose, if not in form) to Islamic finance instruments. To the extent that such religiously compliant borrowing instruments featured a payment equivalent to interest, they should also benefit from tax accommodation provided to Muslim borrowers. Such accommodation is not meant to be available exclusively to Muslim borrowers; in fact, targeting an accommodation solely to members of a single religion would be constitutionally impermissible[65] *and* poor tax policy.

There is no reason to believe that Islamic finance instruments would be acceptable to everybody with religious objections to the payment of interest. After all, though they have no formal interest payment, there is, nonetheless, a payment in addition to the repayment of capital that functions similarly to interest. Imagine, then, a religion that proscribes the payment of interest or of anything that could be recast as interest. Instead, members of the religion pool some amount of money every month, and each month, a different member takes the pool. The putative borrower effectively repays the loan by contributing to the pool in subsequent months; each pool is the same amount of money, and each member gets an opportunity to take the money.[66] Nobody repays more than they borrow – effectively the pool represents time-shifting, allowing an individual to have several months (or years) of savings at once to fund a large purchase.

In that kind of case, although the form of lending is ultimately mandated by an individual's religious beliefs, there is no interest equivalent. Borrowers repay the amount that they borrowed, and nothing more. True, if an individual were to use this kind of financing to purchase a house, they do not enjoy the mortgage interest deduction. But that is because they are not in a similar economic situation to an individual who borrows money to buy a house. Rather, their situation is economically equivalent to an individual who purchases a house for cash. Yes, they have time-shifted their cash, but they are not paying anything extra in exchange for time-shifting their money. That their religion makes it impossible for them to take a mortgage interest deduction does not leave them in a worse economic position than the equivalent person who pays cash, because they do not, in fact, pay a financing charge for access to the money.

Unlike Muslims who finance purchases with *shari'a*-complaint instruments, creating a fake interest payment that they could then deduct would put our believer here in a *better* economic position than a buyer without a religious objections to interest. Moreover, because there is no economic cost to them of borrowing, determining a permissible deduction would be an impossible task for them or for the IRS. The mere fact of a prohibition against paying interest, then, is insufficient to trigger tax accommodation.

Paying Interest to the Government

While there may be a compelling argument for treating some non-interest payments as interest for tax purposes, that does not mean that the IRS should accommodate religious individuals' desire not to pay interest. To understand why, it is necessary to understand that the question of deductibility is not the only way in which the tax law and interest payments intersect. By law, when a taxpayer fails to pay any part of their tax liability on time, they must pay interest on their underpayment. That interest runs from the day the tax was due until the day they pay it off.[67]

The government's purpose in charging interest on underpayments is primarily about incentives. It wants to discourage taxpayers from evading their tax liabilities. But without an interest charge, taxpayers have a financial incentive to delay their payments. Inflation eats away at the purchasing power of money, meaning that having a dollar today is worth more than having that same dollar in a year. To the extent a taxpayer can defer paying their taxes, they reduce the cost of paying them, thus saving money (and reducing government revenue).[68]

Interest eliminates the benefits of deferral, though. If the interest rate the government charges is the same as the inflation rate, deferring my tax payment does not reduce the present value of the payment. If I wait to pay my $100 for a year, the present value of that $100 stays $98.04. But the $2 of interest I must pay a year from now has a present value of $1.96; with interest I end up paying the same present value, whether I pay today or in a year. Interest, then, eliminates the biggest economic benefit taxpayers would otherwise receive from deferring their tax payments.[69]

Interest can also compensate lenders for taking risk. That is, the more likely it is that a borrower will default, the higher the interest rate the lender will charge.[70] When a taxpayer pays their taxes late, they effectively borrow their unpaid taxes, turning the government into an unwilling creditor, and introduce default risk into the picture. Where taxes are paid on time, the government has its money. The longer a taxpayer takes to pay, though, the more likely it becomes that the taxpayer will never pay, increasing the default risk that the government bears. Interest on underpayments of tax does very little, though, to compensate the government for this risk. The tax law imposes interest mechanistically; a taxpayer's interest rate is based on the applicable federal rate, not on any personal characteristics of the taxpayer.[71] That is, both the most and the least credit-worthy taxpayer face the exact same interest rate on underpayments.

Other than the fact that the interest rate is determined statutorily, irrespective of the creditworthiness of the taxpayer, there is no substantive difference between interest on underpayments and interest paid to any other creditor. As a result, presumably the Qur'anic prohibition on *riba* would apply equally to interest on the underpayment of taxes. But the question of paying this interest differs substantially from the question of deducting interest equivalents on the Islamic financing instruments.

Charging interest on underpayments is a central part of administering the tax law. Even if the tax law accommodated Islamic financing instruments, the question of whether it should accommodate delinquent Muslim taxpayers would be entirely separate. For example, should the IRS provide *shari'a-*compliant ways for delinquent taxpayers to repay their taxes? Developing such an interest would be expensive, if it were at all possible – most Islamic financing instruments require collateral, which, in turn, depends on the parties voluntarily entering into the lending agreement. With underpayments, the government becomes an involuntary creditor, and the IRS and taxpayer cannot negotiate the terms of the loan. Moreover, the IRS has no expertise in Islamic finance, and there is no reason to believe that it has the capacity, much less the need, to develop such expertise.

The very mechanistic structure of the interest makes the question of accommodation with respect to interest on underpayments different from the question of paying interest on borrowing. A delinquent taxpayer pays interest at a statutorily defined rate: the federal short-term rate (determined quarterly) plus three percentage points.[72] Although the flat rate is too low for taxpayers who present a credit risk, and may be too high for the most credit-worthy taxpayers, it presents the IRS with a significant benefit: it is easy to apply. The IRS does not have to look at the characteristics of individual taxpayers. Even if the IRS were willing and able to accommodate Muslim taxpayers, it would have to evaluate each delinquent taxpayer individually to determine whether to charge interest or some *sharia*-compliant interest equivalent. Such an individualized inquiry would add significantly to the government's administrative burden and the costs of collecting delinquent taxes.

Finally, the trigger for paying interest on tax underpayments differs religiously from the trigger for borrowing using Islamic finance instruments. What triggers interest on underpayments of tax is not the decision of whether to pay interest. Rather, it is the decision to underpay one's taxes, because it is that underpayment that triggers the interest charge. There is nothing about Islam that requires Muslims to underpay their taxes. And underpaying taxes is the proximate cause of this interest. As a result, unlike questions of deliberate borrowing, there is no religious justification for accommodation.

7

Deductible Contribution or Purchase
of Religious Benefit?

In the late 1940s and early 1950s, L. Ron Hubbard, a prolific author and former naval intelligence officer, began to investigate the "technology of the human mind."[1] He developed a technique he called "auditing" to deal with mental aberrations and, in 1950, published *Dianetics: The Modern Science of Mental Health*, in which he laid out his ideas. They became popular enough that, by the end of the year, he had created the Hubbard Dianetic Research Foundation to train auditors, and he went on a lecture tour of the United States, speaking about the various principles of Dianetics.[2]

As Hubbard continued to train auditors, he became interested not only in the mind, but in "the entity observing the images that the mind was storing" – what he called a "thetan."[3] With this new focus, Hubbard coined the term "Scientology." But in spite of its focus on the soul-like thetan, Scientology did not become a religion until 1954, when some of Hubbard's followers formed the first local Church of Scientology.[4]

From there, the Church of Scientology expanded, forming more local congregations. In addition, in 1955, the Founding Church of Scientology, essentially the parent church of the religious movement, was formed in Washington, D.C., and Hubbard became its executive director. As each congregation was formed, each received a tax exemption as a church.[5] In 1966, though, the IRS began proceedings to revoke the exemption of the Church of Scientology of California and, in 1967, the Church of Scientology of California lost its exemption.[6] At about the same time, the IRS also revoked the Founding Church of Scientology's tax exemption.[7] (The Department of Justice requested that the IRS revoke the exemptions of other Scientology churches, too, but, although the IRS opened investigations into a number of other churches, it ultimately seems to have been content just revoking the exemption of the Founding Church of Scientology and the Church of Scientology of California.[8]) The Church challenged the IRS's decision in federal court. The court agreed with the IRS,[9] and for the next twenty-six years, the Church of Scientology battled the IRS.[10]

And "battled" is undoubtedly the correct description of those two-and-a-half decades. The Church of Scientology did not limit its attacks on the IRS to the courts, although it spent the whole of those twenty-six years in litigation, challenging the IRS's determination that it did not meet the requirements for tax exemption. It also launched operations that would feel at home in a spy thriller. For example, the Church assigned Gerald Wolfe to infiltrate the IRS, which he did in 1974. Within six months, he had stolen 30,000 pages of IRS documents. Around the same time, the Church managed to bug the IRS Chief Counsel Office.[11] The Church also "besiege[ed] the IRS with 200 lawsuits on the part of the church and more than 2,300 suits on behalf of individual parishioners in every jurisdiction in the country."[12]

Why did the Church of Scientology spend so much time and money fighting for a tax exemption? In part, it appears to have been a matter of legitimacy: exemption meant that the federal government recognized it as a legitimate church. And, in fact, immediately after the IRS recognized it as exempt from taxation, Scientology used that recognition to try to gain legitimacy in other countries.[13] It was also undoubtedly a financial decision, on at least two levels. Clearly, if it did not have to pay taxes, it would be left with more money. But, perhaps more importantly, donations to tax-exempt churches are deductible to the donors.

CHURCH DONATIONS

In 2013, Americans gave over $335 billion (or 2 percent of the United States' gross domestic product for 2013) to charitable organizations.[14] To put that in perspective, $335 billion represents about $1,060 for every man, woman, and child, or just over $2,746 per household. In 2013, then, American households donated approximately 5.3 percent of their income to charity.[15]

A significant portion of this generosity can be attributed to religious believers. American's charitable largesse goes to a broad range of organizations with a broad range of goals, including, among other things, nonprofit universities, museums, arts organizations, and hospitals. But the largest recipients of American generosity – by far – are religious institutions. Of the $335 billion Americans gave to charity in 2013, about $106 billion went to churches, synagogues, mosques, and other religious organizations. Educational institutions, the next-largest recipient, received about half as much as religious organizations.[16]

The US government encourages Americans' charitable inclinations through the tax law. Donations to qualifying public charities – including to churches – are deductible by the donor.[17] Deductions reduce an individual's ultimate tax liability. They do not, however, reduce taxes on a dollar-for-dollar basis. Rather, they reduce an individual's taxes by a percentage of the amount of the donation. That is, if I donate $100 to my church, I do not pay $100 less in taxes. Rather, I reduce my taxes by a percentage of that $100. If, for example, I am in the 25 percent tax bracket, I reduce my taxes by 25 percent of $100, or $25.

Economically, this means that when I make a charitable donation, I do not bear its full cost. Because my $100 donation reduces my taxes by $25, the donation only costs me $75 after taxes. So where does the other $25 come from? The government. True, the government does not actually give $25 to the charity; the full amount comes from my pocket. But the government voluntarily gives up revenue that it would otherwise have collected from me.

The US system is not inevitable; other countries have structured their incentives for charitable giving differently. The United Kingdom, for example, does not permit donors to deduct their donations. Under the UK's Gift Aid program, though, the recipient charity can receive an additional grant from the government that amounts to 25 pence for every pound donated by a qualified donor.[18] While the mechanisms for the government grant differ, their economic effect is the same. As discussed above, if I, as a US taxpayer, want to donate to my church and ensure that, as a result of my donation, it has $100, I give it $100. I then take a deduction on my tax return, reducing my taxes by $25, and have borne $75 of the cost.

If, on the other hand, I were a UK taxpayer, and I wanted to donate to my church and ensure that it had £100 after my donation, I would not donate £100. Instead, I would donate £80 to my church. It could then claim another £20 from the government under the Gift Aid program. Again, the church has £100 after my donation, but it only cost me £80 to make that donation. Although the United States uses a deduction for the donor and the UK uses a matching grant, the end result is the same.

Or rather, it would be the same, if all American taxpayers could deduct their charitable donations. But in many cases, they cannot. While the deduction regime is available to *certain* US taxpayers, it is not available to *all* of them. The charitable deduction is an itemized deduction, which means that it is only available to taxpayers who itemize their deductions. And taxpayers get to choose whether to itemize.

And for some taxpayers, not itemizing may be advantageous, even if they donate to charity. As an alternative to taking itemized deductions, the tax law provides taxpayers with a standard deduction. The standard deduction is inflation adjusted, but, in 2017, was $12,700 for a married couple filing jointly.

Unless that couple has itemized deductions in excess of $12,700, they will not itemize. And the vast majority of the US taxpayers do not itemize – in 2013, only 29.6 percent of taxpayers itemized; the rest took the standard deduction.[19]

A significant percentage of charitable donors did not itemize, in fact. Of the $335 billion donated to charity in 2013, individuals (as opposed to corporations and other legal entities) donated about $241 billion.[20] Of that $241 billion, 72 percent came from taxpayers who itemized their deductions, but a full 28 percent of individuals' charitable donations (or $41 billion) came from taxpayers who did not itemize.[21]

Those charitable donors who took the standard deduction derived no tax benefit from their donations; because the standard deduction does not vary in relation to the amount of money they gave to charity, they bore the full cost of any donation they made to their churches. And, while we do not know what percentage of church revenue comes from members who do not itemize, we do know that lower-income taxpayers – the taxpayers who are least likely to itemize – give a higher percentage of their household income to religion than higher-income taxpayers.[22] While it is possible that religions receive more money from high-income congregants, low-income individuals tend to favor religious organizations in making their charitable contributions, while higher-income individuals are more likely to send their charitable dollars to arts and cultural organizations, hospitals, and colleges and universities.[23]

Still, even though the vast majority of donors cannot deduct their donations, and an even larger proportion of donors to churches probably cannot, churches are acutely sensitive to maintaining the deductibility of charitable donations. Why? While not completely clear, it may have something to do with the disconnect between Americans' knowledge of the charitable deduction and their knowledge of its limitation. That is, everybody knows that contributions to charity are deductible. Museums advertise that the cost of a membership is deductible to donors. In NPR pledge drives, the radio hosts soliciting donations make clear to listeners that donors to the radio station can deduct the value of their donations. When a university writes fundraising letters to its alumni, it makes sure that the letters tell alumni that they can deduct any donations they make.

These charitable fundraisers are not lying – donations are, in fact, deductible. But the fundraisers inevitably fail to mention that only itemizers can actually deduct the amount of their donation. There is no reason to believe they are being disingenuous or malicious; the idea of itemized deductions is complicated, and would require significant and complicated explanations from the fundraiser (who, themselves, may not be an expert in taxes). Moreover, a donor would not necessarily know whether they would itemize or not until they prepared their tax return, which would happen after they made the donation. As a result, even if a particular donor is unlikely to itemize, and thus to get the tax benefit of a charitable deduction, the charitable deduction may still influence their decision to make a donation, as well as their decision of how much to donate.[24]

Churches and policymakers seem to believe that religious donors are sensitive to the fact that donations are deductible. In 2011, when the Senate Committee on Finance held a hearing on charitable deductions, Senator Orrin Hatch explained the importance, in his mind, of the current deduction regime. Although Senator Max Baucus had just mentioned that only about a quarter of Americans took deductions for charitable contributions, Senator Hatch affirmed that the deduction was "of critical importance to me, to the people of Utah, and to millions of Americans who give every year to their churches and communities."[25] In that same hearing, Dallin Oaks, an ecclesiastical leader of the Church of Jesus Christ of Latter-day Saints, testified that the charitable deduction transcended religion, politics, and even economics. Instead, it was "a question about the nature and future of America."[26] The charitable deduction, though not unique to churches and their members, is important to them.

AUDITING SCIENTOLOGISTS

Although a taxpayer must itemize before they can take a charitable deduction, even itemizers face certain limitations on the amount of their charitable contributions that they can deduct. For example, irrespective of how generous an individual is, they cannot deduct charitable contributions in excess of half of their adjusted gross income for the year. If their charitable giving exceeds the 50 percent limitation, they can carry any excess forward for up to five years.[27]

Additionally, to qualify as deductible, charitable contributions must actually be gifts; to the extent a donor expects to receive any substantial benefit from the charity, amounts given to a charity do not qualify as deductible charitable contributions.[28] If a donor receives something in exchange for their charitable donation, then, they can only deduct that portion of their donation in excess of the fair market value of the goods and services they receive.[29]

Much of the time, determining the deductible amount of a donation is easy. If, for example, you donate $100 to NPR and receive a canvas tote bag in exchange, you can go to the NPR store and see that it sells a canvas tote bag for $32.[30] Because you got a bag in exchange for your donation, you cannot deduct the $32 that you effectively spent buying a bag. Rather, you can deduct $68 of the $100 you gave to NPR.

Not everything has an easily discernable fair market value, though. Where a charity provides unique, nonmarket goods or services in exchange for charitable contributions, donors can generally rely on the charity's good faith estimate of their value. A donor cannot, however, rely on the charity's estimate where they know – or should know – that the charity's estimate is unreasonable.[31]

As the benefits donors receive get further from the market, though, their monetary value becomes more and more difficult to ascertain. Big-ticket donors, for example, sometimes demand naming rights in exchange for their gifts. In 2015, for example, David Geffen donated $100 million to Avery Fisher Hall in Lincoln Center. To induce Geffen's generosity, Avery Fisher Hall agreed to rename itself after him.[32]

What is the fair market value of naming rights? There must be one, even if it is less than $100 million: the heirs of Avery Fisher were ultimately willing to relinquish their rights to have his name on the hall in exchange for $15 million.[33] That suggests, in this case, that the naming rights were worth at least $15 million. But the IRS generally treats naming rights as having no value;[34] as a result, as long as Geffen has more than $200 million in income in the year he makes his donation to Avery Fisher Hall, he will be able to deduct his full $100 million donation, even though his name will ultimately grace the building.

Where on this spectrum do religious benefits fall? It depends on the benefit. A general tithe or similar donation to a church, synagogue, or mosque is fully deductible. True, religious individuals presumably receive some benefit from those donations. At the very least, they enjoy the "warm glow" of knowing that they have helped a worthy cause. The IRS considers this type of warm glow too indirect, though, to warrant being treated as a quid pro quo.[35] What about the fact that the donation funds an organization that itself benefits the donor (presuming, of course, that the donor attends and enjoys church)? Under current law, that benefit is also too indirect to count as a quid pro quo, in the same way that a donation to one's local opera is. Most individuals who donate to the opera enjoy and attend opera performances; their donations, then, redound (at least a little bit) to their own benefit. But, like the religious individual who makes a nonquid-pro-quo gift to their church, the opera donor can fully deduct their donation, provided it does not entitle them to any tangible benefits.

Not all donations to churches provide only incidental benefits, though. Some provide specific tangible or religious benefits. For example, where an individual's will provides a bequest to their church, that bequest is tax deductible. But what if the bequest is conditioned on the pastor's saying Mass for members of the donor's family who had died? Such chantry Masses, performed on behalf of the souls of the dead in exchange for gifts to the church, date back at least as far as medieval days.[36] The IRS decided that because the donation goes to the church's general fund, and because the Mass would have occurred with or without the bequest, the fact that the pastor says Mass on behalf of the donor's family members does not represent a quid pro quo. As such, the donor's estate can deduct the full amount of the bequest.[37]

The spiritual nature of the benefit was neither necessary nor sufficient for full deductibility, though. Pew rents, for example, entitle donors to sit in specific, advantageous seats during religious services. Some churches used pew rents as a significant source of operating revenue.[38] Even though the right to sit in a specific pew is a tangible and secular benefit, presumably one with a financial value, the IRS views it as nothing more than a way to contribute to a church and, as such, entirely deductible.[39]

Even though the IRS was generous with the treatment of some spiritual and religious quid pro quos, it was skeptical of the religious nature of contributions to Scientology. Scientologists believe that people's survival depends on their "attainment of brotherhood with the universe."[40] Through auditing, a Scientologist can clear away memory traces – what Scientology calls "engrams" – that would otherwise prevent them from achieving this brotherhood. Ultimately, through auditing, an individual can become Clear, which, according to the Church, provides wide-ranging benefits, including increased IQ, better health, and well-being.[41]

Auditing comes with a price tag: in 2009, different levels of auditing could cost hundreds of dollars per hour.[42] The proceeds from auditing represent the primary revenue source for the Church of Scientology.[43] Still, although there is a clear quid pro quo, it does not seem substantively different than pew rent or money in exchange for a special Mass. The benefit is not a market benefit; rather, it is purely a religious benefit.

Still, whether because of its contentious relationship with Scientology or because it felt that payment for auditing represented a clear exchange, the IRS announced that Scientologists could only deduct their payments for auditing if their payments exceeded the fair market value of the services and benefits they received.[44] But because auditing services are not sold on an open market, and have no objectively ascertainable value, the prices charged by the Church of Scientology were presumptively the fair market value.

After the IRS disallowed their deductions, several Scientologists challenged its determinations in court. Eventually, their case made its way to the Supreme Court. The Supreme Court denied that Scientologists had a constitutional right to deduct their payments to the church. Dispensing with the constitutional challenge, the only question the Court had to answer was whether auditing payments qualified under the tax law as deductible donations.

The Scientologists argued that the quid pro quo analysis was inappropriate in this case, because any benefit they received was purely religious; the Court countered that Congress had not chosen to make the religious nature of the benefit received a lynchpin in deciding whether or not the donor received a benefit. The sole question was whether the payments qualified as contributions or gifts, and were therefore deductible. As defined in the tax law, to be a contribution or gift, the payor could not receive any benefit in exchange.

The decision seems odd in light of the IRS's policy with respect to pew rents and other religious donations that provided the donor with a spiritual or religious benefit. And the Supreme Court appears to have recognized the strangeness of that result. Instead of addressing it, though, the Court sidestepped. The Court explained that its quid pro quo analysis was the law, and, while it acknowledged the IRS's policy with respect to other religions, it claimed that it lacked the factual record to address the administrative consistency of the IRS's different policy for Scientology.[45]

The Supreme Court's ruling probably would not have dealt a devastating blow to Scientology. Still, it would have been costly both to the church and to Scientologists themselves. If payments for auditing were not deductible, Scientologists would bear the full cost themselves. They could react to the higher cost in two ways: either they could reduce the amount of auditing they participated in, which would result in the church receiving less revenue, or they could get the same amount of auditing, which would leave them with less money than they had before.

Although courts had consistently sided with the IRS against the Church of Scientology in questions both of tax exemption and deductibility, in 1993 the IRS and the Church engaged in a *rapprochement* of sorts. The tax law explicitly gives the IRS authority to enter into a written agreement (called a "closing agreement") with a taxpayer who settles their tax liabilities.[46] The IRS and the Church of Scientology did exactly that. While the IRS refused to disclose the settlement agreement, even in the face of Freedom of Information Act requests, a copy was eventually leaked to the *Wall Street Journal*.[47]

A significant purpose of the agreement resolved the question of the church's tax exemption. The church agreed to pay $12.5 million in settlement of its tax liabilities (which by then exceeded $1 billion) and to drop its lawsuits. In exchange, the IRS agreed to recognize the church as exempt from taxes, cancel payroll taxes and penalties against several top Scientologists, and drop audits of thirteen Scientology organizations.[48]

In addition, the IRS's closing agreement appeared to effectively overrule the Supreme Court. True, the closing agreement did not challenge the Supreme Court's legal conclusion that payments for auditing were quid pro quo exchanges and thus nondeductible, but it mooted the consequences. The IRS agreed that going forward it would not contest Scientologists' attempts to deduct their auditing payments.[49] It also allowed Scientologists to deduct 80 percent of their pre-1993 payments for auditing.[50] While agreeing not to contest deductions does not mean that the deductions are legitimate, for all practical purposes, as long as the IRS – the enforcer of the tax law – does not contest the deductibility, Scientologists are free to deduct their payments.[51]

It is worth noting that the idea that a clear quid pro quo (which is how the Supreme Court characterized auditing payments) would nonetheless be deductible is not unique to Scientology. Taxpayers who buy a membership to a museum, for example, can treat their purchase as a deductible charitable donation, provided the museum membership costs less than $75. The payment is deductible even though membership allows members to go to the museum for free, which is a clear benefit received by members.[52] And in 1988, Congress enacted an exception to the quid pro quo rule for wealthy university donors. Under the exception, if a donor pays a university for the right to buy tickets to a university athletic event, the donor can deduct 80 percent of the amount they pay, even though the payment is a clear quid pro quo.[53]

In its decision, though, the Supreme Court had not acknowledged how widespread the exceptions from the quid pro quo rule were, even outside of religion. As a result, Scientologists were jubilant with the IRS deal that allowed them to deduct their auditing payments. A week after the closing agreement, David Miscavige, successor to L. Ron Hubbard and leader of the Church of Scientology, publicly celebrated the IRS's decision. He announced that the decision meant "everything. The magnitude of this is greater than you may imagine."[54] A significant part of their excitement came, not from the actual economic effects of the agreement, but from the legitimacy it entailed. The Church of Scientology used the IRS decision to get recognition and tax-exempt status in other countries.[55] With the apparent imprimatur of the US government, it could forcefully argue that it was a true religion, deserving of that status in other countries, too.[56]

But the strategic value of tax-exempt status in gaining legitimacy should not diminish its economic value to the church and its members. In 1998, the Church of Scientology produced a pamphlet for members describing their tax obligations. The pamphlet differentiates donations for training and auditing services, which "generally qualify for deductions against federal personal income tax returns even though the donor obviously receives an intangible religious benefit as a result of the donation" from donations where "the contributor receives a tangible benefit for his or her contribution." According to the pamphlet, the second category includes, among other things, the purchase of books, cassettes, E-Meters, and other religious materials.[57] Essentially, in the closing agreement, the Church of Scientology got exactly what its members argued for, and lost, in the Supreme Court: that the quid pro quo analysis not include purely religious benefits.

PRIVATE RELIGIOUS SCHOOLS

The IRS's closing agreement did not resolve the quid pro quo question. In fact, it actually exacerbated the problem. As far back as 1954, the IRS had ruled that tuition for parochial or other religious schools was not deductible as a charitable contribution.[58] Michael and Marla Sklar were practicing Orthodox Jews who believed that they had a religious obligation to provide an Orthodox Jewish education to their children. As a result, they sent their five children to Orthodox Jewish day schools and, in the process, paid a significant amount of tuition (in 1995, they ended up paying $27,283 in tuition, fees, and an after-school Mishna program).

In 1993, the Sklars heard about the closing agreement between the IRS and the Church of Scientology. Though they would not have known details of the agreement – it was not leaked until 1997 – they apparently found it intriguing that payments to a tax-exempt religious organization could be tax deductible, even if the donor received an intangible benefit as a result. They decided that the closing agreement had conflicted with the IRS's 1954 revenue ruling. They therefore claimed a portion of the tuition they had paid for their children's schooling as a deduction on their 1993 tax returns, and amended their 1991 and 1992 returns to also claim a deduction for a portion of their tuition payments.[59]

The IRS allowed the Sklars' deductions in 1991, under the erroneous assumption that the Sklars were Scientologists. Even though Michael wrote *and* called the IRS to correct its misunderstanding and explain that the deductions were for religious private school tuition, the IRS allowed the Sklars' full refund claim. Similarly, in 1992 and 1993, the IRS allowed the Sklars to deduct the portion of their tuition payments that they claimed as charitable contributions.

That changed in 1994. In 1994 and 1995, the Sklars claimed a deduction for about 55 percent of their children's tuition and fees. (They chose a 55 percent deduction because their children's schools estimated that 45 percent of the children's instruction was secular, while the other 55 percent was religious.)

The IRS rejected their 1994 and 1995 claims for deduction, and the Sklars challenged the IRS's determination in court.[60]

The courts soundly rejected the Sklars' challenge, following, instead, the Supreme Court's ruling in *Hernandez*. The Court of Appeals for the Ninth Circuit held that *Hernandez's* quid pro quo analysis "clearly forecloses the Sklars' argument that there is an exception in the Code for payments for which one receives purely religious benefits."[61] According to the courts, for tax law purposes, there is no difference between receiving religious and nonreligious benefits in exchange for donations to a church; as long as there is a quid pro quo, the donations are not deductible.

But what about the closing agreement? The Sklars argued that if the IRS allowed Scientologists to deduct the cost of auditing and training, it had to permit their deductions for their children's Orthodox Jewish education. Not doing so would violate the Establishment Clause and the principle of administrative consistency.

The court disagreed with both assertions. The Establishment Clause did *not* require the extension of the Scientology deduction to all religions. Such an extension would both violate the tax law and impermissibly entangle the government with religion. But more importantly, while the court appeared uncomfortable with granting a policy benefitting a particular religion, it was even more uncomfortable expanding the policy to benefit *all* religions.

The court also rejected the Sklars' premise that not extending the Scientology policy to all religious payments was administratively inconsistent. While both Scientologists and the Sklars claimed that their payments were for religious benefits, the court disagreed that the Sklars and Scientologists were similarly situated. Rather, it found the education provided by Orthodox Jewish day schools dissimilar to the auditing and training provided by the Church of Scientology. And, said the court, the IRS has no obligation of treating dissimilar things the same.[62] Tuition payments, even to religious schools, are not deductible, and the Scientology closing agreement does nothing to change that. To the extent that the IRS administratively overruled the Supreme Court, it only did so for Scientologists.

COMPLICATIONS WITH DEDUCTIBLE DONATIONS

Although the court grounded its denial of the Sklars' deductions in the idea that differences between instruction in Orthodox Jewish day schools and auditing in Scientology differ substantively, the assertion rings slightly hollow. True, they differ, but both involve a kind of religious education. Treating them differently feels somehow inconsistent.

That inconsistency multiplies when we consider other questions of deductibility. In 1968, Jacob and Leona Oppewal donated $900 to the Whitinsville Society for Christian Instruction and deducted that $900 on their tax return. The Society had been organized to advance the cause of education, and did so by operating a school. The school did not charge tuition; instead, it was funded by the Society. The Society, in turn, raised money by soliciting donations from its members, nonmembers, and local churches. While parents of children at the school provided about 40 percent of its operating budget, no child was turned away because their parents did not or could not pay tuition.[63]

The IRS disallowed $640 of the Oppewals' donation, treating it as, in essence, a tuition payment for their two children, and therefore nondeductible. The courts agreed. Even though payment went into a general fund rather than being earmarked toward the education of the Oppewals' children, the court looked at a more objective test: did the Oppewals receive something of value in exchange? They did, said the court – they received an education for their children.[64] Essentially, the IRS and the courts prevented parents from transforming a nondeductible expense (tuition payments to a religious school) into deductible payments (donations to a religious society) by looking at the substance of the payment.

The First Circuit Court of Appeals, which decided the *Oppewal* case, is not alone in its conclusion. Both the Second Circuit and the Ninth Circuit have also disallowed parents' deductions for donations to Christian educational associations.[65] As a general rule, where donations from the parents of students represent a significant portion of the donations these organizations receive, the IRS and the courts treat the donations as nondeductible disguised tuition payments.

Just because a church member's children get reduced tuition does not mean, however, that the IRS will disallow the parents' charitable deduction for donations to the church. The IRS looked at a church-run school that enrolled both the children of members and the children of nonmembers. Members' children did not have to pay tuition, while nonmembers' children paid.

The IRS could have come to the defensible – and easily administrable – conclusion that when a parent donates to a religious organization and gets a tuition discount at an affiliated school, a portion of the parent's donation must be treated as nondeductible tuition. Instead, though, the IRS looked at how the donations and the fundraising were structured. It noted that most members of the church did not have children in the school, that all members contributed to the church, and that contributions from parents were put in the same general fund as contributions from nonparents. Moreover, the church used the general fund to pay for all of the church's activities, not just school-related expenses. The church did not do any additional fundraising from parents of children at the school. In those circumstances, the IRS said, donations to the church from parents of children in the church-run school were not disguised tuition, and were fully deductible by the parents.[66]

But this conclusion ultimately proved to be very specific to the set of facts the IRS laid out. Another church offered to pay the tuition of members' children who attended a particular school that was formally unrelated to the church. At the same time, it requested that members who took advantage of its tuition offer increase their donations to the church by the amount they would have otherwise paid in tuition. About a quarter of the families in the church took advantage of the tuition offer.

The church's initial request for higher donations was the only time it requested that the families increase their donations. It did not apply any pressure to parents to pay more in donations and, because the church did not publicize the amount that any individual gave, there was also no social pressure for families with children at the school to give more.

Although many members of the church gave generously, donations from those families with children in the school constituted about half of the donations the church received. On average, then, families with children at the school donated three times as much as families without children in the school. The IRS latched onto this outsized average giving, as well as the fact that giving parents' more-generous giving dropped off in the summer, when school was out of session, to hold that this was essentially a failed attempt to fit within the space it had opened up for parents to make fully deductible donations to churches while receiving free tuition for their children.[67]

Of course, the IRS's walking back the space it had opened significantly complicates the question of deductibility. Individual parents who take advantage of the church's tuition program cannot know whether, on average, they are paying more than members who do not use the tuition program, especially where the church does not disclose members' donations. At the margins, then, parents cannot know whether their donations will be treated as tuition substitutes, or whether they will be fully deductible. True, the IRS also bases its determination on the fact that parents know the program cannot continue if they do not contribute, but presumably, even in a permissible tuition program, parents would be aware that without their donations, their children's education could be impacted. Though the IRS did not explicitly reverse its earlier decision, its inconsistent reentries into the question have made the question of deducting donations to private religious schools virtually unworkable administratively.

ADMINISTRATIVE REQUIREMENTS

Although both the Scientologists and the Sklars pointed out the ambiguity that *can* inhere to the deduction for charitable donations, in most cases, there will be no such ambiguity. But even where donations to a church are unquestionably deductible, an individual must meet certain administrative criteria to take the deduction. And those criteria apply to religious donations in precisely the same way they apply to nonreligious charitable contributions.

In addition to donating to a qualifying nonprofit organization, donors who wish to deduct their donations must jump through three hoops. As discussed at the beginning of this chapter, the first hoop donors must jump through is itemization. If a religious individual wants to deduct their donations to their church, they must itemize their deductions. And while charities have occasionally lobbied to make the charitable deduction available to non-itemizers and itemizers alike, they have had no luck in doing so.[68] Even if there had, there have been no calls (no serious ones, at any rate) for religious donations, and religious donations alone, to become available to nonitemizers.

The second hoop charitable donors face is a limitation on how much they can deduct. Roughly speaking, donors to churches cannot take charitable deductions in excess of half of their adjusted gross income, and donors to certain other religious nonchurch charities are limited to 30 percent of their adjusted gross income.[69] The Treasury Department initially recommended this type of limitation on deductibility on the theory that everybody should pay some taxes, and thus that a person should not be able to eliminate their tax liability entirely through charitable donations.[70] Admittedly, limiting charitable deductions to 50 percent, or even to 30 percent, of a person's income does not seem too terribly oppressive. Most people, after all, cannot realistically afford to donate half of their income to charity.

For certain religious individuals, though, such a limitation has real consequences. Effectively, Rev. Fogarty and Sister Schuster, the Jesuit priest and the nun discussed in Chapter 4, owe taxes *even though* they each took a vow of poverty and, in fact, donated all of their income to their orders. The various courts found that the income they earned working for the University of Virginia and the National Health Services Corps respectively was taxable to them, notwithstanding the fact that they never exercised control over the money. Still, in the first instance, the existence of the charitable deduction ameliorates any apparent unfairness here. Though Sister Schuster had to include the amounts the National Health Services Corps paid her in gross income, by donating it to her Order, she could receive a concomitant deduction. If she earned $15,920 and donated $15,920, that is, the deduction would offset her income, leaving her with no net tax liability.

Except that the deduction limitation means that she could not deduct more than $7,960 (that is, half of the income she earned). In spite of donating her full salary to her Order pursuant to her vow of poverty, she would have a tax liability that she would have to pay. But if the intent of the limitation was to prevent taxpayers from zeroing out their tax liability, in this case it works. The limitation does not take into account *why* an individual donates the amount they do to charity, and certainly does not care if their motivation is religious or not. Rather, it imposes a bright-line limitation, and that limitation applies even to those religious individuals who have taken a vow of poverty and have followed through on it.

Finally, the third hoop charitable donors face is a recordkeeping hoop. The burden of proving entitlement to a deduction rests with the taxpayer claiming the deduction. Charitable donors who want to deduct their donation must retain evidence of that donation. Donors should have either cancelled checks or receipts from the charitable organization, but absent those, need some sort of reliable written record that shows the name of the recipient charitable organization, the date of the donation, and the amount of the donation.[71]

These recordkeeping rules apply whether the donation is to a religious or nonreligious charity, and whether the donor is religious or not. Donald and Sandra Wesley, for example, ran Disciples Empowered by Christ Ministries, a community outreach program. Mr. Wesley served as the ministry's pastor, and he controlled the ministry.

In 2011, the Wesleys claimed a charitable deduction of $28,697. To support their claimed deduction, the Wesleys relied on their testimonies and on documents entitled "Contributions Statements." The court found their testimony self-serving and uncorroborated, and chose not to give their testimony significant credence. (In any event, the testimony was not any kind of written record, as required by the Treasury regulations.)

In court, Mr. Wesley admitted that he had fabricated the Contribution Statements three years after the donation. He had also backdated them from 2014 to 2011. Although the Contributions Statements were written records, the court determined that they were not *reliable* written records, and thus denied the Wesleys' charitable deductions.

Religious donors are subject to the same hoops as nonreligious charitable donors, which makes sense. The purpose behind the hoops is to ensure that deductible donations happened and that the taxpayer does not claim a higher deduction than what they are entitled to receive. And the hoops that exist do not seem to offend any kind of religious sensibility. It is not clear, then, that religious taxpayers would need an accommodation from these generally applicable, nor is it clear that any taxpayer (including the Wesleys) has claimed entitlement to such an accommodation.

Under current law, then, the ability of religious individuals to deduct their religious donations follows the same contours, and is subject to the same requirements, as nonreligious individuals. The questions raised by deductibility – including what counts as value received in exchange – face all charitable donors, and, while the answers may be ambiguous, the courts do not recognize them as uniquely religious. The questions, then, are not a matter of accommodation, but a matter of the line-drawing courts and the IRS are constantly called upon to adjudicate.

8

A Right to Tithe?

Generally, when we think about the intersection between tithing and tax, we think about the deductibility issues addressed in the previous chapter. Deductibility is the most salient tax issue surrounding donations to churches. It is not the *only* relevant tax issue, though. Even where donations are clearly deductible, sometimes an individual may not be in a financial position to pay their taxes *and* to pay whatever amount their religion requires them to pay.

For religious believers, these payment obligations are divinely mandated, and thus are not to be taken lightly. And while, in the United States, religions lack the authority of the state to audit their followers, there is reason to believe that the very status of these donations as religiously mandated means that they enjoy a relatively high level of compliance.

While religions in the United States largely depend on the generosity of their members for financial solvency, many do not mandate a particular amount believers should pay.[1] Instead, they leave amounts to their members' generosity and conscience. Where an individual's religion does not require them to donate a set amount to the religion (or to the poor), their financial obligations to state and to God are unlikely to collide. Instead, to the extent their taxes eat up a portion of their disposable income, they can reduce their religious giving by that amount. Even if they would rather use that money to fulfill religious, rather than civic, obligations, ultimately the flexible nature of their religiously motivated financial obligations allows them to avoid irreconcilable conflict.

Some religious traditions, though, impose more specific financial duties on their members, defining the amounts their members need to donate. Many Orthodox Jewish communities, for example, observe the obligation of *ma'aser kesafim*. Jewish law mandates that, if a poor person appears before you asking for charity, you must meet their needs. Ultimately, the practice of *ma'aser kesafim* (literally "a tenth of the money") developed to help people meet this religious-giving obligation. Rather than waiting until a poor person comes asking for help, people separate out an amount in advance, and distribute that to the poor. Generally, rabbis consider paying 10 percent of an individual's income as meeting this obligation, though many set 20 percent as the ideal.[2]

Similarly, a number of other religious traditions require believers to contribute a set percentage of their income or assets toward religious purposes. The Third Pillar of Islam is *zakat*, or almsgiving, and Muslims have a religious obligation to pay these alms. *Zakat* is similar in many ways to *ma'aser kesafim*. Like *ma'aser kesafim*, *zakat* is meant explicitly to redistribute surplus wealth from the rich to the poor, in order both to close the gap between rich and poor and to help the payor purify themselves. Unlike *ma'aser kesafim* (and many Christian versions of tithing), though, Muslims pay *zakat* on wealth, not on income. Though the rates vary depending on the underlying asset, the rate of *zakat* is typically about 2.5 percent of a Muslim's wealth in excess of a base amount. Although the government collects *zakat* as a tax in some Muslim countries, in the United States, Islamic centers are the principal collectors and distributors of *zakat*.[3]

Some Christian religions believe in a formal tithing. When *Christianity Today* asked its readers what tithing meant, 36 percent of the 244 respondents said that tithing meant paying 10 percent of a believer's income to their church, and more than half believed that tithing required a believer to pay 10 percent of their income either to their church or to a religious charity.[4] The online poll was clearly not scientific – its sample was self-selected and relatively small – but it provides anecdotal evidence that some portion of Christians view tithing both as normative and as consisting of a set percentage of a believer's income. The Southern Baptist Convention, for example, teaches "that a 10 percent tithe belongs to God, is due to God, and should be given to God."[5] Similarly, Seventh-Day Adventists and the Church of Jesus Christ of Latter-day Saints teach that 10 percent of an individual's income belongs to God and should be paid as tithing.[6]

For religious believers whose faiths require them to make a set donation, conflict between various financial obligations is a very real possibility. Some of those conflicts, while real and meaningful, do not invoke the state or the law at all. Where a Mormon must choose between their tithing obligation and buying groceries, for example, they face a real financial and spiritual conflict. Ultimately, they will need to decide how to navigate the conflict. They may choose to tithe and go hungry. They may choose to buy food and ignore (or delay) their religious duty. They may split the difference in some way. But their choice ultimately has no legal significance; the state does not require that they spend their money in a particular way.

But there are situations where the conflict between religious and personal financial decisions does implicate the state. The most obvious example is where a religious believer declares bankruptcy. US bankruptcy law allows individuals who cannot meet their financial obligations to restructure their debts. Bankruptcy is not, however, a private restructuring of debt – it is facilitated by the government, and ultimately overseen by the courts. And the restructuring is not bilateral – it involves the debtor and everybody to whom the debtor has a debt.[7]

Because bankruptcy is supposed to protect both debtors and creditors, and because it is supposed to be objective and fair, debtors cannot discriminate between creditors. They cannot choose, for example, to repay a loan from a friend while ignoring their obligations to the bank. As part of this emphasis on fairness to creditors, declaring bankruptcy necessarily affects a religious individual's ability to tithe or make other donations to their religion. Until 1998, in fact, if an insolvent debtor made a donation, the recipient of the donation had to return the money or property so that it could be properly distributed to creditors.[8]

Bankruptcy law did not specifically mention tithing or other religious donations. As a result of Congress's silence, courts could deal with a debtor's desire to tithe while in bankruptcy procedings in one of three ways. They could treat tithing as a proper expense and allow debtors to continue to pay their tithing. If the courts chose to allow tithepaying, the debtor's religious donations would come at the expense of creditors, because the debtor would have fewer assets with which to repay creditors. Alternatively, courts could treat tithing as unreasonable or unnecessary, and thus prohibit bankrupt debtors from meeting their religious financial obligations. Finally, they could treat a portion of a debtor's tithing expense as permissible, but prohibit the debtor from paying the full amount their religious beliefs mandated. Different courts came to each of these three conclusions, depending both on the court and on the debtor.[9]

Prior to the 1980s, although there was no particular protection for debtors' donations to their religions, bankruptcy attorneys largely did not challenge the donations. In the 1980s, however, as larger firms started to enter the area, and looked at the amount of money debtors had transferred to charities. To the chagrin of churches and other charities, these law firms started to revive fraudulent transfer statutes to force the churches and charities to disgorge donations they had received from insolvent parishioners and donors. Churches began to pressure Congress to change the law and in 1998, they succeeded. Congress enacted the Religious Liberty and Charitable Donation Protection Act of 1998, which limits the ability of creditors to attack most charitable and

religious contributions under both federal bankruptcy law and state fraudulent transfer laws. The Act limits the relevance of an individual's charitable
donations in determining whether a debtor is insufficiently distributing their
disposable income. And it explicitly states that it is not meant as a limit on the
Religious Freedom Restoration Act, leaving the door open for churches to use
RFRA to protect donations not covered by the Act.[10]

Although the passage of this bankruptcy accommodation found its genesis in the lobbying of religious groups, its ultimate reach was broader than
just religious individuals. After passage of the Religious Liberty and Charitable Donations Protection Act of 1998, the bankruptcy trustee could no longer
void certain transfers made to a "qualified religious or charitable entity or
organization."[11] For these purposes, qualified religious and charitable entities
are those that are capable of receiving tax-deductible donations.[12] These entities include churches, of course, but also universities, museums, public radio
states, and other so-called public charities.[13]

As with most accommodations, the bankruptcy accommodation for religious donors has winners and losers. The winning side includes insolvent
individuals who face a religious obligation to make donations. It includes
religious organizations. And it includes other individuals who want to make
charitable donations, as well as the recipients of their generosity. Even in
the face of bankruptcy, a religious individual can now meet their religiously
motivated financial obligations, as long as those obligations are to make donations directly to a tax-exempt religious body. And churches, synagogues, and
mosques do not need to worry about the financial status of their members.
They can accept donations without risking the future disgorgement of those
amounts.

The federal government did impose certain limitations on its accommodation, however. The bankruptcy law only protects individuals' donations, for
example; religious and charitable donations by insolvent corporations and
partnerships can be voided. In addition, for a charitable donation to benefit from this protection, the insolvent donor must make the donation to a
tax-exempt entity. A donation directly to the poor, even if such a donation is
made as the result of an individual's religious commitments, does not qualify
for protection. And the amount of protected donations is generally limited to
15 percent of a donor's gross income for the year of the donation, unless the
individual has established a pattern of donating more.[14]

Why limit the amount of religious contributions an individual in
bankruptcy can make? Because the bankruptcy accommodation also has
losers. Every dollar that a bankrupt individual can donate to their religion is
one dollar less that can go to creditors. Any type of religious accommodation

may impose costs (albeit nonfinancial ones sometimes) on those who do not benefit from the accommodation, but this religious accommodation in bankruptcy law underscores the financial burdens that other parties may face. If a bankrupt individual has $50,000 in debts and $25,000 in assets, their creditors will collectively only receive half of what the individual owe them. But if that person pays $5,000 in tithing, on average, creditors will only receive 45 cents on the dollar, or five percentage points less than they would receive if they could void the individual's tithing and require their church to disgorge it.

TAX LAW

The function and form of the tax law differ significantly from those of the bankruptcy law. While both the tax and bankruptcy law attempt to promote fairness, their underlying goals differ. Where bankruptcy law attempts to protect a debtor while providing a fair recovery for creditors, the tax law focuses on raising revenue for government programs.

Unlike the bankruptcy law, tax law contains no general and explicit accommodation of tithe paying. Yes, religious donors can deduct their donations in the same way nonreligious donors deduct their donations to other charities. But, while the government is willing to force other creditors to yield to debtors' religious obligations, it has not chosen to yield itself. A taxpayer who must choose between paying their taxes and paying their tithing does not get a choice: they must pay their taxes on time or face interest and potential penalties when they pay them late.

Most of the time, of course, the amount a taxpayer owes in taxes does not truly conflict with the amount they want to pay in religious offerings. Money is fungible and, if the individual truly wants to make religious offerings, nothing stands in their way. If they owe too much in taxes to make their offerings, they can reduce their spending somewhere else. Or they can reduce their offerings. Or they can pay less in taxes than they owe, and face the legal consequences of doing so. But, unlike the bankruptcy regime, the tax law does not impose limitations on how an individual spends their money.

Or, rather, it does not impose limitations on how an individual spends their money in most cases. There are two situations in which the tax law both takes note of, and circumscribes, how an individual spends their money: installment agreements and offers in compromise.

Installment agreements principally benefit taxpayers who do not have enough cash to pay their tax liabilities and do not have assets that they can borrow against, but who earn enough money to eventually allow them to pay off their tax liabilities. A taxpayer in that situation can request that the IRS allow them to pay their taxes in installments over time. Generally, the IRS has discretion to allow these installment agreements if doing so will facilitate its full or partial collection of the tax.[15] Although interest continues to accrue until the tax liability is paid in full (potentially doubling or tripling the ultimate amount the taxpayer pays to the IRS) the installment agreement is beneficial to taxpayers in several ways. It gives a delinquent taxpayer additional time to pay their tax liability. It permits some degree of planning. And it protects the taxpayer from IRS collection actions (including levies and wage garnishment) as long as the taxpayer is complying with their agreement.[16]

While an installment agreement unquestionably helps taxpayers, it increases the government's risk of not collecting the tax. If the IRS were to institute the more aggressive tools it has at its disposal, it could ensure its collection of the tax debt. By permitting a taxpayer to pay over time, though, an installment agreement increases the chances that the taxpayer will default, whether because they lose their job or because they have time to hide their assets, or just out of carelessness. To try to ameliorate this risk, the IRS requires a taxpayer to include detailed financial information with their application for an installment agreement.[17] Among other things, the taxpayer needs to tell the IRS what personal and real property they own (including the value of the property) and their and their spouse's income (including wages, dividends, interest, and other forms of income). At the same time, the form asks about certain of the taxpayer's monthly living expenses, ranging from food and housing to secured debts.[18]

Not every delinquent taxpayer has a realistic chance of paying their full tax liabilities. Even where a taxpayer does not qualify for an installment agreement, they may qualify to make an offer in compromise. An offer in compromise still may allow a taxpayer to pay their tax liability over time, but will allow them to pay less than the full amount of their liabilities. While there are three grounds to qualify for an offer in compromise – doubt as to liability, doubt as to collectability, or the promotion of effective tax administration – for purposes of looking at religious accommodation, only the doubt as to collectability matters. "Doubt as to collectability" means that a taxpayer does not have enough income or assets to pay the full tax liability.[19] Naturally, to come to this conclusion, the taxpayer requesting an offer in compromise needs to disclose their income, assets, and expenses to the IRS; the IRS requires the same financial disclosures from a taxpayer requesting an offer in compromise as it does from a taxpayer requesting an installment agreement.[20]

While generally there is no actual conflict between a person's religiously motivated financial obligations and their tax obligations, applying for an installment agreement or an offer in compromise can pit a taxpayer's religious obligations against their tax obligations. Even here, the conflict between religious and tax obligations is nowhere near as stark as the conflict engendered under the bankruptcy regime. If a taxpayer whose installment agreement or whose offer in compromise has been accepted by the IRS pays tithing in place of taxes, the recipient church does not have to disgorge the amounts the taxpayer paid. Paying something other than the installment obligation is not a fraudulent transfer. Rather, when a taxpayer violates any of the terms of an offer in compromise or an installment agreement, the IRS can cancel the agreement, with the full amount of taxes owed coming due immediately.[21]

Even without an explicit conflict though, the IRS can ignore most taxpayers' religious contributions in determining how much a taxpayer can pay, and when they can pay it. The IRS uses the financial information it collects to determine whether a taxpayer qualifies for an installment agreement or an offer in compromise. It also uses the information a taxpayer provides about their income, assets, and liabilities to determine how much the taxpayer must pay and, if the liability is to be paid in installments, how much they must pay in each installment. The questions of *when* and *how much* ultimately reside with the IRS; the IRS has significant discretion in determining both whether to permit a taxpayer to defer or avoid their tax liability and the terms under which such deferral or reduction will occur.[22]

For religious individuals, then, the question becomes whether the IRS will take their religious payments into account in determining whether they qualify for an installment agreement or offer in compromise and in determining how much they can pay.

As it decides how much a taxpayer can pay, the IRS classifies the taxpayer's expenses. It will take into account allowable expenses, which it defines as expenses necessary for the taxpayer's health, welfare, and/or production of income. Once it decides which of a taxpayer's expenses are allowable, it then decides the amount of expenses it will recognize. Just because an expense is allowable, that is, does not mean that the taxpayer can reduce their available income by the amount of their actual expense. Food, for example, is an allowable expense, but if a taxpayer is going out to Michelin-rated restaurants every night, the IRS may reduce the amount of the expense it allows. Generally speaking, the IRS uses a national standard to calculate what it will allow for food, clothing, and other similar amounts, while it uses a local standard for housing, transportation, and utilities.[23]

Where do religious offerings fall into this framework? Exactly the same place as any other expense: the IRS takes necessary offerings into account, but disallows unnecessary charitable contributions. The only example the IRS provides of charitable contributions that qualify as necessary expenses are charitable contributions required as a condition of a taxpayer's employment. The IRS illustrates such necessary charitable contributions with the example of a minister who is required by their employment contract to tithe.[24]

Though the IRS's exemplar of a charitable contribution that qualifies as an allowable expense is a religious payment, its inclusion here does not come from an accommodationist framework. Rather, it fits precisely within the secular framework that the IRS has established. The minister in the IRS's example is obligated, under their employment contract, to tithe. Their tithing expense, then, is necessary for their production of income. As such, it fits precisely within the definition of an allowable expense.

And for other religious taxpayers? In evaluating applications for installment agreements, the IRS does not concern itself with taxpayers' eternal souls. If a taxpayer does not have an employment-related obligation to tithe, the IRS's guidelines do not make an exception to its general exclusion of charitable contributions. In nonreligious situations, courts will not second-guess the IRS's procedures in determining the reasonable collection potential of a taxpayer, and rejecting proposed offers where that potential is sufficiently high.[25]

That kind of deference makes sense, of course, where the expense is a nonreligious expense. There is no constitutional obligation for the IRS to take a taxpayer's personal (and possibly idiosyncratic) spending into account in determining how much they can afford to pay. But do the Religion Clauses of the Constitution require the IRS to treat religious contributions differently?

George Thompson and Bradley Pixley argued that the Constitution did mandate different treatment. While there were significant differences between Thompson's and Pixley's situations, each had outstanding tax liabilities, each believed that he had a divinely mandated obligation to tithe, and each requested that the IRS take his tithing obligation into account in determining how much he could pay.

Pixley was an ordained Baptist minister. From 1995 until 2001 he served as pastor of Grace Community Bible Church in Texas, while also working at Cardiology Associates of Houston, Texas. In 2001, he and his wife moved to Los Angeles, where he began a job as an echocardiographer at Children's Hospital.

Shortly before Pixley moved, he received a letter from the IRS. In the letter, the IRS threatened to impose a levy on Pixley because of the almost $60,000 in taxes from 1992 and 1993 that he had failed to pay. In response, Pixley submitted an offer in compromise, in which he proposed to pay less than the full amount he owed in full satisfaction of his tax liabilities.

With his offer in compromise, Pixley submitted the mandated financial disclosure. Among the monthly living expenses he listed was a $520 tithe. The IRS requested evidence that the tithe was a condition of Pixley's employment. When he failed to respond to the IRS request, the IRS determined that Pixley had the ability to fully pay his unpaid tax liabilities, and rejected his offer in compromise.

Pixley challenged the IRS's determination in court, arguing both that paying tithes *was* a condition of Pixley's employment and that disallowing tithing expense violated Pixley's First Amendment rights. The Tax Court demurred in addressing the question of whether Pixley owed the $60,000 the IRS assessed against him. Pixley had not challenged his underlying tax liability, so the only question in front of the court was whether the IRS's rejection of his offer in compromise was permissible. Unless the court found that the IRS Appeals Office had abused its discretion, it could not reverse the IRS's rejection of Pixley's offer in compromise.

And here, the court found that the IRS had clearly not abused its discretion in determining that Pixley did not have to tithe as a condition of his employment. Even assuming that Southern Baptist Convention doctrine requires members to tithe (which it does), if Pixley wanted the IRS to take his tithing into account in determining whether he qualified for an offer in compromise, it was his job to demonstrate that paying tithing was a condition of his employment. And because he never responded to the IRS's request for information, he did not bear that burden. Even if he had produced that evidence at trial – which, from the opinion, it looks like he did not – his failure to produce it upon the IRS's request means that the IRS had not abused its discretion in rejecting his offer in compromise.

The abuse-of-discretion question is ultimately only relevant if the IRS's criteria are constitutionally permissible, though. And Pixley argued that they were not. By refusing to make allowance for tithing expenses Pixley asserted that the IRS had impermissibly reduced the amount of money religious taxpayers had available to support their religion. If that were an accurate understanding of the Free Exercise Clause, the IRS would have to treat any tithing as a necessary expense in evaluating offers in compromise, whether or not the taxpayer was a minister, and whether or not the tithing was somehow necessary for the production of income. Recognizing tithing, according to Pixley, was a necessary accommodation.

The Tax Court rejected Pixley's constitutional claim. He had a point, the Tax Court acknowledged, that paying taxes may reduce the amount of money religious taxpayers have to support their religion. But, the court said, "this is a burden, common to all taxpayers, on their pocketbook, rather than a recognizable burden of the free exercise of their religious beliefs." The First Amendment does not entitle an individual to do everything they want in the pursuit of their religious practices.

Moreover, the court said, even if the IRS's refusal to take tithing into account *did* impose a recognizable burden on Pixley's free exercise of his religion, he would still lose. The burden it imposed would be justified by the government's need to collect tax and administer a workable tax system. The government's interest in collecting taxes is sufficiently compelling to justify its refusal to provide an unlimited accommodation for delinquent taxpayers to reduce their tax liabilities by the amount of religious offerings they want to make.[26]

Almost a decade later, the Tax Court revisited the question of whether and when the IRS must consider the tithing of a delinquent taxpayer. George Thompson was the president of Compliance Innovations, Inc. In addition, Thompson was a practicing Mormon. He regularly paid a tithe of 10 percent of his income. In addition, as part of his religious practice, he volunteered both in the church's Manhattan Temple and with a Mormon Church-affiliated Boy Scout troop.

In 2008, the IRS determined that Compliance Innovations had failed to withhold and pay over to the IRS more than $150,000 in employment taxes between 2004 and 2007. Although it was Compliance Innovations, not Thompson, that had failed to pay the taxes, Congress provided that certain officers and employees of corporations could face personal liability for unpaid withholding taxes.[27] As a result, Thompson became personally liable for the delinquent employment taxes.

This was not the first time that Thompson had been in trouble with the IRS. In fact, it was not even the first time that Compliance Innovations had failed to withhold and pay employment taxes it owed. In addition to corporate tax problems, Thompson and his wife had underpaid their taxes in 1992, 1995, 1996, 1999, and 2000. In all, at the time the Tax Court heard his case, Thompson owed more than $730,000 of unpaid personal taxes in addition to the $150,000 the IRS assessed for 2004–2007.

Faced with more than $880,000 in tax liabilities, Thompson requested a partial payment installment agreement. In his application, he, like Pixley, included the required financial disclosures. He reported monthly income of $27,633 and monthly expenses of $24,416. He offered to pay $3,000 a month toward his tax liabilities. At $3,000, it would take him more than twenty-four years to pay his delinquent tax liability, even if it did not accrue interest (which it would).

As part of his monthly expenses, Thompson included $2,110 of tithing and $232 of other church service expenses. The IRS disallowed his religious expenses, as well as the $2,952 he claimed in college expenses for his children. It determined that he had allowable monthly expenses of $19,244, and that he could afford a monthly payment of $8,389 toward his tax liability. At $8,389, he could pay his full tax liability (again, pretending that it would not accrue interest) in less than nine years. (With interest, of course, repayment would take longer, both under the $3,000 per month and the $8,389 per month plans.)

Like Pixley, Thompson did not challenge his underlying tax liability. Rather, he, too, challenged the IRS's refusal to take his tithing into account as it calculated how much he could afford to pay. Like Pixley, Thompson argued that, under IRS procedures, it should have treated his tithing as a necessary expense. And like Pixley, he argued that even if it was a conditional expense, the Free Exercise Clause of the First Amendment compelled the IRS to take his tithing expense into account. In addition, he argued that treating his tithing as a conditional expense violated RFRA.

Thompson's claim that the IRS violated its procedures in classifying his tithing as a conditional expense was going to be a hard one for him to win. Though Mormonism requires a 10 percent tithe, it has very few paid clergy, and Thompson was not one of those. Still, he argued, he was "employed" by the church, both as a temple shift coordinator and a stake scouting coordinator. And he had to tithe to maintain those positions.

Neither of those positions paid him anything, though, and he acknowledged that his family's financial welfare would be unaffected if he lost his two religious positions. Still, he argued, the IRS's use of the word "employment" was not limited to compensated employment. The Tax Court disagreed. The reason for the *condition of employment* exemption to ignoring charitable contributions, it said, was to ensure that ministers (and others – the court noted that the condition of employment exception for charitable deductions was not limited to ministers) could keep their jobs. True, reducing a minister's monthly payment by the amount of their tithing ultimately reduces federal revenue. But where their employment is conditioned on the payment of a tithe, preventing them from paying tithing would cause them to lose their job, which would significantly harm the IRS's compelling interest in collecting taxes.

Although the court rejected his claim that his volunteer church positions constituted employment, Thompson had other arguments up his sleeve. He also argued that, even if the volunteer work he did for his church did not qualify as *employment*, IRS procedures also treat expenses for taxpayers' health and welfare as necessary expenses. The inability to tithe, as well as the loss of his volunteer positions, would negatively affect his spiritual welfare. In response, the Tax Court said that requiring the IRS or the courts to determine whether tithing was necessary to an individual's spiritual health would represent an inappropriate church–state entanglement.

The Tax Court's decision makes clear that the IRS's accommodation for some ministers' tithing was not a religiously motivated allowance. Rather, it is a concession meant to maximize the government's collection of tax revenue. Where a religious individual is trying to enter into an installment agreement to pay their taxes over time, the IRS does not care whether they can fully practice their religion. The IRS cares, rather, that the individual can pay back as much of their tax liability as possible, as quickly as possible. And its procedures allow certain ministers to treat tithing expenses as necessary expenses because for those ministers, permitting them to pay tithing represents the best route to being paid.

Of course, as in Pixley's case, if the IRS's refusal to treat tithes as a necessary expense were unconstitutional, it would not matter that the IRS had complied with its procedures. But as in the *Pixley* case, the Tax Court did not recognize the IRS's procedures as violating the Free Exercise Clause. It provided two main justifications for its holding. In one, it echoed the Pixley court, reiterating the fact that taxes are a burden common to all Americans, and do not represent a particular infringement on religious belief. Additionally, in response to Thompson's assertion that not paying tithing would require him to resign his church positions, the court pointed out that the IRS neither required him to resign nor pressured his church to make him resign. Rather, if his church would no longer allow him to fulfill his volunteer roles, that was the decision of the Mormon Church, and not of the government.

Thompson made one final argument for why the IRS should be required to treat his tithe as an allowable expense, an argument that Pixley failed to make. He argued that RFRA required the IRS to recognize his tithe.

Thompson argued that the IRS's refusal to treat his tithing as a necessary expense violated RFRA because it imposed a burden on his religious practice, and was not the least restrictive means the IRS could have used. What was his proposed least restrictive means? To allow him to make monthly payments of $3,000.

The court acknowledged that paying $3,000 a month was less restrictive than paying $8,389 a month. But less restrictive, it explained, was only one part of RFRA; the other, it reminded Thompson, was that the less restrictive means proposed by the taxpayer must satisfy the government's compelling interest. The government has a compelling interest in collecting taxpayers' taxes as quickly as possible. So although paying less imposed less on Thompson's ability to pay his tithes, the IRS had no obligation to accept his offer. Even if Thompson were a minister (which the court assumes for the sake of its discussion), his tithing is a conditional expense, one the IRS could ignore in calculating how much he could pay.[28]

Ultimately, neither Pixley's nor Thompson's case was a hard one to decide. Neither demonstrated that his inability to tithe would impact his ability to make a living, which is what IRS procedures focus on. But, beyond that, neither demonstrated that he would be unable to tithe if he made the payments required by the IRS.

Specifically, the amount of expenses the IRS allowed was arbitrary to some extent. The IRS allowed Thompson, for example, to reduce his income by $4,619 a month (or $55,428 a year) for housing and utilities, an amount in excess of its guidelines for New Jersey. If his tax payment plan actually conflicted with his religious donations, and he sincerely wanted to continue to tithe at his previous rate, nothing in the installment agreement prevented him from moving to a less expensive house, or otherwise reducing his consumption.

But what if Thompson had faced an intractable conflict between his tax-paying and his tithes? Even in that situation, there would be no accommodation of his tithepaying. The courts have made clear that delinquent taxpayers have no constitutional or statutory right to have their religious offerings taken into account when calculating their ability to pay their unpaid taxes or when determining the monthly amount they can afford. As such, courts have left the determination of whether to grant an accommodation to the IRS.

And, although no court has directly answered the question of whether the IRS *must* take into account the religious offerings of ministers whose employment contracts require them to tithe, there is no reason to believe that the IRS must accommodate even these ministers. There is no reason that the IRS would be constitutionally compelled to accommodate ministers, but not other religious individuals. And, in fact, the IRS's reason for accommodating certain ministers' tithes has nothing to do with the religious nature of the payments. Rather, it believes that taking such payments into account, while reducing its immediate revenue, ultimately facilitates its collection of these ministers' taxes.

True, the IRS uses the minister as an example of a necessary expense. But the minister example is merely illustrating situations in which a charitable contribution may be a necessary, and therefore an allowable, expense. If the employee of a nonreligious nonprofit organization were required to donate to their organization under the terms of their employment, their donations would also be treated as necessary and allowable. Religious belief neither adds to nor takes away from the IRS's policy.

CONCLUSION

Many religious traditions require their adherents to make some kind of financial contributions, whether to the religious organization, to the poor, or somewhere else. Some even specify, with some degree of specification, how much an individual needs to contribute to be in God's good graces. And meeting that obligation can force religious individuals to make difficult trade offs. Money is fungible, but it is finite. An individual who feels obligated to donate $5 to their church and follows through cannot use that same $5 to buy coffee. If they have $10, they can do both, but if they only have $7, they cannot meet their religious obligation *and* have their coffee. they must choose.

The tradeoff the individual faces is not unique to religious individuals. A nonreligious individual may have to choose between spending $1,000 on rent or on new furniture. If they had $2,000, they could do both, but if they only have $1,500, they cannot both pay the rent and buy a $1,000 sofa.

The government has no obligation to ameliorate these necessary tradeoffs, even when they implicate religion. Under current law, the government has no obligation to accommodate tithepaying at the expense of its revenue. All delinquent taxpayers have expenses outside of their tax obligations, and the government has established an objective hierarchy of those expenses. It allows expenses that taxpayers must incur to live, expenses that will allow delinquent taxpayers to eventually fulfill their tax obligations.

But the need to make religiously motivated payments does not fit within that box. And it is not a financial dilemma unique to the religious, one that demands behavior that is irrational from a tax perspective. Rather, religiously motivated payments are similar to other charitable donations, or even to other consumption: they are perfectly permissible, but the government does not need to jeopardize its ability to collect taxes by allowing religious individuals the ability to choose to make religious contributions in place of making tax payments.

Ultimately, with or without accommodation, delinquent taxpayers can make their religious offerings. The offerings may require them to sacrifice other consumption, but that kind of sacrifice and tradeoff is a natural part of economic life.

9

Without Purse, Scrip, or Taxes

In April of 1984, Bart Davis, a young Mormon attorney, was reading his church's official magazine. As he flipped through its pages, he came across an article that piqued his interest. Entitled "U.S. Court Rules Missionary Support is Tax-Deductible," the article explained that the Court of Appeals for the Tenth Circuit had ruled that money parents sent to their missionary children was for the benefit of the church, and thus qualified as a deductible donation. The article ended with a recommendation: "Members who might be affected by this ruling may want to consult with their tax adviser in filing 1983 income tax returns, and possibly amended returns for prior years."[1]

The article stuck out to Bart because two of his younger brothers had recently finished their missions for the Mormon Church. Benjamin had performed his missionary work in New York and Cecil in New Zealand and the Cook Islands. Bart mentioned the article to his parents. His father Harold, who worked for the Atomic Energy Commission, and his mother Enid, who worked for LDS Family Services, were life-long Mormons, but they had no particular knowledge about the tax law. Still, they were intrigued and consulted with their accountant. After a little investigation, their accountant thought they had a basis for the deductions, so they filed amended returns, expecting to get a refund from the IRS.

Instead, the IRS rejected their deductions. Bart mentioned the rejection to another attorney at his firm. The attorney's response? "Let's sue them."

With his parents' permission, Bart prepared and filed a suit on their behalf. Shortly after filing suit, he got a phone call from Wilford W. Kirton. Kirton introduced himself as the General Counsel for the Church of Jesus Christ of Latter-day Saints, and explained that the issue of the tax treatment of payments to missionaries was important to the Mormon Church.[2]

The issue was very important to the Mormon Church, in fact. Kirton's firm had been looking to establish test cases, even prior to *White v. United States*,[3] the case Bart had read about. The attorneys at Kirton's firm talked about suggesting a particular parent of a Mormon missionary for the IRS to audit, but ultimately decided their case would work better if the parent of a missionary claimed a deduction for payments made to the child and then filed for a refund. Assuming the IRS rejected the claim, they could get the question of deductibility in front of the courts quickly. After the firm located the *White* case – and won at the appellate court level – they started getting calls from other parents of Mormon missionaries who, like the Whites, had also sent money to their missionary children. One of those calls pointed them toward the Davises.[4]

Kirton explained to Bart that there were currently two cases pending at the trial court level in the Ninth Circuit dealing with this question of deductibility. In addition to his parents' case in Idaho, a suit had been filed in California. The church wanted to look at the two cases to see which had cleaner facts, facts that would allow the court to directly address the question of whether payments to missionaries were deductible. Because bad facts can lead to bad law, the church wanted the case with the cleaner set of facts to go forward. Kirton asked Bart whether his clients would be willing to let him audit their case and, if he did not like their facts, whether they would be willing to dismiss their case.

Bart spoke with his parents, who agreed to let the church audit their case. Harold Davis, a stereotypical engineer, had kept all of the receipts documenting the money he had sent, and sent the receipts to Kirton along with other information Kirton requested. A short time later, Bart got another call, and Kirton told him they had chosen his parents' case. He also mentioned that his firm had an excellent tax department, and asked whether Bart had much experience with tax litigation. Bart admitted that he did not, and Kirton offered to represent his parents, *pro bono*. Bart and his parents agreed, and Bart became co-counsel with Kirton.

The Davises lost at the trial level.[5] After the loss, Kirton again contacted Bart and offered to continue his representation in an appeal to the Ninth Circuit then, after losing again, to the Supreme Court.

THE STRANGE WORLD OF MISSIONARY ECONOMICS

Many churches maintain a missionary force, intended to preach their religious doctrines to the world (or, at least, find and convert those who do not belong to the church in question). Missionaries have been a fixture in Christianity since its inception.[6] And today, two millennia later, many Christian churches continue to send missionaries to proselytize their religious beliefs, to convert others to their religion, or to provide aid and service to people who need it.[7]

There likely exist as many iterations of missionary service as there are denominations that send out missionaries, each with subtly (or not-so-subtly) different activities and goals. A missionary may be an 18-year-old boy, walking in tandem with his partner missionary, wearing a white shirt, tie, and black nametag, and knocking on doors. Alternatively, a missionary may be a person standing in the train station by a display of religious literature. Missionaries include Mother Theresa, serving the poor in India, Jesuits in South America, teenagers hosting events at a playground in Chicago, and doctors treating Ebola patients in Africa.

This diversity of missionary activity complicates questions of missionary economics and, by extension, of missionary taxation. Still, for tax purposes, the various kinds of missionaries can be broadly classified in two categories: employee missionaries and volunteer missionaries. The economics of employee missionaries differ substantially from the economics of volunteer missionaries. Likewise, the tax regimes applicable to the two types of missionaries differ significantly, both from each other and, in many ways, from nonmissionaries.

Employee Missionaries

Domestic employee missionaries – that is, missionaries who are employed by a church or church mission and work in the United States – generally pay federal income taxes on their compensation. (The principal exception to this rule is a missionary who belongs to a religious order, has taken a vow of poverty, and who, subject to that vow of poverty, returns their compensation to the order. This exception, though, has been carved out by the IRS, not by Congress, and is discussed in Chapter 4.) Like any other employee, a missionary's wages constitute taxable income, even if they earn their wages working for God. In general, a domestic employee missionary's taxes are exactly like a nonmissionary's.

In some ways, though, working for God as a missionary may be disadvantageous from a tax perspective. An employee missionary must include certain amounts they receive as gifts in their income, although generally the tax law excludes gifts from its definition of "income."[8] While there is no question that gifts do not constitute taxable income, the tax law does not define "gift." Instead, Congress left the definitional question to the Supreme Court, which ultimately decided that a payment's status as a gift for tax purposes depended on the giver's intent. If the giver made the gift out of "detached and disinterested generosity," out of respect or affection, not expecting anything in return, the payment qualified as a gift, and the recipient did not have to pay taxes on it.[9]

Even a gift given out of detached and disinterested generosity does not always qualify as a nontaxable gift, though. Congress, for example, decided that a gift from an employer to an employee almost never qualifies as a gift for tax purposes.[10] For employee missionaries, there is a similar exception to the general rule of tax-free gifts. In 1968, the IRS announced that support payments to employee missionaries, whether the payments come from the mission itself or from third parties, did not qualify as gifts for tax purposes. If the main reason the third-party donors are making payments to the missionaries is because of the service the missionaries are performing, the IRS said, the payments are income, not gifts, irrespective of how the donor labels the payment.[11] The IRS's rule effectively replaces the Supreme Court's general intent rule with respect to gifts to employee missionaries. Rather than looking at the giver's intent – which may be disinterested generosity – the IRS looks instead to the employee–employer relationship and treats the gift as an indirect payment from the religious employer, which never qualifies as a tax gift.

The same broad taxing regime that applies to employee missionaries in the United States also applies to American employee missionaries stationed in foreign countries. The United States' ability to tax income is not limited by geography; it can and does tax any money earned by US citizens, irrespective of where they earn it or, for that matter, where they live.[12] Despite the near limitless potential reach of US taxing power, though, the United States has tempered its worldwide taxation in a number of ways. Among these is an exclusion for foreign earned income.[13] In its original incarnation, enacted in 1926, a US citizen who lived abroad for at least six months would not have to pay taxes on their foreign earned income.[14] While Congress enacted this exclusion to increase foreign trade,[15] its enactment also benefitted foreign missionaries. As long as a missionary lived abroad for at least six months, the income they received for performing missionary work (as opposed, for example, to passive income from an investment portfolio) would not be subject to US tax.

While this exclusion was available to any US citizen who lived and worked abroad, the IRS broadened its applicability for missionaries. Many missionary societies allowed their missionaries to take an occasional "furlough," or home leave. The idea of the furlough may have been borrowed from British military and government officials stationed in colonial India. These British colonial furloughs were rhetorically justified as allowing military and government officials to recuperate from the putative health hazards attendant to being stationed in tropical climates.

Mission furloughs borrowed the idea of physical recuperation, but missionaries on furlough were encouraged to do more than merely recover. Furloughs were an opportunity for missionaries to reconnect with their families and the congregations that sent and supported them. Networking with their families and friends allowed furloughed missionaries to rekindle the missionary spirit of those at home, and allowed missionaries to thank their supporters personally.[16] In addition to resting and networking, missionaries on furlough were expected to study and train, and to prepare for the end of their furlough when they would return to their full-time missionary work.[17]

Whatever their religious and recuperative benefits, furloughs could result in disadvantageous tax results for employee missionaries who took them. Returning to the United States meant that the missionary was no longer a foreign resident, and any furlough allowance they received from their supporters while in the United States would not qualify for the foreign earned income exemption. Furthermore, when they returned to their foreign mission, they would have to reestablish their foreign residency.

Faced with the question of the tax consequences of missionary furloughs, the IRS decided to treat missionaries differently than other foreign employees who returned to the United States. Even though furloughed missionaries lived in the United States, the IRS determined that the furlough did not cause them to lose their foreign residency, as long as they intended to return to their foreign posting at the end of the furlough.

This determination had two significant consequences for foreign missionaries. First, they did not have to reestablish foreign residency when they returned from their furloughs. Instead, they instantly and automatically requalified for the exclusion. But more importantly, the IRS determined that the furlough allowance was foreign source income, attributable to missionaries' foreign residence. In other words, even if a furloughed missionary lived in the United States when they received their furlough allowance, as long as they intended to return to their foreign mission, they did not have to pay US taxes on the money they received.[18]

As the result of some legislative changes, the IRS eventually walked its broad exclusion back slightly. Rather than allowing missionaries to exclude their full furlough allowance, the IRS allowed them to exclude only that amount attributable to their final year in the foreign country. In addition, they had to pay taxes on any amount they received for work they performed in the United States while on furlough.[19] With that, the IRS ensured that the tax treatment of foreign missionaries matched the requirements for nonmissionary expatriates.

Like the IRS's special exclusion for furloughed missionaries, the broader exclusion for expatriates has not stayed static. Since its 1926 enactment, it has gone through several iterations, each with small differences. Today, US citizens living and working abroad do not enjoy a blanket exemption from taxes on all income they earn. Rather, the exclusion has an inflation adjusted ceiling and, if an expatriate earns more than the ceiling (in 2017, $102,100[20]), they owe US taxes on the excess.

For most missionaries, however, this ceiling is probably irrelevant. According to the Bureau of Labor Statistics, in 2014, nonclergy religious workers earned a median income of $34,700. At the ninetieth percentile, they earned $62,880.[21] While the Bureau of Labor Statistics numbers are imperfect for our purposes – they do not break out missionaries in particular, and they provide salaries for religious employees working in the United States, not abroad – they strongly suggest that few religious employees, presumably including foreign missionaries, will earn more than the exclusion amount.

Mostly, then, the federal income tax treatment of employee missionaries tracks the tax treatment of nonmissionary employees, albeit with some small variations. Missionaries and nonmissionaries are not, however, on identical footing for all federal tax purposes. While most US taxpayers who earn money are subject to social security taxes, certain ordained ministers can choose be exempt from paying these self-employment taxes.[22] The IRS decided that ordained missionaries – whether foreign or domestic – are always exempted from these employment taxes, whether or not their missionary work is directed by their religious superiors, and irrespective of the specific services they perform.[23]

Not being subject to social security taxes represents a real reduction in taxes. Currently, these taxes are imposed at a rate of 12.4 percent.[24] That 12.4 percent tax is the most significant federal tax many taxpayers face: most taxpayers earning less than $200,000 pay more in social security taxes than they do in federal income taxes.[25]

The net benefit of avoiding social security taxes must take into account the fact that these missionaries will not receive social security benefits from their current payment of taxes in the future, reducing the current net value of the exemption. Still, the benefit of avoiding paying a tax today likely exceeds the cost of not receiving that same amount of money sometime in the future. Thus, the automatic extension of this exemption to missionaries represents a very real tax savings to them (even accounting for the loss of future income), and a tax savings not available to individuals who are not missionaries, let alone those who are not religious.

The social security tax benefits available to employee missionaries are, not surprisingly, unavailable to missionaries who are neither employees nor otherwise compensated for their work. Because volunteer missionaries do not receive compensation for their missionary work, they do not come within the social security regime. But where otherwise the tax treatment of employee missionaries tracks the tax treatment of nonmissionaries, the tax treatment of volunteer missionaries differs from the standard tax regime in a number of ways.

Though there are many kinds of volunteer missionary work within many different religions,[26] I will focus here on the financial and tax issues affecting Mormon missions. Mormon missions are important for two reasons. First, they are standardized to a remarkable degree, from the age of missionaries to the length of missions to the manner in which Mormon missions are financed. Second, much of the case law and IRS rulings surrounding the tax consequences of volunteer missions derive from questions about Mormon missions.

Almost immediately after the formation of the Mormon Church, missionaries began to evangelize their faith.[27] Originally, Mormon conceptions of missionary work deliberately followed the New Testament model of missionaries preaching "without purse or scrip"; missionaries often left their home to proselytize with little more than clothes they wore. These missionaries relied principally on individual generosity for their support.[28]

Though missionaries nominally travelled without any assets, the congregations where they performed their missionary work often implemented systemic ways to help support them, and the Utah-based church began to subsidize their travel expenses. By 1890, most Mormon missionaries in England – and, presumably, in the rest of Europe – had largely abandoned the ethic of preaching without money and, instead, drew on their own personal resources for their support.[29]

Throughout most of the twentieth century, Mormon missionaries were responsible for funding their own missions. The church generally only paid for transportation to and from the missionary's assigned area.[30] Otherwise, the missionary, their family, and their friends were responsible for the expenses the missionary would incur. Occasionally, the church would support missionaries whose families could not afford to support them out of its General Missionary Fund.[31]

This combination of self- and church-funded missionary work raised a number of tax questions, including whether payments made by the parents of missionaries to their missionary child or to the General Missionary Fund were deductible charitable contributions and whether reimbursements from the church to missionaries constituted income to that missionary.

Deductible Charitable Contributions

In 1962, the IRS answered to those questions. To answer the question of whether donations meant to support missionaries were deductible, the IRS looked to the substance of the donations. If the donations were earmarked to support a particular missionary (and, by extension, if they were given to that particular missionary), the IRS said that they would be treated as gifts to that missionary. The IRS ruling meant that volunteer missionaries did not owe taxes on their support; gifts are not taxable income and, unlike employee missionaries, gifts to volunteer missionaries who were funding their own missions did not substitute for church-provided salaries. The ruling did impact donors, though: while gift recipients do not have to pay taxes on their gifts, givers cannot deduct the value of their gifts. Thus, according to the IRS, donations earmarked for particular missionaries were nondeductible.

By contrast, if the church had control over the donated funds, and discretion over their use, the IRS would treat them as donated to the church, allowing the donor to take a deduction for their charitable contribution. The IRS allowed this result even where the donor's child was a missionary and received reimbursements from the fund. As long as the donating parent had no control over what the missionary fund did with the money, or who it supported, the donation was treated like any other charitable donation.[32]

But the framework that the IRS had laid out did not match the economics of Mormon missions. Because Mormon missionaries were generally responsible for providing their own support, parents often sent money to their missionary children, and their children used that money to support their own missionary efforts. Under the IRS's framework, parents could not deduct these monetary transfers: not only were they earmarked for a particular missionary, but they were given directly to that missionary.

It was not completely clear that parents had to follow the IRS ruling – the framework came in the form of a revenue ruling, a kind of administrative ruling that the IRS uses to answer broad classes of taxpayer questions. Though revenue rulings have some precedential value, their precedential value lies primarily in their persuasiveness and, as a result, their determinations of law are subject to taxpayer challenge.[33]

And so, in the early 1980s, several Mormon families challenged the IRS's framework. Which brings us back to Harold and Enis Davis: their case, chosen by the Mormon Church as a test case, typified the challenges launched by Mormon parents against the IRS's tax framework for volunteer missionaries. While Benjamin and Cecil were on their missions, Harold and Enis deposited money into their sons'checking accounts. In 1980, Harold and Enis deposited $3,480.89 in Benjamin's account, and in 1981, they deposited $4,135. In 1981, they also deposited $1,518 in Cecil's bank account. Benjamin and Cecil used the money primarily to pay for rent, food, transportation, and other personal expenses. (Benjamin also spent money purchasing religious tracts; Cecil, on the other hand, did not.) Neither son accepted donations on behalf of the church, and neither would have been required to give any unspent money to the church when his mission ended, even if one had ended his mission with a surplus.[34]

When the Davises originally filed their tax returns for 1981 and 1982 (the years their sons were missionaries), they did not view their sons' missions as having any tax significance. In 1984, though, they filed amended returns for 1981 and 1982, claiming charitable deductions for the nearly $8,000 they had deposited in their sons' checking accounts during those two years. The IRS disallowed their claimed deductions, and the Davises filed a second set of amended returns. In the second set of returns, they did not claim a deduction for the full $8,000. Instead, they claimed a deduction for about $4,400, which was the amount the Mormon Church indicated for missionaries in New York and the Cook Island would need in the years in question.[35]

The Davises argued that the money they transferred to their sons qualified as charitable contributions. Although they transferred the money directly to their sons, it was "for the use of" the church. (Only contributions made "to or for the use of" a qualified charity are deductible by the donors.[36]) Their sons were providing a service to the church by being missionaries. Although the money was theirs, and they could use it as they wished, the church had requested that the missionaries, their family, or their friends provide their own support and had set the amount to be transferred to the missionaries. Moreover, the church exercised some soft control over the funds – while missionaries did not need to get church approval before spending money, they were required to provide weekly expense sheets, documenting how they had spent their money. To the extent they had surplus funds, they were responsible for asking their parents to reduce the donations sent to them monthly.[37]

Alternatively, the Davises argued, if courts found that the money was not *to or for the use of* the church, they should at least hold that the unreimbursed expenses associated with their sons' missionary work qualified as deductible. While their sons could not deduct the value of the services they provided, the tax law does allow taxpayers who donate services to deduct any expenses they incur in providing their services, as long as the charity does not reimburse them for the expenses.[38] Even if the courts believed that payments made by the Davises directly to their sons were not for the use of the church, the amounts they transferred to their sons were used by their sons to provide services to the church were costs of providing services. Because the church did not reimburse either the Davises or their sons for those costs, the costs were deductible, the Davises argued.

Both the district court in Idaho and the Ninth Circuit Court of Appeals rejected the Davises' arguments. The courts held that the Davises' transfers to their sons did not qualify as *for the use of* the church. Even though ultimately the money went to fund missionary work that benefitted the church, the courts said, the ultimate beneficiary was not the relevant test for these purposes. The relevant test was who had control and possession of the money. And on this count, the Davises lost. Even if the church could direct much of what its missionaries – including the Davis brothers – did on a day-to-day basis, and even if it exercised some after-the-fact supervisory authority over their spending, it lacked actual possession of and control over the funds. Here, the missionaries themselves had both possession and control, and therefore, the transfers were not for the use of the church.[39]

The courts also dismissed the unreimbursed expenses claim, in a fairly summary fashion. Whether or not the costs of missionary work constituted unreimbursed expenses (more on that shortly), the courts held that the deduction is only available to the individual actually performing services on behalf of a charitable organization. Because Benjamin and Cecil, not Harold and Enis, were engaged in volunteer missionary work, Harold and Enis could not deduct the amounts they transferred to their sons as unreimbursed expenses.[40] (The courts' decisions do not discuss the intriguing question of whether Benjamin and Cecil Davis, the missionaries themselves, could deduct some or all of the money they spent on their missions as unreimbursed expenses. Ultimately, though, it probably does not matter significantly; while missionaries, they almost certainly would not have itemized their deductions and, even if they did, they presumably had little, if any, income against which they could have taken deductions.[41])

Though the Davises failed to convince either the district court or the court of appeals that they were entitled to deduct the money they transferred to their missionary sons, two other sets of Mormon parents (whose appeals ultimately lay in courts of appeals other than the Ninth Circuit) fared better. In a nearly identical set of facts, Lyle White, a nineteen year-old Mormon, left his Salt Lake City home in 1978 to perform missionary service in Tampa, Florida. His parents, Don and Alice White, contributed $100 to a private travel agency to defray the cost of their son's transportation to Florida, and also transferred money to their son so that he could pay his living expenses. As with the Davises, the church provided the Whites with a recommended amount, but did nothing to prevent them from transferring more (or, for that matter, less) to Lyle. Also like the Davises, the Whites initially did not claim a deduction for the amounts they sent to their son; they amended their tax return about six months after initially filing it, requesting a refund, claiming a deduction both for the amount they paid to the travel agency and the amounts they deposited in Lyle's bank account.[42]

Similarly, in 1977, Derry Brinley left his home in Texas for the Mormon Church's Salt Lake City missionary training center, where he began his mission. Like the Davises and the Whites, his parents, Eldon and Mary Ann Brinley, sent him money to defray his expenses in the missionary training center. They also paid $170 to the same travel agency as the Whites, and paid $86 in boarding expenses for Derry's time in the missionary training center. Unlike the Whites and the Davises, though, the Brinleys did not need to file amended returns; they claimed a deduction for all of the money they spent on and sent to their son on their initial tax return.[43]

The Whites and the Brinleys made the same arguments as the Davises – that the funds they transferred to their sons were ultimately for the use of the Mormon Church and, in any event, that they represented unreimbursed expenses in the course of providing services to a charity. The appeals courts largely agreed, finding that the Mormon Church did not necessarily have to have control over funds for those funds to qualify as *for the use of* the church, and thus deductible by the parents. (In neither case did that guarantee that the parents could take their full deductions – the courts of appeals held that the trial courts had insufficiently developed the facts, and sent the cases back to fully develop the factual basis. But in both cases, the IRS stipulated that the missionaries' parents would be able to deduct the amounts they transferred to their sons.)[44]

As a result of the different appeals courts' inconsistent understandings of the tax law, the substantive tax law governing deductibility of transfers to missionaries differed, depending on where a missionary's parents lived. That the federal tax law can differ depending on a taxpayer's home, though counterintuitive, is nonetheless unremarkable. A circuit court's decision may be persuasive to other courts, but it is only precedential within its jurisdictional limits. As far back as the 1940s, academics recognized this quirk of the purportedly national tax law, and some called for a single court of tax appeals to replace location-driven appeals and provide national consistency in the interpretation of the tax law.[45]

That call went unheeded. Today, district courts are bound only by the decisions of the circuit court to which their decisions can be appealed. Even the tax court is subject to these jurisdictional inconsistencies. The tax court has nationwide jurisdiction – it can hear tax cases irrespective of where a taxpayer litigant lives.[46] But when it decides an issue where the circuit courts have interpreted the law differently, it must determine the circuit to which the taxpayer can appeal its decision, and follow that circuit's precedent.[47]

As a practical matter, this meant that the question of the deductibility of Mormon parents' transfers to their missionary children was an unresolvable mess. If the parents lived in Alaska, Arizona, California, Hawaii, Idaho, Montana, Nevada, Oregon, or Washington (that is, within the jurisdiction of the Ninth Circuit), they could not deduct transfers they made to their missionary children. On the other hand, parents who lived in Louisiana, Mississippi, or Texas (the Fifth Circuit) or Colorado, Kansas, New Mexico, Oklahoma, Utah, or Wyoming (the Tenth Circuit) could deduct the amount they sent to their missionary children. Moreover, parents who lived in the thirty-two states not covered by one of these circuit courts had no way of knowing whether they could deduct the transfers or not. (It is worth noting that, while the questions arose specifically in the context of Mormon missionaries, the same rules – and inconsistent jurisdictional treatment – would apply to other volunteer missionaries who received money directly from donors, too.)

Resolution: The Supreme Court

The Ninth Circuit Court of Appeals decided the Davises' case in November, 1988. The Davises appealed the decision to the Supreme Court and, a year later, it agreed to hear their appeal.[48]

The Supreme Court heard the parties' oral arguments in March, 1990. When it issued its opinion two months later, it sided with the Ninth Circuit. The Court recognized that "for the use of" was susceptible to a number of different interpretations, including the one proffered by the Davises. However, it said, the best reading, especially in light of the history of the tax law, was that Congress meant for the language to allow taxpayers to deduct donations made to charities in trust or other similar legal arrangements. Transfers to a taxpayer's missionary children, even if such transfers do in fact benefit the church, are neither actually made to the church nor made in trust to the church. Therefore, the Supreme Court said, transfers made directly to missionaries, to be used to pay their mission expenses, are not deductible, no matter how much control the church has over its missionaries' activities.

As a practical matter, the Supreme Court also pointed out that the rule the Davises wanted it to endorse would raise virtually insurmountable administrative difficulties. If a donation could qualify as "for the use of" a charity even if it were made to an individual, taxpayers could theoretically deduct any gifts they made to relatives or friends. Clearly most such gifts would not be for the use of a charity, even under the Davises' interpretation of that phrase. But the IRS would face the expense of finding and evaluating these gifts; even though the Court recognized that there was no suggestion that the Davis sons had improperly used the money, it was clear to the Court that the interpretation they favored "would create an opportunity for tax evasion that others might be eager to exploit."[49]

The Supreme Court also rejected the Davises' argument that the amounts that they transferred to their sons represented unreimbursed expenditures associated with their sons' contributions of services to the church. Again, the Court said, accepting the Davises' position would practically invite tax evasion. But it also "strains the language of the statute." The Supreme Court held that deduction is permissible for unreimbursed costs of one's own donation of services only, not for expenses incurred in a third party's donation of services.[50]

The Aftermath of Davis

In the wake of the Supreme Court's decision, the jurisdictional differences disappeared. Transfers made from parents to their missionary children were not deductible, no matter where the parents lived. Although the Supreme Court did not mention the IRS's 1962 revenue ruling that the Davises and other Mormon parents challenged, it essentially adopted the IRS's view.

Of course, the story of the tax treatment of volunteer missionaries – including Mormon missionaries – does not end with the Supreme Court's decision in *Davis*. About six months after the Supreme Court's decision, the Mormon Church announced a fundamental change in the way missions would be financed going forward. Rather than require missionaries to bear the actual costs of their missions, missionaries would be responsible for a standardized monthly amount (initially $350 a month for missionaries leaving from the United States). The missionaries and their friends and family would contribute that money to missionary funds owned and controlled by the church, and the church would use those funds to pay for missionaries' actual expenses.[51]

The new version of financing Mormon missions was not entirely tax driven, of course. Prior to 1990, the monthly cost of a mission could be anywhere from $100 to $750 a month, depending on where the missionary went.[52] But Mormon missionaries do not choose where they will go – they are assigned, not more than a couple months before their missions begin. That made it virtually impossible for families to know how much they needed to save for their children's eventual missions. They could save for their children's missions, of course, but because they could not know how much it would eventually cost, they had no target for their savings.

Even if there were nontax reasons for the change, it also provided significant tax benefits. Under the post-1990 program (which does not have to be unique to Mormonism), payments are made to the Mormon Church. Because the church receives and controls the funds, and because they are not earmarked to any particular missionary (even though they are made by or on behalf of a particular missionary), these payments are deductible charitable donations under the framework laid out by the IRS and the Supreme Court.

And, from a tax perspective, allowing parents to deduct the amounts they pay *to the church* makes sense. The donors do not have to rely on an interpretation of "for the use of," because the donations are not made in trust. The donations are, in fact, to the church, which itself qualifies them as deductible.

Interestingly, although the Mormon Church's restructuring of its mission finances made the Supreme Court's decision in *Davis* irrelevant for Mormon missionaries, the decision is not entirely irrelevant. Nor, it turns out, did it close the door on deducting donations made to missionaries. In 2010, the Tax Court revisited the question and decided that, in certain circumstances, donations made directly to missionaries could be deducted by the donor, *Davis* notwithstanding.

Jeffrey and Patricia Wilkes belonged to the Church of Jesus Christ, a church without hierarchy, clergy, or even formal leadership. Members get together and form their own autonomous churches. The local churches rely on contributions from their local members, but the Church of Jesus Christ's doctrine prohibits these churches from accepting contributions directly from people who are not local members.

In 2005, the Wilkeses gave money directly to three missionaries, each of whom was developing a different local church. One was in Michigan, one in North Carolina, and the third in South Africa.

The Tax Court recognized that individuals cannot receive tax-deductible contributions; for a contribution to be tax deductible, it must be made to or for the use of a qualified tax-exempt organization. And, under US law, foreign entities are not qualified. Thus, the donation to the missionary establishing a church in South Africa was not deductible.

Likewise, the Tax Court held, as the Supreme Court had before it, that the contributions to the domestic missionaries were not made "for the use of" a church or other qualified entity. It found, though, that the contributions were "to" the churches in Michigan and North Carolina, respectively, and thus the Wilkeses could deduct those contributions.

On its face, the Tax Court's conclusion seems incompatible with the Supreme Court's *Davis* decision. But the Tax Court found that missionaries of the Church of Jesus Christ had a different relationship to the church than Mormon missionaries. Because church doctrine prohibited local churches from accepting donations from individuals who were not members of the local church, the missionaries served as agents of the church; unlike the Mormon missionaries, missionaries of the Church of Jesus Christ solicited, collected, and disbursed funds on behalf of the church. Although the missionaries also used the funds to support their own (modest, according to the Tax Court) living expenses, the Tax Court held that the donations made to the missionaries were, in fact, made to the church. As such, they were deductible.[53]

THE UNADDRESSED QUESTION: COMPENSATION

Essentially, then, the Mormon Church reacted to the Supreme Court's decision by radically changing its missionary funding model. Rather than its original unfunded missions, or its century or so of self-funded missions, under post-1990 policy, Mormon missions became church funded. True, the church requests that missionaries and their families contribute to a centralized, church-controlled fund, but the amount of a missionary's (and her family's) contributions are entirely divorced from the costs of the mission. A missionary sent to New York City contributes the same amount as a missionary sent to the Cook Islands, in spite of the fact that the cost of living – and the actual expenses incurred by missionaries – differs dramatically between the two places.

This shift from self- and parent-funded missions to church-funded missions creates an odd dissonance in the tax law. Although Mormon parents challenged the portion of the IRS's 1962 revenue ruling that disallowed deductions for money earmarked for a particular missionary, they embraced – and continue to embrace – the part of the ruling that deals with the tax consequences *to missionaries* of receiving support. The rule that the IRS laid out – that reimbursements to volunteer missionaries do not constitute taxable income to the missionaries – seems like a clear, simple solution, but, in the context of the tax law generally, is neither simple nor obvious.

While it feels intuitively correct that the money paid to volunteers is not income, the reasoning is ultimately tautological. Essentially, the payments are not income because the missionaries are volunteers, and the missionaries are volunteers because they are uncompensated. If, however, the payments were compensation, it follows that the missionaries were not volunteers. Similarly, if the missionaries are not merely volunteers, the amounts they receive from the church in support of their missionary work is income.

And nothing in the tax law precludes payments from the church to missionaries from constituting income. Under US law, the scope of income that may be subject to the federal income tax is tremendously broad. The tax law defines gross income as "income from whatever source derived."[54] This definition of "income" is, of course, circular, and no other part of the tax law defines the word. The Supreme Court explained that income includes all "undeniable accessions to wealth, clearly realized, and over which the taxpayers have complete dominion" qualify as income for tax purposes.[55] This definition is nearly as broad as the circular statutory definition – unquestionably broad enough to encompass payments to missionaries from a centralized mission fund, even where those payments are in the form of reimbursements for mission-related expenses.

Of course, it is not enough to say merely that the receipt of money by missionaries *could* qualify as income. That would be true of any receipt of money, and yet, not all accessions to wealth are income. In spite of the fact that the tax law *could* include virtually any receipt of money or property as taxable income, the government has carved certain types of receipts out of the world of taxable income.

For example, in addition to the exclusion of gifts from income, some (but not all) employer reimbursements are excluded from the reimbursed employees' income.[56] And perhaps that fact gave missionaries pause: even though the payments from the church to missionaries were styled as "reimbursements," not all reimbursements can be excluded from gross income. To be excluded, a reimbursement must (among other things) be connected to the performance of services by an employee for an employer.[57] Non-employee missionaries, however, are not employees of the church and, as a result, reimbursements for their mission expenses do meet the criteria for exclusion from income.

The IRS recognized that the tax law could easily treat missionary reimbursements as income, but it also believed that there was something different about the reimbursement of missionaries. It looked both at missionaries' motives and what they actually did. A missionary, the IRS said, was "motivated by religious conviction and a desire to donate services to his church"; at the same time, the missionary was, in fact, "rendering gratuitous services" to her church. As a result, neither reimbursements to the missionary nor direct payment by the church of the missionary's expenses constituted income to the missionary.[58]

Do "Volunteer" Missionaries Warrant Accommodation?

Realistically, the reasons the IRS provides for allowing missionaries to exclude reimbursements from their income appears to be a *post hoc* justification for arriving at the conclusion it preferred. And the IRS's conclusion *feels* plausible. Its plausibility, though, rests first on the idea that missionaries are in fact unpaid volunteers, and second on the assertion that there is something materially different about volunteer missionaries and other volunteers.

But does missionary work warrant special tax treatment? Under the Mormon model, it is not clear that it does. Neither the assumption that Mormon missionaries are unpaid volunteers nor the assertion that they are somehow fundamentally different from other taxpayers is entirely plausible, at least since the church responded to the Supreme Court's decision in *Davis*. The IRS's determination that payment to missionaries was not taxable rested on the premise that missionaries' work was voluntary and uncompensated. Prior to 1990, Mormon missionary work was both; while the church covered the expenses of missionaries who could not afford to go otherwise, most missionaries paid for their missions themselves or received help from their parents.

With its 1990 policy change, though, the Mormon Church effectively severed the direct financial link between parents and missionaries, both to improve the fairness between missionaries who were sent to expensive missions and those sent to inexpensive missions and to allow parents to deduct their missionary support. But if the direct relationship between missionary parents and the support of their children is severed for deduction purposes, there is no consistent reason why their payments should be treated as supporting their children for income purposes.

This is not to say that missionaries are deceptive either in their self-presentation or their presentation to the outside world. Certainly, Mormon missionaries think of themselves as unpaid volunteers. Witness Dallin Oaks, a member of the Mormon Church's leadership, commending members for "serving missions at your own expense."[59] On the 2015 version of its official website, the Mormon Church reinforces this vision, asking rhetorically, "Why do these people, most of them under the age of 25, volunteer to leave their homes at their own expense and dedicate a period of their lives to preaching the gospel of Jesus Christ?"[60]

Mormon missionaries undoubtedly feel like they are supporting themselves. In addition to the volunteerism rhetoric they hear from their church,
they are, in fact, required to contribute (or solicit contributions from family)
for their mission. But feelings aside, looking at the actual economic structure
of a Mormon mission belies claims that these missions are self-funded and
uncompensated.

Certainly missionaries, their parents, and their friends are paying in to the
church. But their payments are fully tax deductible charitable contributions;
moreover, the donors have no control over where the funds are used. The
centralized fund takes all of its (entirely fungible) donations, and uses those
collectively to support the full missionary force of the church.

Beyond that, the amount the church asks missionaries to contribute is
entirely unrelated to the actual cost of their missions. They pay a set amount,
irrespective of the actual cost of their mission. If the amount they pay is equal
to the amount their missionary work costs, that is purely serendipitous.

On the other side, the church covers certain of its missionary's expenses
(including housing) out of the Church Missionary Fund – the same fund that
missionaries have paid into – and provides the missionaries with an additional
living allowance that they use to pay for food, transportation, and sundry other
expenses that they encounter on their missions.

It would be difficult to explain how these payments to missionaries differ
from other churches' payments to employee missionaries. True, the Mormon
missionaries donated to the church. But donations do not negate income;
employees of local public radio stations, for example, often donate to their
radio stations, but those donations do not transform them from employees to
volunteers. There may be a difference in scope between the donations made
by public radio employees (presumably in the hundreds of dollars a year) and
those made by Mormon missionaries (currently $400 a month), but realisti-
cally, there often is not. The Davis brothers, Lyle White, and Derry Brinley
were largely, if not entirely, supported by their parents. Though some missionaries do save up and pay the $400 monthly amount themselves, in many cases,
that amount is largely or entirely covered by others. Even where missionaries
fund themselves, though, the deductible donation has no direct connection
to the amount paid to the missionaries.

Even outside the world of Mormon missionaries, it is difficult to articulate a reason missionaries should be treated differently from other taxpayers.
It is true that missionaries preach the gospel (or otherwise proselytize) out of
religious conviction, or, at least, from a sense of duty grounded in religious
belief. And it is true that many missionaries make sacrifices, both financially
and in other respects, in order to proselytize. But for the most part, economic

differences between missionaries and other taxpayers are not the result of religious conviction.

There is no compelling reason, for example, that an employee missionary located outside of the country should get special treatment for furlough purposes. Furloughs available to foreign missionaries are employment perquisites, not religious imperatives. Because the furloughs are a matter of convenience, rather than a religious mandate, they do not represent religious decision making that is economically counterproductive, and there is no reason that they should be accommodated for tax purposes. There is no coherent justification for allowing missionaries to instantly recover their foreign residency status where nonmissionaries would have to first reestablish foreign residency.

And there is even less reason to exempt missionaries, as a blanket class, from social security taxes. It is true, as we have seen, that some religions object to government-provided social safety nets, and do not want to either pay into or receive social security. But Congress has demonstrated that it can narrowly address the objection, singling out those whose religious beliefs actually conflict with the payment of social security taxes. At the same time, Congress and the courts have made it clear that the tax law must explicitly allow for the exemption – there is no implicit accommodation here. In the case of missionaries, though, the IRS did not bother to try to exempt only those who actually object, nor did it point to an underlying doctrinal need to be treated differently. Instead, it merely allowed a blanket exemption to ministers.

Though the IRS did not explain its reasoning in providing these accommodations to employee missionaries, presumably it was similar to the IRS's reasons for allowing non-employee missionaries to exclude receipts from their income. Those reasons, though, are at least slightly odd. The IRS's analysis largely focuses on missionaries' motivations. Because they act altruistically as missionaries, the IRS says, they should not be taxed on the support they receive. But while missionaries' motives may be altruistic and non-economic, the motives of an individual who receives money are generally irrelevant in determining the tax consequences of that receipt. The employee missionary, for example, whose motives may be identically altruistic and heaven-oriented, does pay taxes on their income from the church. (They may be able to exclude reimbursements for certain expenses they incur, but that exclusion is a function of their status as an employee, rather than their motivation for engaging in missionary work.)

Likewise, the fact that an employee missionary works for God, not Mammon, impacts neither their ability nor their legal obligation to pay taxes. They do not work differently just because they are a missionaries. And the altruistic component to missionary work is not unique to missionaries: at least some portion of church employees who have administrative jobs are motivated at least in part by their religious devotion. Others, who work in nonreligious charities, can similarly believe in the good they are doing, having chosen their jobs partially for altruistic purposes. Even individuals in the for-profit world can have altruistic motivations: doctors and attorneys, among others, can work to improve their communities through their professional endeavors. The fact of altruism, by itself, does little to justify unique tax treatment.

Similarly, it is hard to articulate a substantive difference between volunteer missionaries and other volunteers. Services, even provided to a charity at no cost, are not deductible. Even the donor's intention is largely (though not entirely) irrelevant to the tax treatment they receive. An individual who provides services to a church or other charity without charging cannot deduct the value of the services. If two individuals have the exact same selfless and altruistic motivations, the one who donates money or property can deduct the value of their donation,[61] while the one who provides services cannot.[62]

This distinction between donations of tangible property or money and donations of services makes sense – it reflects a real pre-tax difference between the two types of donation. Before a donor can give money or property to a charity, they first need to earn money. Only after they earn money can they donate it to a charity or purchase property that they will subsequently donate to charity. But even if they intend to donate their earned money to the charity at the moment they earn it, they must pay taxes when they receive the money. The deduction they receive for their charitable donation offsets the income that they ultimately do not consume, putting them roughly in the same position they would have been in if they had neither earned nor donated the money.

When they donate services to a charity, on the other hand, they do not earn any money. True, if they were not providing services to the charity, they may have instead used that time to earn money for themselves and paid taxes on that amount. But that would put them in the same position as the money donor, who spent time earning money that the taxpayer eventually gave away. Allowing a taxpayer to deduct the value of services provided would mean that the service donor would not pay taxes on income earned *and* would get an additional deduction, and would provide a double benefit to individuals who donated services. Just as the Supreme Court rightly found that the tax law does not permit a deduction for donations made directly to missionaries for their support, the framework of the tax law necessarily does not allow for missionaries to deduct the value of the services they provide.

CONCLUSION

Though the economics of missionary work are admittedly unique and unusual, the case for tax accommodation under current law is tenuous. For the most part, they are not so unique and unusual that they warrant special accommodation. Nothing about missionary work demands accommodation, and the altruism that missionaries display can also be found in nonmissionaries who choose to act for the betterment of society. As a result, most of the tax accommodations provided to missionaries are unnecessary and overbroad. Except in specific circumstances where missionaries have an actual religious motivation for departing from the economic norm, it makes little sense to create different rules for missionaries.

Still, without any consistent framework with which to think about tax accommodation, it is also hard to articulate a reason why missionaries should not be accommodated. If accommodation will always be an ad hoc decision, guided by salience and sympathetic actors, missionaries seem like as good a candidate as any for accommodation. Still, accommodation for the sake of accommodation does create problems. These problems can be comfortably illustrated by the problems in figuring out how to deal with Mormon missionaries. In the end, although they style themselves as volunteers, they receive payment from the church. That payment may not feel like compensation; after all, they or their parents or friends paid for them to be on the mission. But the direct connection between their, their parents', and their friends' donations and the amounts they receive has now been broken. As a condition of their deductibility, the payments go to the church, and the amount a missionary receives is unrelated to the amount they and their family contribute to the fund.

And yet, the IRS's 1962 ruling explicitly allows them to avoid paying taxes on the amounts they receive as support. That ruling is premised, though, on the idea that these missionaries are volunteers, donating their services to the church. For Mormon missionaries, that was clearly the case prior to 1990, when they were truly self-funded, except where they did not have the resources to support themselves, and needed help from others.

Today, though, the volunteer nature of Mormon missionaries is less clear. It is true that the church provides them with a monthly allowance that essentially covers their housing, food, and transportation needs, without any significant surplus for personal consumption.[63] But that is not unique to missionary work. People who work minimum wage jobs are clearly earning income, and that income may (or may not) cover their living expenses, but in many cases, it does not provide for significant additional consumption.[64] Still, the income they earn is subject to both income and payroll taxes. Though employee missionaries are exempt from payroll taxes, they still must pay taxes on the income they receive as a result of performing missionary work.[65] Volunteer missionaries, on the other hand, earn no income and, therefore, pay no taxes.[66]

Ultimately, the accommodations provided to missionaries are ad hoc, not grounded in any kind of consistent policy judgments. Instead, the arbitrary nature of the accommodations means that the form of missionary compensation matters inordinately. That, in turn, puts considerable pressure on the line dividing volunteer missionaries from employee missionaries. Unfortunately, neither Congress nor the IRS appears to have given any substantive thought to where that line falls. The IRS has simply made clear that some missionaries are employees, and some are volunteers, and each faces different tax burdens, in essence, allowing missionaries to classify themselves. Without a consistent framework, the tax law leaves missionaries in an uncertain world.

10

Religious Communitarians

In the early twentieth century, the Israelite House of David – a Michigan-based religious community – fielded a traveling baseball team. Originally when they travelled east from their home in Benton Harbor, Michigan, they would play Negro League teams. Later, they started to take their opponent (often the Kansas City Monarchs or Satchell Paige's All Stars) with them as they barnstormed around the United States, Mexico, and Canada. It must have made quite an impression when the Israelite House of David baseball team came to town.

The entertainment value of the House of David baseball team likely had as much to do with their appearance as with their playing. Among their religious tenets was an injunction against shaving or cutting their hair. (In 1920, the *Mid-Week Pictorial* included a piece about their baseball team titled "Long-Haired Team That Plays Snappy Baseball." That same year, the Associated News Service announced that the Cubs were seeking a "long-haired pitcher" from the House of David.[1]) As a result, the men on the baseball diamond sported hair past their shoulders and beards to the middle of their chests.

The Israelite House of David was founded by Benjamin and Mary Purnell in 1903. Its baseball team existed both because Benjamin believed in the spiritual and physical benefits of sports and because the religion needed money. Baseball was far from its sole source of revenue, though: in 1908, the House of David opened an amusement park, followed by a zoo and an aviary. They ran a vegetarian restaurant, bottled and sold spring water, and had both an orchestra and a jazz band. They operated hotels in Benton Harbor, owned a logging operation in northern Michigan, and eventually began running the local streetcar company.[2]

Along with the Shakers, the Israelite House of David also served as inspiration for one of the more obscure religious accommodations in the tax law.

The religion's economic and entertainment forces were not merely reflections of its intertwinement with capitalism; rather, they belie just how far the Israelite House of David was from the pervasive twentieth-century capitalism that infused not only the United States but, by the end of the century, almost the whole world. The Israelite House of David was not a subscriber to the economic isolationism that pits each person against all others: it was a communitarian group in the model of the early Apostolic church (as well as many nineteenth-century restorationist religions that tried to recreate the economics of the New Testament).

RELIGIOUS COMMUNITARIANISM

Shortly after Pentecost (that is, fifty days after the Resurrection, when the Holy Ghost came to the Apostles), the New Testament shifts briefly from the religious to the economic. The new Christians, it tells us, had all things in common. Initially, it appears that those who joined the Jesus movement sold their property and distributed the proceeds to other Christians who had need.[3] At some point, the procedure was formalized, and, rather than uncoordinated distributions, members gave the proceeds to the Apostles, who took a centralized responsibility for providing money to those who needed it.[4] In that way, the early Church worked to ensure that none of its members suffered from poverty.

In this Apostolic Church, communitarianism was not just a nice thing that believers did. It was a responsibility of believers, and the Bible illustrated its seriousness in the story of Ananias and Sapphira. Ananias and Sapphira joined the Christian movement and sold their property. Rather than give the full proceeds to the Apostles for distribution to those with needs, Ananias – with Sapphira's knowledge and consent – only delivered a portion of the proceeds to the Apostles, and kept the rest for himself. The Apostle Peter was unimpressed, though, and called him out on his partial compliance.

The New Testament reports that, when Peter accused Ananias of lying both to them and to God, Ananias fell down, dead. Several hours later, Sapphira came to the Apostles, and Peter entrapped her into repeating Ananias's lie. When she, too, had lied, Peter accused her of conspiracy with her husband and she, too, fell down, dead.[5]

In spite of the morbidity framing this early Christian communitarianism, American Christianity, especially in the early nineteenth century, had a distinctive air of restorationism about it. Many Christian movements attempted to slough off the accumulated trappings of two thousand years of experience and instead return to New Testament Christianity. While *New Testament*

Christianity meant different things to different believers, a number of these restorationist movements embraced the economic communitarianism of the Apostolic church laid out in the Acts of the Apostles.[6]

This is not to say that only nineteenth-century restorationist Christianity embraced communitarianism; it existed both before and after that century, and has been adopted by various religions and nonreligions. Still, many of the major adopters of religious communitarianism adopted it in the nineteenth century.

SEXUAL EXPERIMENTATION

And who were these prominent nineteenth-century communitarians? Three of the most famous were the Oneida Perfectionists, the Shakers, and the Mormons. Interestingly, all three movements are probably better known for their marital and sexual experimentation than for their economic experimentation.

The Oneida community embraced "complex marriage." Under this alternative marital regime, all of the roughly 200 adult members considered themselves heterosexually married to the other adult members. They frequently traded sexual partners, and worked to break up exclusive romantic pairings as inimical to their religious commitments.[7]

The Shakers, too, saw romantic pairings as inimical to their religious beliefs. Unlike the Oneida Perfectionists, though, the Shaker solution was not to expand the pool of potential sexual partners to the entire community. Rather, the Shakers, who wanted to follow the example of their "androgynous God that transcended all physicality," practiced and enforced celibacy. Shaker orthodoxy proscribed both marriage and sex.[8]

Nineteenth-century Mormon marital and sexual beliefs fell between these extremes. Mormon restorationism adopted the polygamy of Hebrew Bible patriarchs (and of a God that nineteenth-century Mormons believed was physical, married, and even polygamous).[9] More than merely an option, nineteenth-century Mormon theology saw polygamy as prerequisite for salvation.

Nineteenth-century Americans did not react to these groups with alacrity; rather, they responded with hostility and alarm. The Republican party rose on a platform of ending slavery and polygamy, and the federal government ultimately stamped out the Mormon's practice of it. Once criminalized, Mormon polygamists were jailed and disenfranchised, and ultimately the Mormon church was disincorporated, its property escheating to the government.[10]

The Oneida community's group marriage inspired less outrage, but they, too, experienced hostile neighbors. In 1851, grand juries in the counties surrounding the Oneida community heard complaints about them. The Utica grand jury ultimately called men and women from the community to testify, "asking obscene and insulting questions about their most personal experiences." The harassment and pressure they faced caused Oneida leaders to start looking for places to move.[11]

Even the Shakers faced public hostility for their rejection of sex and marriage. In part, this hostility is understandable, given the Shakers' outspoken (and unsubtle) condemnation of the marriage and sex they rejected. Partly, too, it stemmed from the Shakers' assault on marriage and family. Among other things, critics of the Shakers attempted to pass laws that joining the Shakers "was equivalent to a legal divorce."[12]

ECONOMIC EXPERIMENTATION

The most salient and salacious aspect of these various restorationist Christian movements is unquestionably their rejection of American sexual mores. But these groups experimented with far more than just sex and marriage: they also adopted various versions of the communitarianism of the New Testament.[13] Salaciousness aside, their economic experimentations were equally radical and foreign to the surrounding American culture. In the end, nineteenth-century American legal institutions were just as hostile to these new religious movements' economic experiments as they were to their sexual and marital experiments.

The Mormons faced this hostility within a year of their organizing a church. In 1831, founder Joseph Smith asked all existing members and converts to deed their property to the church's bishop. The bishop would then divide this deeded property among members according to their wants and needs, and give a "stewardship" to each member. The stewardships were formed out of whatever real and personal property the bishop had received, and could constitute anything from a farm to a store to a mill to a workshop. To the extent that the deeded property exceeded the stewardships, the bishop may have additional assets to give to poorer and younger members of the church who had no property to deed to the church.

This initial economic organization hewed closely to the pattern established by the Apostolic church. The New Testament did not discuss how this communalism functioned beyond the initial contribution of property, though. Undeterred, the Mormons expanded the scope of Apostolic communalism. After the initial economic leveling inherent in deeding property to the bishop and receiving stewardships in return, Mormons were to return any surpluses in excess of their wants and needs to the bishop. The bishop would initially distribute the surplus to those who had, for whatever reason, failed to produce enough to support their families.[14]

Religiously and conceptually, this type of communalism (which the Mormons called "consecration") is both interesting and, perhaps, laudable. Legally, though, it turned out to be relatively unenforceable. At least some wealthy members of the community became disillusioned and successfully sued for the return of the property they had initially donated to the bishop.

The Mormons tried again. On their second attempt, the bishop only granted Mormons with a conditional title to the stewardship property that he granted to them. This conditional title would allow the bishop to take property back if it turned out that his stewardships were too big to accommodate all of the Mormons who arrived in Missouri. Again, though, this new communitarian property system "deprecated traditional notions of property rights." Individuals who wanted to leave again successfully sued for the return of their property; "the law would not accommodate" the Mormons' alternative economic vision, and the Mormons found their attempts at communalism constrained by the laws of the United States.[15]

Over time, this legal hostility toward communitarian property schemes has dissipated. The Hutterites, a branch of the Anabaptists, trace their roots as far back as 1528. They began moving to the United States and Canada in the 1870s.[16] The Hutterites have continued to grow, from 230 colonies as recently as 1974 to 475 in the United States and Canada in 2010.[17] Although their exact property system differs from the nineteenth-century Mormons, Hutterites, too, believe in Apostolic communitarianism. Substantially all of the property in a Hutterite colony belongs to the church, which allocates a monthly allowance, as well as food, clothes, and necessaries, to the members. While members have the right to use those things allocated to them, they only own whatever personal property they buy with their monthly allowance.[18] While Hutterites have historically experienced very low rates of defection, they have had defectors throughout their history.[19] Unlike the nineteenth-century Mormons, though, Hutterite defectors "leave with little more than their clothes."[20] The twentieth- and twenty-first century Hutterites have not been plagued by a loss of communal property through defection. Whether because the defectors have chosen not to sue or because the courts have recognized the validity of private economic ordering, the Mormons' experience of losing communal property to defectors no longer appears to hold.

Of course Mormons and Hutterites (and Shakers and Oneida Community and the Israelite House of David) were not the only communitarian groups to exist. These kinds of Christian communitarian religions flourished in nineteenth-century America. By the beginning of the twentieth century, communitarianism had retreated, with many groups dissipating or embracing the broader culture's individualistic capitalism. Retreat, though, did not mean there were no communitarians at the beginning of the twentieth century. Rather, it meant that they were less visible and less flamboyant than they had previously been. Dozens of Christian communitarian groups persisted, with new ones (including the Israelite House of David and the Fundamentalist Church of Jesus Christ of Latter-Day Saints) emerging.

Although Christians found their communitarian impetus in the New Testament, the communitarian impulse did not find its sole expression in Christianity. A number of new African American religions, collectively known as "black Judaism," emerged, some of which embraced communitarianism. And the Vedanta Society established a number of communitarian colonies in the United States around this time period.

Communitarianism in the United States diminished as the twentieth century progressed, but it saw a resurgence in the hippie movement of the 1960s (though it is not clear whether they knew about the long history of religious communitarianism or if they believed they were creating something new). Today, US communitarian groups run the gamut from Christian groups to intentional communities built around retirement.[21]

Nor is communitarianism limited to the United States. I will not try to comprehensively detail all of the communitarian groups around the globe (or, for that matter, try to distinguish communitarianism from socialism). For my purposes, it is enough to mention Israel's kibbutzim. The first kibbutz was founded in what is now Israel in 1910, although the majority began in the 1930s and 1940s, shortly before the founding of Israel. The kibbutzim rejected capitalism and, instead, formed communities intent on rejecting the selfish individualism central to capitalism. In its place they created societies that resembled American Christian communitarians in many ways (while differing in other ways). Members of kibbutzim shared income equally, eschewed private property, and provided public goods to members. Members worked for the kibbutz, and the kibbutz did not hire outsiders, believing that hiring outside labor was exploitative.[22]

As we look at how US tax law has accommodated religious communitarians, it is worth keeping in mind the kibbutz. While the original kibbutzim were fiercely secular, by 1931, religious kibbutzim began to exist.[23] And kibbutzim are important enough to the Israeli identity that the Israeli income tax has a special regime for taxing them, a regime that treats kibbutzkim differently from ordinary corporations.[24]

TAXING COMMUNITARIANISM

Personal Income Tax

While communitarian religious groups have always contended with the culture at large – their religious beliefs mandating that they organize their economic lives differently from the surrounding society – initially, tax did not contribute to that contention. Prior to the twentieth century, the federal government's revenue came primarily from customs duties and excise taxes on alcohol and tobacco.[25] These excise and customs taxes applied to religious communitarians in precisely the same manner it applied to atomized economic individualists. The end consumer did not directly pay the tax; rather, the importer or the seller paid, and passed that cost on to the consumer by charging a higher price for the goods. The tax law at the time had no direct impact on the religious practices of communitarian religious groups.

Twice in the nineteenth century, the federal government tried to increase its revenue (and cause the rich to bear a higher percentage of the cost of government) by moving to a progressive income tax. The first, enacted to fund the Civil War, existed for ten years, but likely did not affect religious communitarians. It provided a sufficiently large exemption amount that only the wealthy actually paid the income tax, and religious communitarians generally did not figure among the wealthy.[26] The second, enacted in the 1890s, was declared unconstitutional by the Supreme Court before it went into effect.[27]

Initially, even the enactment of the modern income tax in 1913 would have had little (if any) impact on religious communitarians. Modeled partly on the Civil War income tax, the 1913 tax clearly fell into the model of the class tax. Initially, it only drew revenue from the wealthiest 2 percent of Americans. And, in fact, it took almost three decades for the income tax to consistently reach the poor and middle-class.[28] Because of the exemption amount, for the personal income tax to apply to religious communitarians, they (like all Americans) would have had to earn greater than median wages.[29]

But the federal income tax consisted of more than just the *personal* income tax, and the corporate income tax, it turned out, did impact religious communitarians, at least indirectly, as a direct result of their religious practice of holding all property in common.

Corporate Income Tax

In the first decade of the modern income tax's existence, the Bureau of Internal Revenue (which later became the IRS) pursued taxes from several different communitarian religious groups. In response, three of these groups – the Israelite House of David and two Hutterite colonies – sued the IRS, asserting that they were exempt from taxation and therefore owed no corporate income tax. All three groups lost.

Although I focus in this book on the taxation of religious individuals, not entities, for purposes of the development of an accommodation for religious communitarians, we must take a quick look at how the exemption of religious organizations from the corporate income tax functions. The tax law has recognized that some corporations should be free from paying income taxes for more than a century. The abortive 1890s federal income tax recognized that entities organized and operated for charitable, religious, or educational purposes could qualify as exempt from taxes, and the income tax since then has consistently adopted, and built upon, this foundation.

Solely because an organization has a charitable, religious, or educational purpose does not mean it qualifies as tax-exempt, of course. In addition to having a qualifying purpose, since at least the end of the nineteenth century, the tax law has prohibited would-be exempt organizations from providing private inurement. That is, individuals related to the organization cannot use the organization's income for their own benefit.[30]

Why did both the Bureau of Internal Revenue and the courts decide that religious communitarian groups did not qualify as exempt? The court's decision in the Israelite House of David case does nothing to help understand their legal analysis. In that case, the Israelite House of David sued for a refund of the $947.06 (plus penalties) in taxes the Bureau collected for 1924. It also claimed an exemption the Bureau had denied it, and requested that the court prohibit the Bureau from collecting taxes going forward.

In its decision, the court avoided the substantive questions of whether the Israelite House of David qualified as exempt, and whether the Bureau could collect taxes from it, either in the past or going forward. Two things prevented the court from arriving at the merits of the Israelite House of David's complaint. First, the Israelite House of David brought the case in the wrong kind of court – a court of equity could not enjoin the collection of taxes, where a court of law could have done so.

While that distinction is hard to understand, and the distinction between courts of law and courts of equity has limited relevance today, at the time, the forum selection would have been sufficient grounds on its own for dismissing the Israelite House of David's complaint. Nonetheless, the court found another procedural ground for dismissing the complaint: the Israelite House of David had not filed an appeal with the Commissioner of Internal Revenue. The law, according to the court, clearly required a taxpayer to file an appeal with the Commissioner *before* it could take the case to court. As a result of the Israelite House of David failing to pass these two procedural hurdles, it did not qualify for any relief, and the court was able to dismiss the case without addressing the substantive question of whether a communitarian religious group qualified for exemption from tax.[31]

While the court dismissed the Israelite House of David's case on procedural grounds, two other cases brought by communitarian religious groups were adjudicated on the merits. Both of these cases involved Hutterite colonies. The first concerned Hutterische Gemeinde Elmspring, a South Dakota corporation formed in 1897. By 1917, Elmspring consisted of four separate Hutterite colonies. Members of these colonies engaged in a number of agricultural pursuits on behalf of the corporation, including raising corn, oats, rye, and wheat, as well as poultry, sheep, hogs, horses, and cattle. Among other properties, Elmspring owned farmland, farm implements, flour mills, a bakery, and blacksmith shops.

Remember, Hutterites eschew private ownership of property; property belongs to the church, which provides members with work and with necessaries. As a result, it was the church – a religious organization that would apparently have qualified for tax exemption – that owned the property and that earned money from the various goods and services produced by Elmspring members.

In 1917, Elmspring earned net income of $145,969.50 from its various agricultural and factory endeavors. It used its income to support its members, to maintain its property, and to reinvest in more property. At the same time, as a result of its religious nature, Elmspring claimed an exemption from taxes.

The Court of Claims disagreed. And the court's holding would have repercussions for any other communitarian group. The first strike against Elmspring was its purpose. According to the court, its extensive business activities indicated that it was not organized and operated exclusively for religious purposes. Commerce made up a significant portion of its purpose and operation, and engaging in commerce did not qualify as a tax-exempt purpose.

The second strike was *how* it used its money. In large part, its income went to support its members. The problem? Supporting its members violated the prohibition on private inurement. These two strikes disqualified Elmspring – and, by extension, any communitarian religious group that supported its members – from qualifying for a tax exemption.[32]

At the same time, the Board of Tax Appeals (a predecessor to today's US Tax Court) considered the exemption of another South Dakota Hutterite corporation. Hutterische Bruder Gemeinde was incorporated in 1905, and functioned in much the same way as Elmspring. Geneinde did not issue stock, and it had no shareholders. Instead, its members were those individuals who subscribed to its beliefs. To join, a potential member had to transfer their property to Gemeinde. They then began to work for the corporation. Like Elmspring, Gemeinde was largely agricultural; in addition, it owned and operated grist mills, a broom factory, a machine shop, a ferry, and a carpenter shop. It sold to the general public, and charged market prices for its goods.

Like the claims court, the Board of Tax Appeals found that Gemeinde did not qualify as a tax-exempt charitable organization. As with Elmspring, Gemeinde's profits solely benefited its members, not the public at large. But while that alone would probably have been sufficient to deny Gemeinde its tax-exempt status, the Board of Tax Appeals went even further: it looked at the scope of Gemeinde's commercial activities. With 10,000 acres of farm-land, which not only supported the members, but provided a surplus that Gemeinde then sold to the general public at market rates, the Board held that Gemeinde did not operate exclusively for religious purposes. Rather, it competed with for-profit endeavors, and would be treated for tax purposes as for-profit (and thus taxable).[33]

This inability for communitarian religious organizations to qualify as tax-exempt could have dealt them an insurmountable blow. Members of communitarian religious groups believed that absent an exemption, the tax law would crush their way of life.[34]

Though such fears seem overblown, the tax structure did substantially affect religious communitarians, and in a manner and scope far in excess of its effect on noncommunitarians. Remember, most of these communitarian religious groups held property in lieu of their members; upon joining the religion, members would give their property to the group and, in exchange, would receive a job and various necessaries.

In the early years of the federal income tax, the biggest tax impediment communitarian religions faced was the accumulated earnings tax. Communitarian religious corporations had no shareholders or other equity owners, so they could not pay dividends. Any profits they earned, in excess of their costs and the support they provided members, had to either be retained or reinvested. In the early twentieth century, though, American society was skeptical of the value of retaining earnings, and had set up tax mechanisms to discourage it. By the 1920s, corporations subject to the undistributed income tax had to pay 50 percent of their net income, on top of the standard corporate income tax that they owed.[35]

This loss through taxation of *half* of a communitarian religious organization's income demonstrated the disconnect between the standard economic story of America and the religious economics of the Apostolic communitarians. It is true that these communitarian religious corporations did not fit into the category of tax-exempt organizations. The rule against private inurement alone ensured that.

At the same time, though, these communitarian religions did not belong to the category of taxable corporations. The US legal system was putatively more accepting of communitarians by the twentieth century – certainly courts were not allowing dissenters to leave with the property they had previously contributed – but it showed the same lack of understanding about what was actually happening in communitarian religions. Without shareholders (and with members having eschewed private property), it was literally and religiously impossible for communitarian corporations to avoid the accumulated earnings tax. Courts, though, ignored the substance of these groups' economics and instead looked solely at the formal organization. They did not examine the actual economics of these groups.

ACCOMMODATING RELIGIOUS COMMUNITARIAN ORGANIZATIONS

It took about a decade for Congress to step in, but, in 1936, it created a special tax regime for communitarian religious groups. Under that regime, qualifying religious communitarian organizations do not have to pay corporate income tax; instead, members of a communitarian religious group pay personal income taxes on their pro rata share of money earned by the organization. And, although the provision applies on its surface to communitarian *organizations*, because of the unique economics of communitarianism, it functions as an accommodation for individuals, not for organizations.

The new accommodation exempts qualifying "religious and apostolic organizations" from tax. To qualify, a religious communitarian organization must be incorporated. It must have a religious or apostolic "character," and it must have a common or community treasury.[36]

There is little extant that explains why Congress enacted this accommodation. Its reasons are not entirely shrouded in silence, but the legislative history behind the provision consists of a single paragraph introduced into the Congressional Record by Senator David I. Walsh. Senator Walsh explained that

> [i]t has been brought to the attention of the [Senate Finance Committee] that certain religious and apostolic associations and corporations, such as the House of David and the Shakers, have been taxed as corporations, and that since their rules prevent their members from being holders of property in an individual capacity the corporations would be subject to the undistributed-profits tax. These organizations have a small agricultural or other business. The effect of the proposed amendment is to exempt these corporations from the normal corporation tax and the undistributed-profits tax, if their members

take up their shares of the corporations' income on their own individual returns. It is believed that this provision will give them relief, and their members will be subject to a fair tax.[37]

This legislative history makes clear that Congress was sympathetic to the plight of religious communitarians, and intended to reverse the courts' determinations that religious communitarian organizations were subject to both the corporate income and the undistributed earnings tax. It also shows some awareness of the plight of the Israelite House of David, though it is interesting that instead of mentioning the Hutterites, who had been the subject of two losing cases the prior decade, Congress chose instead to highlight the Shakers. (The choice may be related to the size of Shaker agricultural and other businesses – the courts explicitly found that the Hutterite agricultural operations were enormous.)

Even that background helps little with the actual interpretation of the statute. Although the Code conditions the accommodation on the existence of a *religious* or *apostolic* corporation with a *common* or *community treasury*, none of those terms have easily discernable meanings, and neither the Internal Revenue Code nor the Treasury regulations define them. Moreover, according to the Tax Court, "we find it difficult to view Senator Walsh's comment as defining a religious or apostolic association or corporation, let alone as defining the terms 'common treasury' or 'community treasury.'"[38]

That definitional hole makes the accommodation more ambiguous – and thus less valuable – than it might have been. Still, between the text of the law, courts' interpretations, and the legislative history, we can find hints at what a communitarian religious organization must do to qualify.

For example, while "religious or apostolic" remains undefined, the legislative history did point to the Israelite House of David and the Shakers as examples, presumably, of religious organizations that would qualify. And both religious organizations taught that believers had a religious mandate to give up private property and, instead, work for and receive support from the religious community. Presumably, any religion with similar teachings and practices would meet the "religious or apostolic" requirements. But even assuming the legislative history means that religions like the Israelite House of David and the Shakers qualify as "religious or apostolic," their use leaves significant ambiguity. Did Congress intend its list to be exhaustive or illustrative, for example? If exhaustive, could they really have intended the provision to apply solely to the Shakers and the Israelite House of David? Or was it meant to cover every communitarian religion that looked enough like the Shakers or the Israelite House of David?

If the examples were merely meant to be illustrative, what is the outer limit of *religious or apostolic*? Could any religious organization qualify? Does it require some sort of charismatic leadership? There are a wealth of ways a communitarian religion could function. The accommodation Congress provided does not lay out how to determine the outer boundary for the type of economic practices that will fit into the accommodation.

Even if we can decide the contours of *religious or apostolic*, we are not out of the definitional woods. We still need a communal or community treasury. Again, the Internal Revenue Code does not provide a definition. The Tax Court has provided a gloss on the communal or community treasury requirement. It does not, according to the Tax Court, require members to take a vow of poverty or otherwise to give up private property. It does, on the other hand, mean that the treasuries of qualifying religious organizations should be used to support members, and the members should have equal interests in the property.[39]

The final ambiguity in this accommodation is the meaning of "pro rata shares." Although the tax law exempts the organization itself from paying taxes, it requires members to include their pro rata share of the organization's income in their gross income.[40] Generally, pro rata share is conceptually easy to understand: if an individual owns 10 percent of a partnership or corporation, her pro rata share of entity income is 10 percent. (When she pays taxes on that share depends on the type of entity and when it makes distributions.)

But in determining pro rata share of income, communitarian religious organizations differ from ordinary for-profit partnerships and corporations in one profound way: they have no owners. Members have given up some or all ownership of private property, and the amount of support members receive could depend on how hard they work, how much they need, or any other criteria determined by the religion.

If communitarian religious organizations distributed all of their income to members, this ambiguity would not raise any significant problem. The tax law could assume that any amount received by a member constituted that member's pro rata share. But to the extent that the organization does not distribute all of its income – and, because the Hutterites and the Israelite House of David faced the accumulated earnings tax, it is clear that at least some of these religious groups do not distribute all of their income – suddenly, the meaning of "pro rata share" becomes important and ambiguous. These groups do not necessarily distribute a fixed amount or percentage to members. Rather, many distribute according to need. And needs can change from year to year, as can the percentage of its income that the organization keeps rather than distributing to members. Figuring out what percentage of income to allocate to each member necessarily becomes an administratively difficult, and potentially unfair, endeavor.

Moreover, taxing individuals on their pro rata share (however calculated) of entity income creates an additional practical problem: if members of religious and apostolic organizations have given up personal property, where will they get the money to pay their tax bill? Presumably, the religious/apostolic organization provides them with the necessary cash, but there is no reason to believe that all such organizations do.

Personal Accommodation

On its surface, seeing this special tax provision as a personal religious accommodation appears to be a stretch. After all, members of a religious communitarian organization ultimately pay taxes on income that the organization does not distribute to them. And yet the accommodation ultimately benefits the members more than the organization.

And how does it benefit members? In the first instance, by allowing the organization to keep more assets. Because communitarian religions use their assets and income to support their members (who have given up some or all of their private property), increasing the amount of after-tax assets that the religion can keep directly translates into having more assets available to support members.

When originally enacted, the accommodation for communitarian religious organizations functioned primarily by freeing those organizations from paying the accumulated earnings tax. Because the pre-World War II individual income tax reached only the upper echelons of income-earners, this accommodation was not about eliminating a second level of taxation.

Today, the concerns addressed by the accommodation have flipped. Technically, the accumulated earnings tax still exists, but it has become easy enough for corporations to avoid that it is, at best, vestigial.[41] The problem today is that without accommodation, the religious organization would pay the corporate income tax on its income, and then members would pay personal income tax on their receipts from the organization.

Of course, that is the situation facing most employees. Their (corporate) employer pays taxes on its income, then employees pay taxes on their compensation (and their employer gets a deduction for salaries paid). But in the context of communitarian religious organizations, the interpolation of an entity is an unusual step. But for their religious beliefs, members could own property directly. Instead of a religious entity owning farmland, the farmer would own it directly. And only the farmer would pay taxes on income from the farm, because no entity would exist between the farmer and the land.

Even if the farmer needed an entity, moreover, they could choose a partnership or a limited liability company. Unlike a corporation, partnerships and limited liability companies do not pay taxes. Instead, the owners of a partnership or limited liability company pay taxes on their share of the entity's income. Either way, though, the fact communitarians' religious beliefs require entity ownership of property means that members of these religious groups potentially face a second layer of taxation.

Kibbutzim

The disconnect between communitarian organizations and modern liberal capitalism is not limited to Christian communitarians operating in the United States. Israel, for example, has a similar communitarian movement, and Israel has had to make concessions for the same disconnect in its income tax.

In Israel, the communitarian story beings in about 1910, when the first kibbutz was formed in Palestine. Like members of Christian communitarian groups, members of a kibbutz (called "kibbutzniks") eschew most private property. The Israeli government owns the kibbutz's land, and leases it to the kibbutz. All of the nonreal property, in turn, is owned collectively by the kibbutzim, other, perhaps, than small personal effects that kibbutzniks can purchase with an annual allowance the kibbutz provides them. But the kibbutz provides its members with housing, food, clothing, and even medical care.

Although the economics of the kibbutz shares much in common with the economics of Christian communitarians, the origins of the two differ significantly. Unsurprisingly, Jewish settlers in Palestine were not attempting to recreate and reclaim an Apostolic society based on the New Testament. Rather, kibbutzniks based their communitarian vision on two main ideals. First, they believed in "the religion of labor." Kibbutzim elevated physical labor, looked down upon in the shtetls from which kibbutzniks had emigrated, to a moral good.

In addition to the value of labor, kibbutzniks believed in social and economic equality. Kibbutzim believe that private property, combined with the profit motive, creates class distinctions, which, in turn, destroys fraternity and equality. Communal ownership, in contrast, tears down classes and builds up equality. And equality was an important enough principal that, originally, at least, kibbutzim emphasized *formal* equality, where (under most circumstances) each kibbutznik would receive the same allotment of clothing and other goods as every other member.[42]

Like the United States, Israel has a corporate and an individual income tax.[43] And, like the United States, its tax system is a poor fit for members of communitarian groups who eschew private property. Still, even though the fit is poor, Israeli lawmakers, like US lawmakers, recognized that kibbutzniks should not avoid paying taxes altogether. Israel's solution, however, differs from the US accommodation in one significant way: Israel essentially exempts kibbutzniks from paying taxes, instead imposing tax at the kibbutz level.

As demonstrated earlier, the United States' taxation of individuals on entity-level income is complicated, raising significant practical and theoretical questions. It turns out, though, that Israel's taxation of kibbutzniks at the kibbutz level is no less complicated. First, the kibbutz must calculate its income, including both the amount of money it earned and the amount its members earned working outside of the kibbutz. It then allocates that money evenly between each member, and calculates the theoretical tax liability of each of them, taking into account their credits, deductions, and other benefits. Finally, the kibbutz adds these amounts together and pays that total amount as an entity-level tax.[44]

Like the US accommodation for religious and apostolic organization, Israel effectively eliminates the second level of taxation. And like the United States, Israel views the members of a communitarian group, rather than the communitarian group itself, as the appropriate taxpayer. In the United States the belief that individual members, rather than the organization, should pay the taxes is reflected in the fact that the religious and apostolic organizations are exempted from tax. Instead, members are treated (and taxed) as if they had received the income themselves. Administratively, this may prove somewhat problematic, as members' religious beliefs have caused them to give up private ownership of property, including, presumably, money with which to pay their taxes. Still, the entity that holds property exists solely because of members' religious beliefs, and but for those beliefs, would not exist in that same form.

In Israel, the kibbutz is, in fact, the taxpayer. Still, Israel's tax law demonstrates that it, too, views the individual kibbutzniks as the proper taxpayers. That conclusion is obscured slightly by the fact that the kibbutz itself pays the tax, but it does not pay tax calculated on its income. Rather, it pays tax based on the income of its members. This might seem like a distinction without a difference but, as long as individuals face different tax rates than entities, and have different deductions and other tax attributes, the identity of the taxpayer makes a substantive difference in the amount of tax paid. And the amount of tax paid by a kibbutz is the collective individual taxes of its members, not the amount a nonkibbutz entity would pay.

RELIGIOUS AND APOSTOLIC ACCOMMODATION TODAY

Although both the United States and Israel recognize that communitarian organizations do not fit comfortably with the assumptions underlying their tax systems, it is fair to ask whether the US accommodations have any ongoing relevance today. After all, the current federal income tax differs significantly from its early twentieth-century iteration. Importantly, the accumulated earnings tax, while extant, is mostly irrelevant, and, unlike the first decades of the income tax, there is no longer a bar on tax-exempt organizations engaging in commercial transactions.

Even without a bar to engaging in commercial transactions, most communitarian religious organizations – or at least those that engage in commerce with the outside world – still could not qualify as tax exempt under ordinary exemption provisions. The courts in the 1920s disqualified Hutterite colonies not only because they engaged in significant agricultural commerce, but because the money they earned went to the private inurement of members. Because communitarian religious groups still support their members, they would still fail the private inurement test, and would not qualify as tax exempt.

The virtual death of the accumulated earnings tax also does not mean that today communitarians should be indifferent to the tax status of the organization. Until 2017, US corporations paid taxes at marginal rates ranging from 15 percent (on corporate income up to $50,000) to 35 percent (on corporate income in excess of $10 million). (As of 2018, Congress amended the corporate rate and made it a flat 21 percent.) As long as the entity's income exceeds $75,000, though, it will pay taxes at a marginal rate of at least 34 percent.[45]

For an individual to pay taxes at a 34 percent rate, they would have to earn at least $416,700 in 2017.[46] In 2014, income of $416,700 would have put a US household well above the cutoff for the top 5 percent of income.[47] There is no reason to believe that communitarian organizations tend to be particularly wealthy, so taxing their income at corporate, rather than individual, rates is almost certain to cause them to pay more, collectively, in taxes.

It would be possible to avoid the higher corporate tax, but it would require the corporation to make tax-deductible expenditures (including, especially, wages to its member-employees). Even though a taxable communitarian corporation could deduct the amount it paid in wages to members, though, as a practical matter it faces significant impediments to making enough deductible payments. In part, that is because members have a religious imperative not to receive money or property in excess of their needs, so the organization cannot distribute all of its revenue (unless it only earns enough to support its members' immediate needs).

Even if the members *could* own private property, though, the organization would have to keep a certain amount of its income. It must have money to maintain its property and expand, at the very least. To the extent, then, that the entity keeps some portion of its income, chances are that the collective tax burden of the entity plus its members will be higher than the collective tax burden of the members under the current accommodation scheme.

Accommodating religious communitarians ultimately imposes very little cost on the federal government. In 2015, there were only 217 groups that claimed this accommodation. Compare that to the more than 1.5 million organizations exempt under other provisions of the tax law.[48]

That the accommodation for religious communitarians is not overly expensive does not mean it is perfect, of course. Its vagueness and ambiguity present problems, but they are problems that Congress or the Treasury could solve relatively easily. And, while communitarian groups are generally poor vehicles for tax evasion, there are certain holes that Congress can and should fill.[49] Overall, though, the accommodation for religious and apostolic organizations still benefits religious communitarians, and feels like the kind of accommodation that the tax law should provide.

11

A Framework for Religious Tax Accommodation

As we have seen in the preceding chapters, Congress has proven willing to accommodate religious practice in the tax law. In fact, it is willing to create tax accommodations for religious taxpayers even without thinking systemically about the *why* and the *how* of tax accommodation. Given Congress's demonstrated willingness to accommodate, is there any reason to create a framework?

I believe there is. As I have discussed throughout the book, Congress, the IRS, and the courts sometimes provide accommodations that *feel* right. As discussed in previous chapters, Congress has exempted self-employed Amish from paying self-employment taxes. It has allowed religious individuals who have taken vows of poverty to exclude certain income they earn from their gross income, and has allowed ministers of the gospel to broadly exclude housing benefits from their income. It has provided a special tax regime for religious communitarians. The IRS has ignored the value of religious benefits received in exchange for donations.

It may be that Congress and the IRS should have granted some or all of these tax accommodations. But without some kind of standard to measure them against, we cannot say that they *are* right. In fact, the *ad hoc* nature of tax accommodation sometimes leads the government to accommodate religious practices that do not need accommodation and to refuse to accommodate religious practices that warrant accommodation. And because the government provides and denies accommodations on a case-by-case basis, without situating these accommodations in a broader context, religious individuals cannot make an informed prediction about whether their religiously dictated practices will be accommodated.

In this chapter, I will demonstrate why tax accommodation is inevitable, and why such accommodation is consistent with good tax policy. I will build and explain a framework that tax policymakers should use to evaluate potential tax accommodations. In short, though, the framework I propose asks three questions:

1. Does an individual's religion cause them to act in a tax-disadvantaged way?
2. If so, what type of accommodation would put them in a similar after-tax position as other taxpayers without the same religious constraints?
3. Are there extrinsic reasons that the tax law should not provide that accommodation?

The answers to these three questions will help tax policymakers determine whether a particular religious practice warrants a tax accommodation and, if so, how that accommodation should look. After explaining how the questions work, the chapter will end by showing how the framework applies to the various accommodations discussed in previous chapters, as well as how it could apply to hypothetical religious beliefs.

THE COST OF ACCOMMODATION

The idea of accommodations for religious practices and beliefs finds its genesis in the Religion Clauses of the First Amendment. Although the Free Exercise Clause and the Establishment Clause necessarily conflict at times, there is widespread (though not universal) agreement that the Constitution mandates protection for religion from state interference and that this protection sometimes requires accommodation.[1]

Before we can address tax accommodation specifically, it is worth looking at the scope of religious accommodation more generally. In its broadest scope, religious accommodation aims to exempt religious individuals "from generally applicable governmental regulation" when their "religious beliefs and practices would otherwise thereby be infringed."[2]

The question of accommodation "dominates the field of law and religion today."[3] And this domination makes sense. In spite of the frequency with which the Free Exercise Clause and the Establishment Clause potentially conflict, the courts have rarely found these conflicts required mandatory accommodation. Between 1963 and 1990, the Supreme Court read the Constitution to require the state to provide special protection from generally applicable laws to religious individuals and organizations. In 1990, the Court walked that special protection back, holding that laws only unconstitutionally impinged on free exercise – and thus only had to provide for accommodation – when they discriminated (facially or purposively) against religion.

Congress passed the Religious Freedom Restoration Act to reverse the Court's 1990 holding and return Establishment Clause law to its pre-1990 state. For purposes of accommodation, though, that return appears to have been more show than substance; even under the earlier standard, claims for mandatory religious accommodation rarely succeeded.[4] (Claims for mandatory accommodation may be on the upswing – some district courts have been solicitous of employers who claim that the contraception mandate in the Affordable Care Act violates their religious beliefs. The Supreme Court has yet to weigh in on whether the contraception mandate is sufficiently burdensome to require the government to provide an accommodation, though.[5])

Thus, most of the intellectual work surrounding religious accommodation necessarily addresses permissible accommodations. Sometimes that work attempts to find the line dividing permissible from impermissible accommodations. But its more interesting aspect is the normative one; permissible accommodations, after all, are accommodations that the legislature *can*, but is under no obligation to, grant, and thus requires the legislature's judgment.

And that normative judgment requires the legislature to weigh the views of both observant religious individuals and individuals who do not embrace the religious practices at issue. Accommodation, after all, often does more than merely remove obstacles from an individual's religious observance – many times, accommodations impose costs on third parties. Not all do, of course: exempting Jehovah's Witness children from an obligation to say the pledge of allegiance at school[6] does not somehow require the other children to pledge *more* allegiance to make up for their abstaining classmates. It does not, in other words, impose additional costs on the other children. What if the objector were a kindergarten teacher who refused to teach their students the pledge of allegiance?[7] There is some cost – either the children would not learn the pledge or the school would have to find someone else to do it – but the costs imposed on others would still be marginal.

But not all costs of accommodation are marginal. If the United States can draft men and women into the military, but excuses Quakers from the draft to allow them to follow their peace testimony, it must nonetheless fill the ranks of the military with nonQuakers. Those who are drafted in lieu of the conscientious objectors bear the cost, financial and physical, of the government's accommodating Quakers.

The negative externalities of accommodation do not have to be as dramatic as war, though. Under Title VII of the Civil Rights Act of 1964, employers must accommodate employees' religious beliefs and practices unless such accommodation would produce undue hardship. Such statutorily required accommodations may include anything from permitting religious employees to avoid working on their Sabbath to allowing them to wear a religiously mandated beard in violation of workplace safety rules. Providing these accommodations imposes costs on the employer; quite often, it also requires the employer to treat other employees less favorably.[8] That less favorable treatment may not be as dramatic as going to war, but it is, nonetheless, an additional cost borne by unaccommodated parties.

Assuming that there is a middle ground of permissible, but not mandatory, accommodation, a central question becomes how much cost should nonreligious individuals have to bear? This equilibrium point – where the benefits to the religious individuals do not impose too steep costs on their nonreligious fellow citizens – should ultimately be the target for permissible accommodation.

Scholars and policymakers have not come to a consensus on where that equilibrium point lies. They have not even come to a consensus on whether permissible accommodations should exist. It is clear, though, that the Free Exercise Clause will sometimes conflict with the Establishment Clause and, in those cases, accommodation will be allowed in at least some circumstances.

Should the Tax Law Accommodate Religion, Redux

Of course, all of this talk of an accommodation framework is moot if we believe that the tax law should not accommodate religious practice. And the fact that the tax law *does* in fact accommodate some religious practices is not, by itself, a strong argument in favor of accommodation.

In the context of tax laws, the Constitution does not require accommodation. Courts have consistently found that the government's interest in an administrable system for raising revenue outweighs the free exercise interests an individual may have in not paying some or all of their tax.[9] Tax accommodations may be permissible, but they cannot be mandatory.

To justify any tax accommodation requires more than a mere reference to the Religion Clauses, then. Any such accommodation must overcome general normative objections to accommodation. And there certainly are normative objections.

The principal, and most compelling, objection is this: absent a constitutional mandate, why should religious beliefs be treated differently from nonreligious moral beliefs? Outside of the realm of constitutional protection, what is so special about religion? Why, that is, should legal accommodations allow a "religiously motivated individual [to] run a food kitchen in defiance of contrary zoning ordinances where an individual whose humane impulses were not in any recognizable way grounded in religion could not"?[10]

Philosophically, that is a difficult question. True, religion has served an integral role in providing individuals with values, identity, and even integrity.[11] But religion is hardly unique in that regard. There are plenty of nonreligious philosophical systems that similarly provide moral guidance and behavioral imperatives, and "there is no apparent moral reason why states should carve out special protections" that apply solely to the religious.[12] What makes a religiously motivated belief different from one motivated by a sincere irreligious philosophical belief? There may be some difference, but that difference is difficult to pin down, and, even pinned down, may be more difficult to justify. Still, as I discussed in Chapter 1, scholars have made compelling arguments for the philosophical relevance of treating religion as a substantive and separate legal category.

Notwithstanding the philosophical conundrum, the fact remains that the law *does* treat religion differently. The Religion Clauses of the First Amendment provide religion with a "special status."[13] And that special status is not merely an American invention. Though the level of religious freedom differs from country to country, "it seems clear that existing human rights documents and recent international jurisprudence *do* give the right to religious freedom a certain kind of special status."[14]

Still, even if no philosophical basis existed for treating religion differently, that absence would not moot the necessary discussion of tax accommodation. In spite of tax policy's preference to treat similarly situated taxpayers in a similar manner, the tax law already treats similar taxpayers differently. Though "accommodation," with its connotation of religious practice, may not be the perfect word, it is fair to say that the tax law already accommodates certain behaviors. For example, a homeowner can generally deduct the mortgage interest they pay, whereas a renter who is otherwise identical financially cannot deduct any portion of the rent they pay. An expatriate will pay less in US taxes than a US resident with the same income. Someone with extreme medical expenses can deduct a portion of those expenses, where an individual with lower medical expenses cannot deduct them.

Even taking religion out of the picture, then, legislators are willing to look at taxpayers' individual situations. Where their personal situations include a difference that legislators consider relevant, the legislators will provide carve outs from the generally applicable tax law. It makes sense that legislators would approach questions of religion (or, at least, questions of religion that intersect with taxes) in a similar way.

Moreover, these bespoke regimes – including religious tax accommodations – can comfortably exist without a philosophical foundation. Over time, they build on themselves. Tax policy is subject to path dependency and inertia, and "decisions made in response to specific historical circumstances became difficult to change – even after the circumstances themselves changed or were no longer relevant."[15]

And without some sort of active political will on the part of Congress to eliminate all religious tax accommodations, there is basically no way to interrupt this path dependency. A number of constitutional and statutory regimes protect current tax accommodations – both of a religious and a nonreligious nature – from judicial challenges by taxpayers.

The principal impediment to taxpayers' challenging an accommodation is the Constitution's standing requirement. Essentially, the Constitution only allows a potential litigant access to the federal judiciary where they have suffered an "injury in fact," the injury was caused by the person the litigant is suing, and the injury can be redressed by the courts. Generally speaking, a potential litigant who cannot demonstrate that they meet these three criteria lacks standing, and therefore, cannot access the courts. And the harm of seeing somebody else get an inappropriate tax benefit is too attenuated to qualify as an injury in fact.

The standing requirement is not absolute impediment to uninjured plaintiffs, though. In 1934, Congress passed the Declaratory Judgments Act, which allows courts to resolve certain legal questions in advance of a litigant suffering an injury in fact. The scope of the Declaratory Judgments Act, though, is circumscribed and, notably, the Act explicitly excluded rulings on the tax law.[16] The Declaratory Judgments Act's exclusion of tax controversies is further buttressed by the Tax Anti-Injunction Act, which expressly prevents courts from hearing cases challenging the tax law unless the challenged tax has been assessed against the taxpayer who is suing.[17]

While the combination of the constitutional standing requirement and the special treatment afforded tax law by the Declaratory Judgment and Tax Anti-Injunction Acts appear to effectively cabin taxpayers' ability to directly address tax accommodation, taxpayers have one additional avenue to avoid the constitutional standing requirement. Courts have created "Establishment Clause standing," which allows taxpayers to challenge government support of religion in their capacity as taxpayers, even if they have not suffered from individualized harm. The Establishment Clause standing doctrine would appear to be the perfect vehicle to allow individuals to police Congress and the IRS when they create tax accommodations that go too far.

Under current Supreme Court jurisprudence, would-be tax accommodation police do not have access to Establishment Clause standing. It is not enough that the government action provide a benefit to religion. To invoke Establishment Clause standing, the challenged action must involve taxing *and* spending. Tax accommodation does not involve spending, though; instead, tax accommodation allows affected religious taxpayers to reduce their tax bill. Even though direct spending is economically identical to a reduction in taxes, for purposes of determining Establishment Clause standing, courts ignore economic reality and instead look for actual literal spending.[18] Because tax accommodations do not involve government spending or injury in fact, taxpayers have no standing (Establishment Clause or regular) to challenge tax accommodation.[19]

What to Do With Inevitable Accommodation

At this point, tax accommodation appears inevitable. The privileged position religion occupies in the US Constitution and federal law, combined with the inertia of historic accommodation and the virtual impossibility of the public directly challenging tax accommodations, means that accommodation is unlikely to go away. Moreover, without any policing mechanism, and given the *ad hoc* nature of past tax accommodation deliberations, there is reason to believe that Congress will continue to enact new religious tax accommodations in the future.

The inevitability of religious tax accommodations does not by itself argue for providing a framework with which to think about them, of course. If accommodation were entirely undesirable, perhaps the *ad hoc* nature would be for the best; it would raise the cost to legislators of creating accommodations (because they would have to start from scratch each time), and it would raise the cost to religions of pursuing accommodations (because they would have to lobby independently for each one).

Tax accommodation is not always bad policy, though. As we have seen in prior chapters, sometimes it recognizes and responds to actual economic differences caused by religious practice, and the tax law already takes into account certain actual economic differences.

Still, the fact that the tax law takes into account some economic difference does not itself mean that the tax law *should* take into account religiously based economic difference. Every accommodation in the tax law increases the law's complexity. And as the tax law's complexity increases, it becomes more difficult for taxpayers to understand. As a result, taxpayers have less understanding of their own tax obligations. It also becomes easier for the legislature to hide tax benefits for select groups of taxpayers in a complex tax regime without other taxpayers understanding the giveaway.

Complexity is not per se bad tax policy. In addition to its inevitability, complexity can provide "a desirable trade-off for other, more important goals, namely fairness and efficiency."[20] And, as we have seen, in at least certain circumstances, accommodating religious practice is desirable to achieve tax fairness.

Which leads to the strongest argument for designing and implementing a policy framework: it can act as a restraint on government. Not every request for accommodation deserves accommodation; some requests represent frivolous claims about religious beliefs or practice. Some represent sincere religious beliefs, albeit beliefs with no economic consequences. And some represent beliefs with significant economic consequences. Without a framework to guide policymakers, though, they must evaluate each requested accommodation from scratch, not only determining whether to accommodate, but deciding what criteria they will use in evaluating the accommodation. The results of such an *ad hoc* and unconstrained process almost certainly lean toward more accommodation that is optimal – in general, legislation that favors religion tends to be popular among elected officials.[21]

It is important to note that a framework would be the beginning, not the end, of the process. A framework would provide tax policymakers with a heuristic to think about whether and how to design a particular accommodation, but would not prescribe any particular end result. In the end, the legislature or the IRS would have to decide, after analyzing the proposed accommodation, whether to implement it and, if implemented, how they should design it.

Whether one favors religious accommodation or not, if it is ultimately inevitable, at the very least policymakers need to think about the design of accommodation. Professors Ira C. Lupu and Robert W. Tuttle have identified three criteria that should guide the enactment of discretionary accommodation. Such an accommodation should be designed to (a) relieve burdens felt distinctively by religion (and be proportionate to those burdens), (b) avoid significantly impacting third parties, and (c) be available to members of any religious denomination.[22] Although these criteria are not tax-specific, with little adjustment, they establish a good set of guideposts for tax-specific accommodation.

The framework I propose is conceptually simple, comprising three cascading questions: first, does a taxpayer's religious belief cause her to act in a tax-disadvantaged way? If it does, what kind of accommodation would put her in a similar after-tax position as nonreligious individuals in the same position? And finally, is there any reason not to provide that accommodation? The simplicity of these questions belies their relevance, though. Not only do these three questions provide lawmakers with a coherent way to think about tax accommodation, they also meet Professors Lupu and Tuttle's criteria for the enactment of discretionary accommodation.

The application of the first and the third of Professors Lupu and Tuttle's criteria is self-evident: the accommodated tax burden should be significant, as well as religiously motivated. Accommodation should not allow for deducting every religious cost, no matter how small. And where Congress grants an accommodation, that accommodation should be available to all taxpayers with similar practices, rather than limited to taxpayers of a particular denomination.

The relevance of the second criterion is less immediately obvious, but it functions to limit the breadth of a particular accommodation. About 84 percent of Americans claim some religious affiliation; even a small accommodation for 84 percent of Americans would significantly burden the 16 percent who claim no religious affiliation.[23] Accommodations should only be made to outlier practices, then, so that the costs are low and diffused through more taxpayers.

PRELIMINARY OBJECTIONS

At the risk of being overly repetitive, it is essential to keep in mind that the proposed accommodation framework does not automate the work of tax policymakers. The answers to these three questions do not, by themselves, determine whether the tax law should grant an accommodation, much less how the accommodation should be designed, but it does provide policymakers with a starting point in looking at a potential accommodation. To understand the value of these three questions, though, we must first unpack them.

As an initial matter, we need to ask why it matters that an individual's religious beliefs cause them to act in a tax-disadvantaged manner. There are at least two plausible objections to using this as a criterion in determining accommodation. First, religious practice implicates personal preferences. The tax law itself does not expressly discriminate against any religious view (except, perhaps, the view that an individual's religion proscribes the payment of some or all taxes, an argument the courts have uniformly – and rightly – dismissed as irrelevant). For most religious taxpayers, paying taxes is not the same thing as being required to say the pledge of allegiance or fight in a war in violation of one's religious beliefs. Second, a number of academics have argued that horizontal equity – the idea that similarly situated taxpayers should pay the same amount of tax – is any empty concept, and that we cannot and should not use it as a tax policy baseline.

As a practical matter, both objections are beside the point – the tax law does, in fact, provide accommodations to religious practice, and as a result, there is value in having a robust process to determine when and how to provide those accommodations. As a theoretical matter, though, it is necessary to address them.

The first is inarguably true. While the decision to practice religion may (or may not) be different in kind from other personal decisions, it ultimately represents an individual's personal preferences for how to interact with the world. The fact that personal preference underlies religious practice does not determine the appropriate tax treatment, though. As I discussed earlier, the tax law takes some personal preferences into account. For example, the tax treatment of renters differs from the tax treatment of homeowners with mortgages. (Renters cannot deduct any portion of their rent payments, while homeowners who itemize their deductions can deduct their mortgage interest payments.[24]) Similarly, the tax law treats married couples differently from unmarried couples.[25] Even if religious practice is purely a personal preference, there is no intrinsic tax policy that would prevent the tax law from providing special treatment for it.

As for horizontal equity: while its value is contested, it nonetheless appears to be salient and important to ordinary taxpayers. And, while its popularity does not, by itself, justify horizontal equity as a foundational tax policy perspective, it does create a necessary foundation. Tax fairness is important, but people can and do disagree about the criteria making up a fair tax. Horizontal equity, then, can serve to limit the government's ability to provide special tax breaks.[26] That is, privileging the idea that similarly situated taxpayers should pay a similar amount of tax makes it much more difficult for the government to give a substantive tax break to men (or people who live in the city, or people who have an expensive hobby) without giving that same break to others in a similar situation. And, while I suggest that horizontal equity argues in favor of tax accommodations, it also constrains the scope of the accommodation.

ACTING IN A TAX-DISADVANTAGED MANNER

The basic simplicity of the tax accommodation framework does not mean that it can be applied mechanically, or applied carelessly. Rather, policymakers must understand the questions first before they can apply the framework to a potential accommodation. The first question – whether an individual's religion causes them to act in a tax-disadvantaged manner – requires that policymakers first examine what constitutes religion and religious practice, and then that policymakers determine what it means to act in a tax-disadvantaged manner.

Defining "Religion"

Even taking the first step here risks falling into a rabbit hole, and dragging the whole tax accommodation project down that hole. In many ways, attempting to define *religion* brings to mind Justice Stewart's famous stab at defining *obscenity*: it may be indefinable, but we know it when we see it.[27] That said, despite the difficulty of defining *religion*, courts have proven adept at recognizing religious claims, and the question of whether a claim is religious is almost never litigated.[28]

An I-know-it-when-I-see-it approach leaves too many gaps to be helpful here, though. It pushes the question of whether a practice is religious back on the policymakers without giving them any guidance for how to answer it. That lack of guidance means that religions with significant political power, history, and numbers of adherents – for example, Christianity, Judaism, and Islam – would undoubtedly be considered "religions" for tax accommodation purposes. But policymakers would be less likely to view new and minority religions, and those with strange or idiosyncratic beliefs and practices, as "religions" for these purposes, even though, in many cases, it would be the practices of these new and strange religions that triggered the need for accommodation.

At the same time, a bright-line set of rules would be equally prejudicial toward new and minority religions. To put together a list of what constitutes religion is to put together a list of what historic (and often majority) religion looks like.

The courts recognize these problems with defining religion, both in the First Amendment and in statutory areas. More than two decades ago, Judge Brimmer, a Wyoming district court judge, looked at various federal courts' attempts to grapple with the definition, and came up with a series of criteria that a judge could use to determine whether a set of beliefs and practices qualifies as a religion or not. His criteria represent what the tax law calls a facts-and-circumstances test: it provides a number of criteria that go into a definition without assigning weights or priorities to the criteria. Under the judge's facts-and-circumstances test, a policymaker must thus take a holistic approach to determine whether the beliefs and practices in question qualify as a religion.

This kind of facts-and-circumstances is not perfect. It lacks the clarity that a bright-line rule would have, and still puts a thumb on the scale for things that look like Christianity, Judaism, and Islam, but it nonetheless provides guidance while, at the same time, allows flexibility to include new religions in its ambit.

In his opinion, Judge Brimmer laid out the following as indicia of a religion: religion concerns itself with ultimate ideas. It includes metaphysical beliefs and provides some kind of moral or ethical system. Its beliefs are comprehensive. It has certain "accoutrements" of religion, including founders/prophets/teachers, writings, gathering places, ceremonies, structure, holidays, and particular diets or fasting.

Judge Brimmer highlighted that his facts-and-circumstances test would include both traditional religions and a number of new religious movements, and even some more obscure beliefs. It would not, however, encompass the whole of philosophical movements: he argued that it would exclude the purely personal, purely political, purely ideological, and purely secular.[29]

This is not, of course, the only possible test for defining religion. But it works – it provides some idea of how to separate religion from nonreligion, while at the same time allowing for new religions to be treated as religion. At the same time that it adds structure, it also meets the I-know-it-when-I-see-it test.

What is "Religious Practice"?

Once *religion* is defined, policymakers have to determine what qualifies as *religious practice*. It is, after all, religious practices, not merely beliefs, that potentially lead to disadvantageous tax treatment that could qualify for accommodation. Fortunately, it is easier to define religious practice than it is to define religion. For purposes of the Religious Land Use and Institutionalized Persons Act, Congress defined "religious exercise" (which, for our purposes, is essentially the same thing as religious practice) as "any exercise of religion, whether or not compelled by, or central to, a system of religious belief."[30] This definition works equally well in the tax accommodation area.

Accommodated religious practices, then, need not be central to an individual's belief system. Rather, tax policymakers should look to the potential bad tax treatment of religious individuals and determine whether that treatment is related to a religiously motivated economic decision. If there is no religious hook, there should be no tax accommodation. If the behavior in question *is* motivated by an individual's religious belief, though, policymakers do not need to look at the relative importance of that particular belief in relation to the taxpayer's other religious beliefs. (In fact, the government is rightfully cautious of inquiring into the relative importance of an individual's particular religious beliefs.[31]) Instead of centrality, tax policymakers (and, eventually, tax administrators) should look to whether the religious practice in question would derive from a religious individual's "honest belief that the practice is important to his free exercise of religion."[32]

Tax Disadvantage

Under the first prong of the framework, while religion and behavior motivated by that religion are necessary for accommodation, they are insufficient. The first prong also requires a tax disadvantage, and a causal relationship between the religious practice and the tax disadvantage.

Tax disadvantage does not just mean that a religious taxpayer has less money, after taxes, than a nonreligious taxpayer. A religious taxpayer could have less after-tax money than a nonreligious taxpayer for any number of reasons, most of which have nothing to do with disadvantageous tax treatment.

In many cases, religious practices require some kind of consumption that nonreligious individuals do not need. Some of that consumption is almost unnoticeable. An individual who goes to church every week, for example, in many cases must drive or take public transportation. An individual who does not go to weekly religious services would not incur the cost of gas or bus fare that their Christian neighbor incurs going to and from the religious services.

Not all costs will be marginal, though. A person's religion may require them to purchase religious literature, ceremonial clothing, or even take expensive pilgrimages to holy sites. Presumably, our religious individual would not have incurred these particular costs but for their religious observance, and their nonreligious neighbor presumably does not incur these costs, leaving the religious individual with less money after taxes.

The fact that a religious individual may have less money than their nonreligious counterpart as a result of these religion-linked expenses does not, I suspect, lead most people to conclude that the government should somehow absorb the cost of these religious actions. On an intuitive level, it does not feel like the kind of thing into which the government should interpose itself.

And that intuitive conclusion is correct. Not every cost borne by religious individuals represents tax disadvantage, even if that cost is religiously mandated *and* leaves the religious person with less wealth than a nonreligious individual. There are at least three reasons (interconnected, to be sure) why the tax law should not take these differences that do not represent tax disadvantages into account. First, the differences in wealth have nothing to do with government policy, tax or otherwise. The fact that an individual's religion compels them to buy a book that they otherwise would not have bought is completely disconnected from the government. The government neither required nor forbade that purchase.

The second is closely related to the first: these types of religious expenses represent personal consumption. For purposes of tax policy, "consumption" means something different than merely eating and drinking – it means using up resources, often by spending money.[33] In general, the federal income tax is indifferent to personal consumption: individuals pay taxes on their income, irrespective of how they spend that income. If my neighbor and I each earn $100,000 of taxable income, we should pay the same amount of taxes, even if they buy a used Honda and I buy a new BMW. The tax law does not care whether taxpayers are frugal or spendthrift. There is no reason that the tax law should treat religious consumption differently than it treats nonreligious consumption.

Finally, if the government accommodated religious spending generally, whether in part or in whole, that would represent a subsidy for religious individuals. Subsidizing religious practice is constitutionally problematic, and from a tax policy perspective would be suspect. (It is important here to acknowledge that the tax law *does* subsidize individuals' donations to churches and other religious institutions by allowing some donors to deduct their donations.[34] That subsidy, though, is less problematic because it is available to anybody, religious or not, who donates to tax-exempt public charities.)

If *tax disadvantage* does not just mean that a religious individual has less money after taxes and spending than a nonreligious individual, what does it mean? For purposes of this accommodation framework, it means that, for religious reasons, an individual cannot do a transaction in the simplest, most common manner. Rather, their religious beliefs obligate them to structure their transaction in an alternative manner. (Note that I will be using the word "transaction" in a broad sense. I do not mean to limit it to actions taken in the formal economic sector. Instead, I use it to describe any series of actions an individual takes that have tax consequences. For example, borrowing money to buy a home would meet the definition of *transaction* I use here, because taxpayers can deduct mortgage interest. Marrying would also qualify as a *transaction*, because marriage affects many parts of a taxpayer's tax liability, including their tax bracket and the tax consequences of gratuitous transfers they make.)

Not only must the transaction be structured in an unusual way, but the tax treatment of the transaction must be different from the tax treatment of structuring the transaction in the standard way. That is, for religious tax accommodation, policymakers should remain indifferent to after-tax wealth. Instead, they should focus on tax liability – if religious practice creates a higher tax liability, the practice may justify some sort of tax accommodation.

Again, although this first prong of the inquiry is conceptually simple, it is not automatic. As a preliminary matter, policymakers must identify what the comparable standard transaction would be, and then must determine the tax consequences of the alternative religiously inspired transaction. By focusing on religiously mandated transactions, the framework rightly ignores the question of *what* is being bought.

For example, it should not matter whether a bookstore owner is buying and selling religious books and tchotchkes, or is selling academic books and tchotchkes: the religious nature of the goods being bought and sold has no tax consequence. If, however, the bookstore owner's religious beliefs prevented them from paying interest (and so they had to finance their inventory with an Islamic financing instrument, paying a nondeductible interest equivalent), it would not matter whether they were selling religious or academic literature. Either way, their religious beliefs would require them to act in a tax-disadvantageous manner. If their religious beliefs would require them to act in a tax-disadvantageous manner, the tax provision in question meets the first prong of the tax accommodation framework.

ACCOMMODATION AND SIMILAR AFTER-TAX POSITIONS

It is not enough merely to say that the tax law should accommodate a particular religious practice, all things being equal. Policymakers must also decide whether and how to remedy the unequal treatment. Designing the proper remedy will generally be even harder than determining whether a particular religious practice merits tax accommodation. It must walk the line between too generous and not generous enough. On the one hand, a too-generous accommodation will introduce additional distortions into the tax law, encouraging people who otherwise would prefer to use the standard transaction form to instead use a religiously mandated form. As taxpayers arbitrage the tax difference between the standard transaction and the accommodated form, the government will lose more revenue than it should.

On the other hand, if the accommodation is insufficiently generous, it will not accomplish its basic goal – religious individuals will still face additional tax liabilities as a result of their religious practice. In theory, that may not be bad, but as a practical matter, as I have demonstrated, Congress does (and likely will continue to) provide accommodations for religion in the tax law. And as long as the law provides for accommodation, that accommodation should be well designed. Any accommodation will increase the complexity of the tax law, as well as the complexity of complying with the tax law. While increased complexity is not *per se* bad tax policy, to the extent the cost of the additional complexity outweighs the benefits of the accommodation, any accommodation will have been counterproductive.

The simplest way to walk that line is to ignore the religiously mandated form and, instead, look at the substance and motivation of the transaction. That requires tax policymakers to ask three questions. First, they must ascertain what the religiously motivated taxpayer is trying to accomplish. Second, they need to determine whether the form prescribed by the taxpayer's religion differs from the form a nonreligious taxpayer would use. Finally, they must determine whether the religiously motivated form used results on a different tax burden than the form a nonreligious taxpayer would use.[35]

If the tax burden of the religiously prescribed transaction differs from the tax burden a nonreligious taxpayer would bear, then step two of the framework would suggest that Congress ignore the form and sweep the religiously motivated transaction into the regime applicable to the standard transaction. If a taxpayer pursuing a particular result generally gets a deduction in the course of her transaction, religious individuals who are pursuing the same result should also get that deduction, even if formally they do not qualify for it. (I will provide illustrative examples of how this would work in the next two sections.)

But will this type of accommodation ensure that religious accommodations are neither too generous nor too meager? It probably cannot – a motivated taxpayer (or, at least, a motivated taxpayer who can afford the right tax attorney or accountant) will likely be able to find gaps to exploit, irrespective of how the government designs tax accommodation. Taxpayers take advantage of discontinuities in the tax law anywhere that they can find such discontinuities,[36] and it is unlikely that any kind of accommodation – or lack of accommodation – can entirely eliminate this kind of tax arbitrage. A well-designed set of rules can, however, constrain religious tax arbitrage, and the IRS and the courts can work to police the margins.[37]

An accommodation also does not necessarily mean that religious and non-religious taxpayers will arrive at economically identical places. The religiously motivated form may include different (and presumably higher) transaction costs than the standard form does, or may face a higher degree of risk. The purpose of accommodation is not for the government to absorb the extra costs of religious practice; rather, its purpose is to equalize the costs imposed by the government.

Just because a religious practice meets the first two prongs of the framework does not mean that an accommodation should automatically be granted, of course. It merely means that it could be appropriate to grant an accommodation. As the Supreme Court has emphasized, there exists a "broad public interest in maintaining a sound tax system."[38] Even where a potential accommodation meets the first two prongs of the framework, if its implementation would disrupt the soundness of the tax system, the accommodation should not be granted.

Under what circumstances would an accommodation fail this third prong? Easy cases include where the accommodation is too expensive or too complicated for the IRS to administer.[39] Even as the government tries to implement and administer more policies and programs through the tax law, its principal purpose continues to be raising enough revenue for the government to meet its obligations.[40] A tax accommodation that meets the first two prongs of the framework, but causes federal revenues to drop precipitously, is an accommodation that tax policymakers should reject.

Similarly, the IRS is responsible for processing hundreds of millions of tax returns annually.[41] But even as Congress is using the IRS to administer more programs, its budget has fallen precipitously over the last decade.[42] An accommodation that imposes substantial additional administrative duties on the IRS will burden the tax system broadly; even where the religious taxpayers are sincere and face real additional tax liabilities, those additional administrative costs may weigh against providing accommodation.

And burdens on the tax system may not be the only relevant extrinsic considerations. Congress may want to consider other questions of fairness. For example, an accommodation that meets the first two prongs may still be undesirable where it singles out a single religion – or a discrete subset of religions – for accommodation. Remember, the Lupu and Tuttle criteria for discretionary accommodation requires that an accommodation be available widely to all members of a religion. A tax accommodation available solely to one or two religions looks like a special-interest provision, and potentially undermines other taxpayers' faith in a fair system. As a result, in some circumstances, the government may want to reject an accommodation that is too narrowly focused.

There may be other reasons tax policymakers choose to reject a potential accommodation, too. Any viable framework must allow for that possibility, as this one does. The value in making this type of extrinsic consideration a formal part of the framework is that it will encourage policymakers to articulate the reason they reject an accommodation that meets the first two steps. That formal articulation should guard against rejections based in animus or disdain toward a particular religious group.

APPLYING THE FRAMEWORK TO EXTANT ACCOMMODATIONS

How would the framework function in practice? One way we can find out is to look backward at the various tax accommodations that have or have not been granted. We would evaluate how those accommodations would come out under the framework, and how the results correspond to our notions of tax fairness. Looking backward is not perfect for evaluating the framework's prospective functionality, since there is already a thumb on the accommodation scale, but, had they not already been decided, the framework could have guided policymakers in looking at these religious practices.

And the framework may still have some purchase, even in cases where Congress or the IRS has already made a decision regarding tax accommodation. While fundamental tax reform remains rare, the tax law is in a constant state of flux, with Congress debating and enacting large and small changes every session.[43] At some point, Congress may revisit any of the accommodations it has currently made.

So how would the current accommodations fare under the framework? Some religious practices would continue to be accommodated. Other practices would lose their accommodation. And some practices that are not currently accommodated would, under the framework, qualify for accommodation. Although this section will proceed in the order various religious practices appeared in the book, it is worth highlighting two extreme examples of purported accommodation. On the one hand, the clearest case for tax accommodation under the framework is the case of Muslim homeowners who finance their home purchase using instruments that do not charge interest. Conversely, perhaps the clearest example of a tax accommodation that would fail the framework is the parsonage allowance. (It is interesting to note that, in both cases, the framework proposed in this book would reverse the state of accommodation under current law.)

Conscientious Objectors and Pastors

Should the tax law accommodate individuals with religious objections to paying taxes? Unquestionably, the ability to follow one's conscience is central both to liberty and to democracy; one Florida court expressively argued that a "liberated conscience is as essential to a robust democracy as blood is to the human body."[44] As such, individuals have an interest in preventing majoritarian veto over matters of conscience.[45]

What should the tax law do, then, when an individual's religious beliefs – a subset, perhaps, of conscience[46] – conflicts with the manner in which government spends its money? As I have discussed earlier, as a legal matter, the government has no obligation to accommodate these kinds of conscientious tax objectors. The Supreme Court has held that the government's interest in raising revenue outweighs religious individuals' religious rights to not fund religiously objectionable government actions.

That answers a question we have not asked, though. Here, the question is not whether the government *must* accommodate matters of religious conscience (clearly it has no obligation to do so), but rather, whether it should accommodate religious conscience. And this is where the framework can help tax policymakers get a fix on the proper answer.

The first prong asks whether a religious taxpayer's religious practice puts them in a tax-disadvantageous position. The answer, whether it is in regard to Catholics opposed to abortion, Quakers opposed to war, or Amish opposed to social security, is no. Their religious objections to spending do not alter their economic choices in any tax-relevant manner. That is, there is no difference from a tax perspective between a Quaker who embraces the Peace Testimony and a Baptist who is indifferent to federal spending on defense. If both earn the same amount of money, and both engage in the same business transactions, both will pay approximately the same amount in taxes, irrespective of their religious beliefs.

Moreover, even if policymakers were to ignore the first prong, the second prong would be impossible to meet. Because there is no difference in the after-tax position of these religious objectors and others, there is no accommodation the government could make that would put the religious conscientious objectors in the same position as individuals without the same religious objections. They are already in the same financial position. Any kind of accommodation would put religious conscientious objectors in a better position than non-objectors.

The result may be harsh: without accommodation, religious taxpayers may see their money go to support programs they object to on religious grounds.[47] Certainly, to the extent it is reasonable, we want to leave room for individuals to follow their conscience, religious or otherwise. But at the same time, even if we were to jump past the first two prongs, the third prong indicates why this would not work: presumably, every taxpayer objects to some kind of government spending. But if the tax law took into account all objections – or even just all religious objections – it would be unadministrable. Essentially, taxpayers would have the ability to determine their own tax liability, announcing religious objections to this government program or that one. Perhaps, with an unlimited budget and an unlimited workforce, the IRS could evaluate each taxpayer's sincerity. But in a world of finite budgets and shrinking staff, allowing any taxpayer to cut their tax bill by any amount they claimed was objectionable would be utterly unworkable, providing an extrinsic reason to refuse to provide the accommodation.

It is important to note that this full analysis is unnecessary: the accommodation failed at the first prong. Because this is the book's first accommodation analysis, though, I thought it valuable to look at every step in the process.

Conscientious objectors were not the only taxpayers with a claim on not paying some or all of their taxes as a result of their religious status. The book started with clergy who took vows of poverty, whether sincere or not.

As a starting point, a vow of poverty does not, by itself, meet the first prong of the accommodation framework. Nothing about a vow of poverty, on its own, puts a religious individual in a different after-tax position from an individual who is poor because they do not have a job. The potential difference arises where the clergy earns money, which they remit to their religion.

Where the vow of poverty is illusory – as is the case with the mail-order ministers – there should be no question of accommodation. True, they eschew money they have earned in favor of their ministry, but that transactional difference is illusory. These mail-order ministers exercise complete control over their ministries. The imposition of a ministry that holds the money is form without substance. Because there is no substantive difference between these mail-order ministers and nonclergy, their plea for accommodation fails the first prong.

Rev. Fogarty and Sister Schuster, on the other hand, earn money which they immediately remit to their respective Orders. They exercise no control over it, and are unable to control what happens with it. Moreover, because of the limitations taxpayers face on deducting charitable donations (they must itemize and, even if they itemize, they can deduct half of their donation at most), they must pay taxes on a portion of their money that they do not really control. As long as they actually do not exercise control over the money, they meet the first prong of the accommodation framework.

The second prong is analytically more difficult. Who is the proper comparable? If it were an individual who did not earn any money at all, the correct accommodation would be to treat Rev. Fogarty and Sister Schuster as if they also did not earn any money, and thus exempt them entirely from taxation. (Such an exemption could take the form of treating their income as if it had been paid directly to their orders, or it could take the form of exempting them from the deductibility limitations.)

Non-earners are not the best comparable, though. Rev. Fogarty was employed by the Society of Jesus, and Sister Schuster by the Order of the Adorers of the Blood of Christ. Their Orders may have provided them with little or with no cash compensation, but the Orders did provide them with housing, with food, with clothing, and with other necessaries.

It would make sense to allow them to exclude from income any money that they turned over to their Orders. At the same time, though, the tax law should tax them on the compensation they receive from their Orders, whether in cash or in kind. That kind of accommodation would put them in the same after-tax position as individuals without the same religious practices.

There are no extrinsic reasons to deny this kind of accommodation. It would involve some additional administrative work, but that work would largely not fall on the government. Rather, religious employers would have to value the in-kind compensation they provided to employees who had taken vows of poverty, and provide information returns to the employee and the IRS. And, while it is true that these religious employees could face liquidity problems if they were paid entirely in kind, that liquidity problem would be no worse than what they currently face.

Under the tax accommodation framework, religious objections to government spending would not warrant any kind of accommodation. Vows of poverty, however, would, at least where the vow of poverty encompassed the religious individual's actually giving up control over the money they earned. Note, though, that under the framework, the accommodation did not function solely to reduce their taxes. Rather, it tried to match their taxes to what a similarly situated nonreligious taxpayer would pay. As a result, it eliminated taxes on one class of income, but imposed taxes on another class.

Parsonages

As discussed above, the parsonage allowance represents perhaps the clearest example of a religious tax accommodation provision that would not qualify under the tax accommodation framework. The parsonage allowance is the ability of "ministers of the gospel" to receive in-kind housing *or* a cash housing allowance tax free. The parsonage allowance has a long history – the in-kind exclusion dates to 1921 and the cash exclusion to 1954 – but longevity alone tells us little about the policy wisdom of a particular provision.

In its original incarnation, Congress enacted the parsonage allowance to reverse the Treasury Department's determination that "ministers of the gospel" could never qualify for the more general exclusion for some employer-provided housing. Today, however, there is no reason to believe that ministers continue to be excluded from the general regime. The codification of the exemption for employer-provided housing does not exclude ministers of the gospel who otherwise meet the exemption's criteria.[48] The question, then, is not whether the parsonage allowance *ever* should have been granted, but rather whether it should exist today.

The answer is a resounding no. The parsonage allowance fails the framework's initial prong. That failure does not mean, of course, that it should never have existed. It is possible that, in its original incarnation, the parsonage allowance could have passed the first prong. With ministers categorically excluded from the Treasury-created exemption for employer-provided housing, their religious status put them at a disadvantage compared with other employees who lived in employer-provided housing, and who were allowed to exclude housing from their gross income.

However, today's parsonage allowance fails the first prong of the framework. To the extent that a minister must live in employer-provided housing for the convenience of their employer, they qualify for the general exemption. And there is nothing about a minister's (or cantor's or imam's) religious beliefs that require them to live in nonqualified employer-provided housing, or to accept a housing stipend as part of their pay package. The fact that such individuals are religious does not increase or decrease their need for housing.

Losing the parsonage allowance may prove costly to churches, and that cost may fall disproportionately on poorer churches. The parsonage allowance permits churches to pay lower cash salaries to their ministers than the ministers otherwise might demand. It may be true that poorer churches cannot afford to pay market wages to their ministers. It may even be true that ministers are generally underpaid. But neither churches' nor ministers' poverty has anything to do with the tax law. That is, the fact that a minister's after-tax income is low is not the result of a minister's engaging in a tax-disadvantageous transaction. Rather, it is because the minister's pre-tax income is also low. Any supposed tax accommodation represents a wage subsidy, not the correction of a religiously motivated transactional form. And it fails the first prong whether the tax-free housing is provided in kind or as an allowance.

(It is worth noting that, even if the parsonage allowance's original incarnation would have met the first prong of the framework, its execution would have failed the second. Congress crafted a rule that did not merely put ministers of the gospel on an equal footing with nonreligious individuals. Rather, because the parsonage allowance did not include a convenience-of-the-employer or a premises-of-the-employer requirement, it was more permissive than the general rule, and thus put ministers of the gospel in a *better* position than non-religious individuals. And the second prong would never have allowed a cash allowance as an accommodation, since no other domestic housing allowance is free from taxation. So, while the original version could have been designed in a manner that qualified under the framework, it was not designed in that way.)[49]

Although the preceding analysis shows how the framework could have guided Congress as it considered whether to accommodate ministers of the gospel, it can also illustrate how the framework could help the IRS make effective decisions with respect to religious individuals. As discussed in Chapter 5, the Freedom From Religion Foundation attempted to challenge the parsonage allowance's constitutionality in court. The Seventh Circuit dismissed its challenge for lack of standing, but also provided a roadmap for how the Foundation could get standing.

And the Freedom From Religion Foundation followed that roadmap – it designated a housing allowance as part of the salary it paid three of its executives. They then amended their tax returns to reflect a tax-free housing allowance and requested a tax refund.[50] As of the publication of this book, the district court has found the exemption for cash housing stipends to clergy unconstitutional.[51] Even if that stands, the framework will be important, for at least two reasons. The first is that the court's decision has no effect on a religion's provision of in-kind housing to clergy. Clergy still do not have to include that value in gross income. Moreover, if the Seventh Circuit upholds the district court's decision, Congress may want to reconsider how it treats clergy housing for tax purposes, and, to the extent it rethinks a potential accommodation, it should use the framework to decide and determine how such an accommodation would look.

Islamic Finance Instruments

As mentioned above, the clearest example of an accommodation that should be granted under the framework is the case of Islamic finance. Under the first prong of the framework, tax policymakers must decide whether an individual's religion causes them to act in a tax-disadvantaged way. At least some portion of Muslims believe that Islam forbids them from charging or paying interest. Nonetheless, like most other Americans, Muslims often cannot afford to buy a house for cash.[52] To meet the need of Muslim home buyers, banks have developed *shari'a*-compliant finance instruments. Those finance instruments essentially replicate a standard mortgage, but rather than interest, borrowers pay a non-interest amount in additional to principal.

So their religion causes Muslims to act *differently* than nonMuslims. Difference, however, is insufficient to trigger accommodation. The difference must be tax disadvantageous. And here it is: under standard mortgages, any borrower who itemizes can deduct their mortgage interest. Because Islamic finance instruments charge no interest, though, the cost of borrowing through them is not deductible. Analyzing the first prong, then, we see that the after-tax cost of borrowing is higher for Muslim borrowers. This additional cost is the result of the tax treatment of the nonstandard transaction they use to borrow money. And they use this nonstandard transaction for religious reasons.

Moreover, the consumption here is not consumption of religious benefits. It is the consumption of housing. An accommodation would not represent a government subsidy of the Muslim borrower's religious practice – it would represent a subsidy of their owner-occupied housing. And, for better or worse, that subsidy is currently a feature of US tax law. Muslim borrowing, then, meets the first prong of the tax accommodation framework.

Because Muslim borrowing meets the first prong, Congress can move on to the second: what is the solution? To find the appropriate solution, first policymakers need to figure out the transaction. In this case, the transaction is clear: the Muslim taxpayer wants to purchase a house using some mix of their own money and borrowed money. There is an equivalent transaction: purchasing a house using a standard mortgage. A taxpayer who purchases a house using a standard mortgage can deduct the interest they pay, subject to certain constraints.[53]

The solution, then, that would put the Muslim homeowner in an equal position with the nonMuslim homeowner is to allow them to deduct the interest-equivalent amount (subject to the same limitations that a nonMuslim homeowner would face). And what is the interest-equivalent amount? It is at least a portion of the amount they pay in excess of principal.

An accommodation here would meet the framework's requirement. At the subjective level, I see no compelling reason not to grant an accommodation. Muslims make up less than 1 percent of the American population;[54] allowing them to deduct the interest-equivalent amount they pay would not significantly impact federal revenues. And the tax law already treats some non-interest payments as the functional equivalent of interest.[55] There is no reason that it could not do the same here.

It may be necessary that the government set a ceiling on the interest-equivalent amount, to prevent Muslim homeowners from deducting fees and other nondeductible costs. The IRS has the ability to do this, though: it already determines a baseline interest rate, and could use that to set a ceiling.

Importantly, any accommodation should only allow a deduction for interest-equivalent amounts actually paid by the Muslim homeowner. Currently, Islamic finance instruments are at least marginally more expensive than traditional mortgages, but this additional expense is irrelevant to the tax law. Muslim borrowers have chosen to use a religious form, and must themselves bear any additional nontax expense.

Deductions and Religious Quid Pro Quos

In some cases, even with a guiding framework, determining whether to grant an accommodation is a harder call. For example, even with a framework, the question of accommodating deductions for religious costs can be tricky. In most cases, of course, there will be no question of the deductibility – like any donation to public charity, unencumbered donations should be deductible. Permitting the deductibility of these donations does not need to be filtered through a framework because it does not represent a tax accommodation – it merely treats religious taxpayers exactly the same as it treats other taxpayers.

The question becomes more difficult, though, where the religious taxpayer gets some kind of religious *quo* in exchange for their *quid*. While this book focused on Scientologists' payment for auditing, they are not alone among the religious in getting some sort of religious value in exchange for their donations. Mormons cannot enter their temples, for example, unless they tithe. Some Christians get reserved pews at church in exchange for certain donations. Some synagogues auction religious honors, including publicly reading scripture and tickets for high holy day services. Catholics can purchase specific Masses for a stipend. Religious parents pay tuition for their children to attend religious schools.[56]

On the one hand, these *quid pro quo* donations do not meet the first prong of the framework. Receiving goods or services in exchange for a supposed donation is not structuring a transaction in a tax-disadvantaged manner. Rather, it is plain vanilla consumption.

In creating the charitable deduction, Congress explicitly considered and rejected the idea that donations to a public charity could be deductible where the donor expected a benefit in return.[57] And the courts embraced Congress's legislative history, holding that where a donor received something in exchange for their charitable donation, they could not deduct that donation.[58]

This *quid pro quo* rule is why an individual who donates $100 to NPR and, in exchange, receives a tote bag, can only deduct perhaps $68.[59] Their donation is treated as partly a donation, but partly the purchase of a tote bag. And they cannot deduct that amount of the donation that is purchasing the tote bag (which is generally measured by the value of the tote bag they receive).

The rule is clear and relatively simple. Its application is inconsistent when the benefits received in exchange for the donation are intangible, though. For example, in 2016, the basic one-year membership to the Art Institute of Chicago cost $95. That membership provided for admission for two adults and all children under the age of 18 in the member's household.[60] For Chicago residents, admission cost $20 for adults, and $14 for teenagers.[61] Without a membership, a family of four (two adults, two teenagers) would pay $68 each time they visited the Art Institute. For that family of four, then, membership pays for itself in two visits.

The ability to enter the Art Institute costlessly is an intangible benefit, so it would make sense that some, if not all, of the cost of membership was not deductible. According to the Art Institute (and, for that matter, many other museums), though, the cost of membership is *fully tax-deductible*.[62] (Not every museum pretends that the members' unlimited admission has no value; for instance, Chicago's Field Museum acknowledges that membership comes with financial value, and that members cannot deduct the full amount that they pay for membership.[63])

It is not clear, then, that the IRS's decision to allow Scientologists to deduct the amount they pay for auditing represents a religious tax accommodation. Certainly there is some aspect of consumption involved, and that consumption means that the donation has some level of *quid pro quo*. But it is hard to argue that the value of the religious consumption should have offset the religious taxpayer's deductible donation, while the value of entering the museum should not offset the art-lover's deductible donation.

It is true that the Supreme Court held that the IRS could disallow at least a portion of Scientologists' auditing payments as *quid pro quos*. The IRS's ultimate decision not to do so, though, is not really an accommodation, and thus is not amenable to analyzing against the proposed tax accommodation framework. Instead, the IRS's decision can be seen as a recognition of the chaotic state of the law regarding intangible *quid pro quos*, as well as a recognition of the difficulty of valuing many types of intangibles. In light of the treatment of museum members, it is hard to say that the IRS's current treatment of Scientologists is wrong.

If the IRS cracks down on the treatment of museum members, though, allowing religious donors to ignore the religious consumption they receive in exchange for their donations would become an accommodation that failed to meet the first prong of the framework. In fact, that may be the best way to understand the difference between the IRS's allowing Scientologists to deduct the amount they pay for auditing and its (and the courts') refusal to allow religious parents to deduct the cost of tuition at a religious school.

Like churches, private schools can easily qualify for exemption from tax,[64] and that tax-exempt status allows donors to deduct their donations. Parents cannot deduct the tuition they pay for their children to attend nonreligious schools, however. Tuition is paid purely in exchange for the ability to attend the school and gain the education the school provides. Even an individual whose religion required them to send their children to a private religious school is not acting in a tax-disadvantaged manner. Rather, they are paying for consumption, and are receiving the benefit. They thus fail the first prong of the framework.

Even if they were to meet that prong, any supposed accommodation of the cost of private school would put them in a *better* position than taxpayers whose children attended a nonreligious private school. This kind of government subsidy of religious consumption would certainly fail the second prong. The third prong may be implicated, as well: it is easier to place a value on education than it is to place a value on the benefits of a Scientology audit. If one reason that the IRS does not pursue these religious *quid pro quos* is the difficulty of valuation, that difficulty does not apply in the case of a religious private school, and the IRS has an extrinsic reason not to grant an accommodation.

The Right to Tithe

In contrast to the question of deducting donations that contain an element of religious *quid pro quo*, there is nothing complicated about the question of accommodating somebody's ability to make religious donations in the first place. On the portion of this question that the IRS and the courts addressed, they arrived at the right answer. Using the proposed framework, they could also address the question that they have avoided until now.

As discussed previously, the question that the IRS and the courts addressed was not whether the IRS had to permit religious taxpayers to make religious donations. A law specifically forbidding donations to religions would violate the Free Exercise Clause of the Constitution. Rather, some taxpayers have requested accommodations that would allow them to tithe instead of (or before) paying some portion of their taxes.

Such requests are rare. For most taxpayers, the only tax relevance of religious donations is their deduction. For a handful of taxpayers who have not paid all of the taxes they owe, though, the question of religious donations becomes relevant. When these taxpayers request an offer in compromise or negotiate an installment agreement to pay their delinquent taxes, the IRS determines how much they need to pay each month based on their income, reduced by a certain amount of permissible expenses. Some religious taxpayers have argued that the IRS should take into account their tithing obligations in determining how much they can afford to pay.

The IRS and the courts are correct in refusing to accommodate these taxpayers. Accommodating delinquent religious taxpayers here would fail the first prong of the framework. Making religious donations does not cause an individual to act in a tax-disadvantaged manner. True, tithing represents a cost to them, but the government has no obligation to subsidize their costs, religious or otherwise. (And even delaying their taxpaying represents a benefit to the taxpayer and a cost to the government.) For any taxpayer who itemizes, in fact, paying tithes and other religious donations represents an *advantageous* tax position, since they can deduct the tithes and thus only bears a portion of the cost.

While the courts have refused accommodation requests from religious individuals generally, though, they have so far avoided the question about how to treat tithe-paying by individuals whose employment requires them to pay tithes. Should such individuals receive a special accommodation requiring the IRS to take their tithing obligations into account in determining how much they can afford to pay?

No. Again, these religious individuals are not acting in a tax-disadvantaged manner. They face a budgeting issue and, where their employment depends on their making religious donations, that budgeting is important and salient. It is not the government's job, though, to ensure that any given individual can keep their job. Even for religious employees whose jobs depend on their paying tithing, an accommodation would do more than merely put them in a similar position as nonreligious taxpayers; it would put them in a materially better position.

It is important to reiterate that the IRS's refusal to take religious financial obligations into account in calculating how much a delinquent taxpayer must pay each month does not prevent that taxpayer from making their donations. The permissible living expenses do not represent the spending they are required to make. Rather, they must meet all of their financial obligations (including tithe paying) from the pool of money the IRS allows them to exclude in calculating their monthly payments.

It is also important to emphasize that not granting an accommodation here is not meant to be punitive. The proposed accommodation does not meet the first prong of the framework, not because the taxpayer failed to pay taxes that they owed, but because their religion has not caused them to act in a tax-disadvantaged manner. In other words, their religious beliefs do not prevent them from engaging in a standard transaction available to other taxpayers, because there is no such standard transaction.

Missionaries

In the abstract, there is reason to provide religious tax accommodations to missionaries. While it is true that, as they perform their missionary work, they are working both for their church and for God, as with clergy, the distinction between working for God and working for a secular employer has no tax relevance.

As with many of the existing accommodations, missionary work (again, in the abstract) fails the first prong of the framework. Whatever the differences between engaging in missionary work and engaging in nonmissionary work, missionary work does not put a taxpayer at a tax disadvantage. Certainly missionaries may earn less than their compatriots in the for-profit sector, but lower pay has no tax significance, and, in fact, the government should not subsidize religious pay.

It is worth noting, too, that in the abstract, even if we were to ignore the first prong, it would be virtually impossible for an accommodation for missionaries to pass the second prong. It would require defining the elusive tax disadvantage, and crafting a remedy that put missionaries in a similar after-tax position as nonmissionaries. Because there is no tax disadvantage, though, any accommodation would inherently put missionaries in a *better* position than nonmissionaries.

It is easier to see why accommodation is inappropriate by looking at the examples of missionary accommodations from Chapter 9. The first was the accommodation for foreign missionaries who took furloughs in the United States. The IRS administratively allowed these foreign employee-missionaries to ignore their furloughs to the United States in reestablishing foreign residence and regaining the advantageous US tax benefits of such residence.

A missionary's furlough in the United States does not meet the first prong. Although there may be practical reasons for a missionary to return to the United States, including recuperation and networking, those practical reasons are indistinguishable from the reasons a nonprofit or for-profit expatriate might return periodically to the United States. That is, missionaries do not return to the United States for religious reasons, and thus, treating them differently from (and better than) other expatriates violates the norm of tax fairness.

At the other end of the spectrum, allowing missionaries from the Church of Jesus Christ who accept donations from noncongregants to exclude that money from their gross income does not represent a religious accommodation. While those missionaries possessed the money, they were acting as agents for the church. The money never belonged to the missionaries, but the missionaries were a necessary conduit for the church to receive the money. Courts have long held that, where an agent receives money on behalf of their principal (and, of course, passes it on to the principal), that money is included in the principal's gross income, not the agent's.[65] Allowing the Church of Jesus Christ missionaries to exclude the donations they received follows the standard tax law, and is not a religious accommodation.

That leaves the Mormon missionaries. As with mission furloughs, their quasi-volunteer missionary work cannot get past the first hurdle. There may be economic disadvantage that Mormon missionaries face – presumably, such economic disadvantage includes the opportunity cost of not taking other, more lucrative, employment – but they face no tax disadvantage that accommodation could or should resolve. Mormon missionaries do not get past the first prong of the framework.

And yet, the tax law accommodates Mormon missionaries, if not explicitly, at least as applied. Mormon missions are not self-funded; rather, the missionaries or their parents pay into a central fund that the church controls. As long as the missionaries or parents itemize and otherwise are eligible, they can deduct their contributions. This deductibility is appropriate, of course, and it does not represent any kind of accommodation. Because they are donating to a qualifying tax-exempt organization, they can deduct the donations in the same way any donor to a tax-exempt organization can deduct the donations.

But IRS rulings (that predate the current funding regime of Mormon missions) also allow Mormon missionaries to exclude from income the support they receive in their missionary work. Under the first prong of the framework, allowing missionaries to exclude their support does not make sense. They use their support for housing, for food, for transportation, and for other consumption. Admittedly, much of that consumption is necessary, but it is not necessary for religious reasons – it is necessary for human reasons. Both religious and nonreligious individuals need housing, food, and transportation. Nothing about Mormon missionaries' religious practices somehow transforms the consumption of necessaries into tax disadvantage.

Moreover, even if it did, the accommodation currently in place fails the second prong. By allowing Mormon missionaries to exclude payments from gross income, it puts them in a better after-tax position than nonreligious taxpayers. Other taxpayers cannot exclude compensatory payments from their gross income, and there is no compelling reason to provide that benefit to missionaries.

Religious Communitarians

Religious communitarianism provides another example of religious practice that the government should accommodate. Communitarians' religious beliefs require them to eschew personal, private property. Instead of owning property individually, they contribute their property to a religious entity, albeit one in which they have no ownership interest. The entity then provides them with necessaries and, often, with a job.

From a tax perspective, it is disadvantageous for religious communitarians to put their property into an entity. If they owned their productive property individually, they would pay taxes on their own income. Because the property stays at the entity level, though, they face two levels of taxation: first, the entity must pay taxes on its income, then the communitarians must pay taxes when they receive money from the entity.[66] As a result of the transactional form required by their religious beliefs, religious communitarians face a tax burden in excess of the tax burden borne by those who are not members of a communitarian religion.

Applying the second prong highlights the kind of discretion this accommodation framework leaves with tax policymakers. Under current law, the accommodation for communitarian religious groups exempts the entity from taxes, but requires members to pay taxes on their pro rata share of the entity's income. While current accommodation would benefit from some clarification (particularly defining what the tax law means by *pro rata share*), it is perfectly serviceable in eliminating the additional tax cost created by following a religious form that requires the interposition of an entity.

At the same time, the solution Israel has come up with for the same problem – determining how much each member would pay at their marginal tax rate, adding those amounts together, and requiring the entity to pay that amount – is equally serviceable. It eliminates double taxation by exempting individuals from paying.

I personally prefer the Israeli version of dealing with communitarianism. In my opinion, it is cleaner and less complicated. It also solves the liquidity problem that communitarians face. That is, if they contribute all of their property to the religion, they may not have money with which to pay their imputed tax bill. The entity, however, has assets and the ability to pay.

Ultimately, though, that is a personal preference. Either type of accommodation would serve to put religious communitarians on an equal footing

with other taxpayers. Although there certainly are wrong ways to accommodate religious communitarians (for example, exempting both individuals and
the entity from taxation would not meet the second prong), there are different
paths to accommodation.

Finally, there is no compelling extrinsic reason for not granting the accommodation. The IRS already administers the current accommodation. With
just over 200 religious groups that qualify for the accommodation, it does
not cost the government significant revenue. And, in any event, the revenue
that it does cost the government merely puts religious communitarians on an
equal footing with their neighbors who can hold property in their individual
capacities.

APPLYING THE FRAMEWORK: PAULITES AND POLYGAMISTS

Of course, if the framework were only good for looking backwards at accommodations the government had already granted (or failed to grant), it would
have limited value. But the framework also works on a prospective basis. Imagine, for example, a religion that forbids civil marriage, perhaps based on Paul's
advice that "it is well for [the unmarried and widows] to remain unmarried
as I am."[67] Rather than marriage, this Paulite church has its own coupling
ceremony, one not recognized as marriage for civil purposes, but one which
functions in essentially the same manner.

Marriage may seem completely divorced from the tax issues this book has
focused on, but it fits comfortably within the definition of "transaction" I
use in this chapter. Though a detailed examination of the tax consequences
of marriage go well beyond the scope of this book, marriage significantly
affects couples' tax liabilities. Depending on the spouses' income, marrying
may increase or reduce their collective tax obligation. Marriage affects low-
income taxpayers' ability to qualify for the earned income tax credit. Spouses
do not have to pay gift taxes on transfers to each other, but also cannot realize
losses on transfers to each other.[68] The inability to marry, then, has real tax
consequences.

And should the tax system accommodate the Paulites, whose religion forbids them from marrying? Their religious practices seem to largely meet the
first prong of the framework: their religious beliefs require at least some of
them to act in a tax-disadvantaged manner.

Why only some? Because marriage is more complicated than merely a
question of whether the transaction results in increased or decreased tax. The
actual consequences depend on, among other things, both spouses' income –
some couples will pay more in taxes as a result of marriage, while others will

pay less. Still, a religious proscription on civil marriage will result in at least some adherents paying more in taxes than similarly situated taxpayers without the religious proscription.

Which leads to the second prong: how should this religious practice be accommodated? The answer to the second prong is simpler than the answer to the first. Even though the Paulite religion forbids civil marriage, the adherents' religious coupling serves essentially the same purpose; the Paulites' end goal is to live together in a partnered union. The tax law can accommodate their religious beliefs by treating their religious coupling as marriage for tax purposes.

This simple accommodation will not always reduce a couple's taxes, of course: a couple that paid less in taxes unmarried would, in theory, face a tax *increase*.[69] And that would be the appropriate result: the point of the accommodation is not simply to reduce religious taxpayers' taxes. Rather, the point is to treat religious taxpayers in the same manner as other taxpayers. In most cases, that means reducing religious taxpayers' taxes, but in situations where the accommodation could decrease *or* increase taxes, it is imperative that both results remain viable, and respond to the transaction the taxpayer pursues.

The accommodation of Paulite taxpayers' inability to marry would also meet the framework's third prong. It would create very little administrative burden. The IRS already knows how to deal with marriage. Accommodation could reduce federal revenue, but that reduction should not get in the way of providing the accommodation. But for their religious beliefs, a significant portion of those who couple in accordance with Paulite religious proscriptions would have married civilly, and would qualify for the tax treatment afforded married couples. Although tax revenues could be lower than the current (hypothetical) world, they would not be lower than a world without the Paulite religion.

That Paulites would qualify for accommodation under my framework does not mean, though, that the tax system should accommodate every taxpayer who eschews civil marriage for religious reasons. The framework would not require the accommodation of Fundamentalist Mormons who practice polygamy, for example.

For purposes of tax accommodation, Fundamentalist Mormons have some commonalities with my hypothetical Paulites. Although they believe in a religious duty to practice polygamy, because polygamy is illegal in every state in the United States, Fundamentalist Mormon men cannot legally marry multiple women. Instead, they marry their first wife civilly. Any subsequent wives they marry in religious ceremonies that the state does not recognize.

Like the Paulites, Fundamentalist Mormons meet the first prong of my framework. In fact, under current law, there is almost no circumstance where three or more individuals would pay less married than they do unmarried. Fundamentalist Mormons, then, face higher taxes as a result of their religious practices. And the second prong would allow for the tax law to treat them as married.

But how? Except for the bottom couple brackets, federal income tax brackets for married couples are not double the size of unmarried taxpayers' brackets. There is no way to simply create additional brackets for every spouse. Accommodating polygamy would require significant legislative and administrative thought and actions.[70] It may be that the tax law should take account of polygamy. Under current law, though, the tax law faces no imperative to account for polygamous marriage. Imposing such an obligation would be tremendously administratively complex. Thus, an accommodation for religiously motivated polygamists would fail the third prong. The legislative and administrative complexity of polygamy make it a poor candidate for tax accommodation, notwithstanding its roots in religious belief and practice.

GOING FORWARD

Since its inception in the early twentieth century, the reach of the federal income tax has expanded exponentially. Today, most Americans have or will interact with it (and most will touch the income tax, directly or indirectly, every year). This broad reach means, obviously, that religious and nonreligious Americans alike pay taxes.

Given the broad purchase religion has on the lives of those who subscribe to it, it is inevitable that some individuals' religious obligations will, at times, interact with their tax obligations. And it is similarly inevitable that Congress, the courts, and the IRS will accommodate those religious obligations at times.

So how do we do accommodation? As this book has demonstrated, we currently do it in an *ad hoc*, relatively incoherent manner, accommodating beliefs that are salient or popular, and refusing to accommodate those that are not. And in large part, the incoherence underlying tax accommodations stems from the fact that nobody has thought about them in a sustained manner, much less developed a systemic way to think about them.

I hope that this book has filled that gap, both by demonstrating the disconnected nature of current tax accommodations and by proposing a workable framework with which to think about them. The book's proposals have been aimed primarily at the government – policymakers and tax administrators in particular – because the primary job of accountants and tax attorneys is not to create tax law, but to help taxpayers comply with it.

Still, the framework can help tax professionals and the general public, too. In particular, to the extent policymakers adopt the framework, it allows religious taxpayers, watchdog groups like the Freedom From Religion Foundation and Americans United for the Separation of Church and State, and the government a common language with which to talk about current and future accommodations. Instead of requesting an accommodation every time their religion imposes costs on them, a religious taxpayer can evaluate whether the cost is of a type that the government should accommodate. Similarly, rather than attacking accommodations wholesale, the watchdog groups can evaluate whether there is an objective economic reason for those accommodations. In both cases, by focusing on the policy questions, groups can put more effort and resources into the fights that they can and should win, and less into the fights that they should not.

As we have seen, the framework I propose is skeptical toward accommodation – under it, the tax law would provide for very few accommodations. But that, I believe, is the right answer: although the tax law is, in some circumstances, bespoke, it must also apply to 150 million taxpayers. That breadth requires a baseline sameness, one which applies to men and women and children, to the religious and the nonreligious, to the wealthy and to the poor. And that level of generality requires that exceptions happen only in important and compelling situations. Those situations exist, though, and policymakers both can and must think through them carefully.

Notes

Introduction

1. My entry into the Twitter discussion appears at https://twitter.com/smbrnsn/status/ 537743400364437504 [https://perma.cc/96MB-P5KU]. A side note: today, with so much information online, no book can afford to ignore online sources, and this book is no exception. At the same time, link rot threatens readers' ability to go to online sources that I cite. And link rot is a real risk: a 2013 study discovered that nearly half of the links in Supreme Court opinions no longer lead to the intended site, and 70 percent of law review links suffered the same fate. (Link rot has personal implications, too: in the time it took me to write this book, one website I cited reorganized, dropping the language I quoted; I was lucky to find it preserved at the Internet Archive.) To combat link rot, the Harvard Library Innovation Lab launched perma.cc, which preserves cited websites as they looked when cited, and creates a unique URL for the sites. Jonathan Zittrain, "Perma: Scoping and Addressing the Problem of 'Link Rot,'" *Future of the Internet – And How to Stop It.*, September 22, 2013, http://blogs.harvard.edu/futureoftheinternet/2013/09/ 22/perma/ [https://perma.cc/U59H-Y9AS]. In the endnotes of this book, every time I cite a website, I will also include perma.cc link in brackets after the actual URL; that way, even if the original website disappears or changes, you will be able to see my source.
2. While the idea that Hovind's prosecution for tax evasion was pretextual to the actual crime of promoting a Christian worldview seems absurd on its face, it is not entirely unusual. In fact, Christianity has a long history of viewing itself as persecuted by a world that not only does not accept its precepts, but is actually hostile to its mission. This sense of persecution can help Christians situate themselves on the side of good in an eternal struggle between good and evil. *See* Candida Moss, *The Myth of Persecution: How Early Christians Invented a Story of Martyrdom* (New York: HarperOne, 2013), 8–9.
3. Ashley Powers, "Eve and T. Rex: Giant Roadside Dinosaur Attractions Are Used By a New Breed of Creationists as Pulpits to Spread Their Version of Earth's Origins," *Los Angeles Times*, August 7, 2005, sec. A.
4. In 1998, Congress forbade the IRS from designating individuals "illegal tax protestors," or any other similar designation, purportedly because Congress was

worried that such designation would stigmatize illegal tax protestors. Tax Restructuring and Reform Act of 1998, Pub. L. No. 105–206, § 3707, 112 Stat. 685. Congress's misplaced concern does nothing to change the fact that Hovind was, in fact, a tax protestor and, fortunately, does nothing to impede my ability to call him one.

5. www.irs.gov/Tax-Professionals/The-Truth-About-Frivolous-Tax-Arguments-Introduction [https://perma.cc/4BHQ-F7Z2].
6. *See* In re Hovind, 197 B.R. 157 (1989–1995); *Hovind v. Comm'r*, T.C. Memo 2006–143 (1995–1997), *Hovind v. Comm'r*, T.C. Memo 2012–281 (1998–2006).
7. *Hovind v. Schneider*, 2002US Dist. LEXIS 22918.
8. *Hovind v. Comm'r*, T.C. Memo 2012–281.
9. *Kent E. Hovind v. Commissioner*, Tax Ct. Mem. Dec. (CCH) 56,562(M).
10. In re Hovind, 197 B.R. 157.
11. Stephanie Hoffer and Christopher J. Walker, "The Death of Tax Court Exceptionalism," *Minnesota Law Review* 99, no. 1 (2014): 222; *Mayo Found. for Med. Educ. & Research v. United States*, 562 US 44, 55 (2011).
12. *Corp. of Presiding Bishop of Church of Jesus Christ of Latter-day Saints v. Amos*, 483US 327, 334 (1987).
13. Warren Buffett, "Stop Coddling the Super-Rich," *New York Times*, August 15, 2011, sec. A.

1 Religion and the State

1. While it is an imperfect proxy for religious violence in the United States, law enforcement reported 5,850 hate crimes to the FBI. Of those hate crimes, 1,354 were motivated by the victim's religion. This number likely undercounts the number of hate crimes during the year, but, at the same time, not all hate crimes involved physical violence. 2015 Hate Crime Statistics, https://ucr.fbi.gov/hate-crime/2015/topic-pages/incidentsandoffenses_final [https://perma.cc/5VB7-W25D].
2. For analytical purposes, I am treating the Establishment Clause separately from the Free Exercise Clause. While most scholars address the two separately, such treatment is not entirely uncontroversial. Some scholars believe that they are inseparably intertwined, and that non-establishment makes no sense without free exercise, and vice-versa. Richard John Neuhaus, "A New Order of Religious Freedom," in *Law & Religion: A Critical Anthology*, ed. Stephen M. Feldman (New York, NY: New York University Press, 2000), 93.
3. *Lemon v. Kurtzman*, 403 US 602, 614 (1971).
4. *Church of the Lukumi Babalu Aye, Inc. v. City of Hialeah*, 508 US 520, 523 (1993).
5. *Lynch v. Donnelly*, 465 US 668, 673 (1984).
6. Scott C. Idleman, "Why the State Must Subordinate Religion," in *Law & Religion: A Critical Anthology*, ed. Stephen M. Feldman (New York, NY: New York University Press, 2000), 179–180.
7. Arlin M. Adams and Charles J. Emmerich, *A Nation Dedicated to Religious Liberty: The Constitutional Heritage of the Religion Clause* (Philadelphia, PA: University of Pennsylvania Press, 1990), 14–15.

8. Thomas J. Curry, *The First Freedoms: Church and State in America to the Passage of the First Amendment* (New York, NY: Oxford University Press, 1986), 194–195.

9. Ibid., 198–199.

10. Philip B. Kurland, "The Origins of the Religion Clauses of the Constitution," *William and Mary Law Review* 27, no. 5 (1986), 839–861, 851–853.

11. Michael W. McConnell, "The Origins and Historical Understanding of Free Exercise of Religion," *Harvard Law Review* 103, no. 7 (1990), 1503.

12. *Permoli v. Municipality No. I*, 44 US 589, 610 (1845). Remember that the protections of the Religion Clauses of the First Amendment were not incorporated against the states by the Fourteenth Amendment for nearly another century.

13. John Norton Moore, "The Supreme Court and the Relationship Between the 'Establishment' and the 'Free Exercise' Clauses," *Texas Law Review* 42, no. 2 (1963), 143.

14. *Reynolds v. US*, 98 US 145, 166 (1878).

15. Ibid.

16. Ibid., 167. Interestingly enough, in their briefs, Reynolds's attorneys focused on procedural problems with his conviction, and spent very little time discussing the First Amendment question. Edwin Brown Firmage and Richard Collin Mangrum, *Zion in the Courts: A Legal History of the Church of Jesus Christ of Latter-Day Saints, 1830–1900* (Urbana, IL: University of Illinois Press, 1988), 153.

17. *Davis v. Beason*, 133 US 333, 346–347 (1890).

18. Ibid., 342–343.

19. Ronald F. Thiemann, "The Constitutional Tradition: A Perplexing Legacy," in *Law & Religion: A Critical Anthology*, ed. Stephen M. Feldman (New York, NY: New York University Press, 2000), 357–358.

20. John T. Noonan Jr., "The End of Free Exercise," *DePaul Law Review* 42, no. 2 (1993), 573–574.

21. *Sherbert v. Verner*, 374 US 398, 403 (1963).

22. Stephen M. Feldman, "Critical Questions in Law and Religion: An Introduction," in *Law & Religion: A Critical Anthology*, ed. Stephen M. Feldman (New York, NY: New York University Press, 2000), 3.

23. *Employment Div., Dep't of Human Res. of Oregon v. Smith*, 494 US 872 (1990).

24. Terri R. Day, Leticia M. Diaz, and Danielle Weatherby, "A Primer on Hobby Lobby: For-Profit Corporate Entities' Challenge to the HHS Mandate, Free Exercise Rights, RFRA's Scope, and the Non-Delegation Doctrine," *Pepperdine Law Review* 42, no. 1 (2014), 70.

25. John Witte, Jr. and Joel A. Nichols, *Religion and the American Constitutional Experiment*, 3rd edition (Boulder, CO: Westview Press, 2011), 138–139.

26. www.ncsl.org/research/civil-and-criminal-justice/2016-state-religious-freedom-restoration-act-legislation.aspx [https://perma.cc/UA48-CL5G].

27. J John Witte, Jr. and Joel A. Nichols, *Religion and the American Constitutional Experiment*, 3rd edition (Boulder, CO: Westview Press, 2011), 12–17.

28. Richard J. Regan, *The American Constitution and Religion* (Washington, DC: The Catholic University of America Press, 2013), 30–32.

29. Andrew Koppelman, *Defending American Religious Neutrality* (Cambridge, MA: Harvard University Press, 2013), 49, 56–57.

2252

30. John C. Jeffries Jr. and James E. Ryan, "The Political History of the Establishment Clause," *Michigan Law Review* 100, no. 2 (2001), 284–289.

31. *Lemon v. Kurtzman*, 403 US 602, 612–613 (1971).

32. Ibid., 612.

33. Frederick Mark Gedicks and Rebecca G. Van Tassell, "RFRA Exceptions From the Contraception Mandate: An Unconstitutional Accommodation of Religion," *Harvard Civil Rights-Civil Liberties Law Review* 49, no. 2 (2014), 9–10.

34. *See, e.g., Washington v. Trump*, 847 F.3d 1151, 1167 (9th Cir. 2017).

35. Brian Leiter, *Why Tolerate Religion?* (Princeton, NJ: Princeton University Press, 2013), 63–64.

36. Christopher L. Eisgruber and Lawrence G. Sager, "The Vulnerability of Conscience: The Constitutional Basis for Protecting Religious Conduct," *University of Chicago Law Review* 61, no. 4 (1994), 1315.

37. William P. Marshall, "In Defense of Smith and Free Exercise Revisionism," *University of Chicago Law Review* 58, no. 1 (1991), 326–327. Professor Marshall's final point is, ultimately, unconvincing. Notwithstanding popular belief in our meritocratic society, we use the law to support individuals and institutions ranging from poor to large Wall Street investment banks. The fact that religion may not be able to function without subsidy in the marketplace does not demean it any more than affirmative action demeans those for whom it is provided.

38. Jane Rutherford, "Religion, Rationality, and Special Treatment," *William & Mary Bill of Rights Journal* 9, no. 2 (2001), 305.

39. Michael W. McConnell, "A Response to Professor Marshall," *University of Chicago Law Review* 58, no. 1 (1991), 329–330.

40. 7), 499.

41. Ibid., 524.

42. Andrew Koppelman, "How Could Religious Liberty Be a Human Right?" Draft August 11, 2016, at 3. https://papers.ssrn.com/sol3/papers.cfm?abstract_id=x2995605

43. Ibid., ___ [22–23 of the draft].

44. Andrew Koppelman, "Is It Fair to Give Religion Special Treatment?," *University of Illinois Law Review*, no. 3 (2006), 603.

45. Ira C. Lupu and Robert W. Tuttle, *Secular Government, Religious People* (Grand Rapids, MI: Eerdmans, 2014), 213.

46. Michael W. McConnell, "Accommodation of Religion," *The Supreme Court Review* (1985), 3.

47. Mark Tushnet, "Accommodation of Religion Thirty Years On," *Harvard Journal of Law and Gender* 38, no. 1 (2015), 9.

48. Ibid., 27.

49. Samuel D. Brunson, "Dear IRS, It Is Time to Enforce the Campaigning Prohibition. Even Against Churches," *University of Colorado Law Review* 87, no. 1 (2016), 161.

50. *Littlefield v. Forney Indep. Sch. Dist.*, 268 F.3d 275, 294 n.31 (5th Cir. 2001); *Murray v. City of Austin. Tex.*, 947 F.2d 147, 151 (1991); *Saladin v. City of Milledgeville*, 812 F.2d 687, 692–693 (11th Cir. 1987).

51. *Suhre* v. *Haywood Cty.*, 131 F.3d 1083, 1086 (4th Cir. 1997); *Am. Civil Liberties Union of Georgia* v. *Rabun Cty. Chamber of Commerce, Inc.*, 698 F.2d 1098, 1102 (11th Cir. 1983).

2 On Making the Tax Law

1. David Frishberg, "I'm Just a Bill," The Best of Schoolhouse Rock, 1998, compact disc.
2. Steven A. Bank, Kirk J. Stark, and Joseph J. Thorndike, *War and Taxes* (Washington, DC: Rowman & Littlefield Publishers, 2008), 3–7.
3. Ibid., 21, 24.
4. Romain D. Huret, *American Tax Resisters* (Cambridge, MA: Harvard University Press, 2014), 19–20.
5. Joseph A. Hill, "The Civil War Income Tax," *The Quarterly Journal of Economics* 8, no. 4 (July 1, 1894), 450.
6. Christopher Shepard, *The Civil War Income Tax and the Republican Party 1861–1872* (New York: Algora Publishing, 2010), 129–133.
7. *Pollock* v. *Farmers' Loan & Trust Co.*, 157 US 429 (1895).
8. US Const. art. I, § 9.
9. Joseph Bankman and Daniel Shaviro, "Piketty in America: A Tale of Two Literatures Symposium on Thomas Piketty's Capital in the Twenty-First Century," *Tax Law Review* 68 (2015), 489.
10. Robert Stanley, *Dimensions of Law in the Service of Order: Origins of the Federal Income Tax, 1861–1913* (New York: Oxford University Press, 1993), 112–113, 136.
11. Ajay K. Mehrotra, "'More Mighty than the Waves of the Sea': Toilers, Tariffs, and the Income Tax Movement, 1880–1913," *Labor History* 45, no. 2 (May 1, 2004), 167.
12. *See* Joseph M. Dodge, "What Federal Taxes Are Subject to the Rule of Apportionment under the Constitution," *University of Pennsylvania Journal of Constitutional Law* 11 (2009): 839–956, 842–843.
13. *Brown* v. *Allen*, 344 US 443, 540 (1953) (Jackson, J. concurring).
14. Stanley, Dimensions of Law, 178.
15. Mehrota, "'More Mighty,'" 167.
16. Center on Budget and Policy Priorities, "Where Do Federal Tax Revenues Come From?" (Mar. 11, 2015), www.cbpp.org/sites/default/files/atoms/files/PolicyBasics_WhereDoFederalTaxRevsComeFrom_08–20–12.pdf [https://perma.cc/74KS-2W9U].
17. John F. Manley, "Congressional Staff and Public Policy-Making: The Joint Committee on Internal Revenue Taxation," *The Journal of Politics* 30, no. 4 (November 1, 1968), 1048–1049.
18. George K. Yin, "James Couzens, Andrew Mellon, the Greatest Tax Suit in the History of the World, and the Creation of the Joint Committee on Taxation and Its Staff NYU/UCLA Tax Policy Symposium: Taxation and Politics," *Tax Law Review* 66 (2013), 789; Walter J. Oleszek, "House-Senate Relationships: Comity and Conflict," *The ANNALS of the American Academy of Political and Social Science* 411, no. 1 (January 1, 1974), 81.

19. Michael Livingston, "Congress, the Courts, and the Code: Legislative History and the Interpretation of Tax Statutes," *Texas Law Review* 69, no. 4 (1991), 832–836.
20. "Writing and Enacting Tax Legislation." Resource Center. December 5, 2010. www.treasury.gov/resource-center/faqs/Taxes/Pages/writing.aspx [https://perma .cc/Y7LF-32M2].
21. Brandice Canes-Wrone, "The President's Legislative Influence from Public Appeals," *American Journal of Political Science* 45, no. 2 (2001), 317.
22. Alan Murray and Jeffrey Birnbaum, *Showdown at Gucci Gulch: Lawmakers, Lobbyists, and the Unlikely Triumph of Tax Reform* (New York, NY: Vintage, 1988), 22, 51.
23. Sheldon D. Pollack, "Farewell to Tax Reform: The 1993 Act in Historical Perspective," *Tax Notes* 64 no. 8 (1994), 1082, 1085–1089; Sheldon D. Pollack, "A New Dynamics of Tax Policy," *American Journal of Tax Policy* 12 (1995), 95–96.
24. Richard W. Stevenson, "Bush Tax Plan: The Debate Takes Shape," *New York Times*, August 26, 2000, www.nytimes.com/2000/08/26/us/the-2000-campaign-the-tax-plan-bush-tax-plan-the-debate-takes-shape.html [https://perma.cc/DV93-VJTJ].
25. Alan J. Auerbach, William G. Gale and Peter R. Orszag, "Bush Administration Tax Policy: Introduction and Background," *Tax Notes* 104 no. 12 (2004), 1291.
26. Alistar M. Nevius, "President's Budget Proposes Many Tax Changes," *Journal of Accountancy*, February 9, 2016, www.journalofaccountancy.com/news/2016/feb/budget-proposes-many-tax-changes-201613856.html [https://perma.cc/LQB3-CYAD].
27. Joseph J. Thorndike, "Reforming the Internal Revenue Service: A Comparative History Annual Regulation of Business Focus: Reorganization of the Internal Revenue Service," *Administrative Law Review* 53, no. 2 (2001), 763.
28. Bryan T. Camp, "Tax Administration as Inquisitorial Process and the Partial Paradigm Shift in the IRS Restructuring and Reform Act of 1998," *Florida Law Review* 56, no. 1 (2004), 8.
29. Leonard E. Burman and Joel Slemrod, *Taxes in America: What Everyone Needs to Know* (New York, NJ: Oxford University Press, 2012), 203–204.
30. For example, investment fund managers treat a part of their compensation, known as "carried interest," as capital gain, taxable at a lower tax rate than other types of compensation. The preferential tax treatment of carried interest rests, in large part, not on the Internal Revenue Code, but from a 1993 IRS administrative decision. Samuel D. Brunson, "Taxing Investment Fund Managers Using a Simplified Mark-to-Market Approach," *Wake Forest Law Review* 45, no. 1 (2010), 90.
31. I.R.C. § 4252(b)(1) (2012).
32. Samuel D. Brunson, "Watching the Watchers: Preventing I.R.S. Abuse of the Tax System," *Florida Tax Review* 14, no. 6 (2013), 229–230.
33. Samuel D. Brunson, "Dear IRS, It Is Time to Enforce the Campaigning Prohibition. Even Against Churches," *University of Colorado Law Review* 87, no. 1 (2016), 163–164.
34. Jonathan Barry Forman and Roberta F. Mann, "Making the Internal Revenue Service Work," *Florida Tax Review* 17, no. 10 (2015), 814.
35. Brunson, "Dear IRS," 163–165.

36. US Const. art. III, § 2.
37. *Jackson v. Northern Cent. Ry.*, 13 F. Cas. 232, 233 (D. Maryland 1865).
38. *Collector v. Day*, 78 US 113, 127 (1870).
39. *Clark v. Sickel*, 5 F. Cas. 981, 981 (E.D. Penn. 1871).
40. Ex parte *Ives*, 13 F. Cas. 179, 180–81 (D. Conn. 1865).
41. *Bank for Sav. v. Collector*, 70 US 495, 508 (1866).
42. Harold Dubroff, *The United States Tax Court: An Historical Analysis*, CCH Tax Court Reports (Chicago, IL.: Commerce Clearing House, 1979), 32.
43. *Flora v. United States*, 362 US 145, 177 (1960).
44. *Procedure and Practice Before the United States Board of Tax Appeals* 6th ed. (Chicago, IL: Commerce Clearing House, 1937), 23.
45. Dubroff, *The United States Tax Court*, 165.
46. *Eisner v. Macomber*, 252 US 189, 213 (1920).
47. Linda D. Jellum, "Codifying and Miscodifying Judicial Anti-Abuse Tax Doctrines," *Virginia Tax Review* 33, no. 4 (2014), 590.

3 Accommodation in the Intersection of Religious Practice and the Tax Law

1. Edward A. Zelinsky, "Do Religious Tax Exemptions Entangle in Violation of the Establishment Clause – The Constitutionality of the Parsonage Allowance Exclusion and the Religious Exemptions of the Individual Health Care Mandate and the FICA and Self-Employment Taxes," *Cardozo Law Review* 33, no. 4 (2012), 1635.
2. *US v. Lee*, 455 US 252, 260 (1982).
3. US Const. art. III, § 2.
4. *Lujan v. Def. of Wildlife*, 504 US 555, 560 (1992).
5. Donald L. Doernberg and Michael B. Mushlin, "Trojan Horse: How the Declaratory Judgment Act Created a Cause of Action and Expanded Federal Jurisdiction While the Supreme Court Wasn't Looking," *UCLA Law Review* 36, no. 3 (1989), 531–532.
6. Samuel D. Brunson, "Dear IRS, It Is Time to Enforce the Campaigning Prohibition. Even Against Churches," *University of Colorado Law Review* 87, no. 1 (2016), 163.
7. Josh Barro, "The Tax Code Can Be Simpler. But Not Three Pages.," *The New York Times*, November 13, 2015, www.nytimes.com/2015/11/15/upshot/a-three-page-tax-code-not-exactly-simple.html [https://perma.cc/JZW4-ZBN3].
8. Professor Lawrence Zelenack has argued that advances in tax return software could actually make a complex, personalized income tax computationally administrable. He argues, though, that such complexity would make the income tax incomprehensible to taxpayers, undermining its legitimacy. Lawrence Zelenak, "Complex Tax Legislation in the TurboTax Era," *Columbia Journal of Tax Law* 1, no. 1 (2010), 118–119.
9. Michael J. Graetz, "100 Million Unnecessary Returns: A Fresh Start for the U.S. Tax System," *The Yale Law Journal* 112, no. 2 (2002), 273–274.
10. Consolidated Appropriations Act, 2016, H.R. 2029, 114th Cong. § 304.
11. I.R.C. § 139F(a) (2016).

12. National Registry of Exonerations, "Exonerations in 2014," January 27, 2015, www .law.umich.edu/special/exoneration/Documents/Exonerations_in_2014_report .pdf [https://perma.cc/RG5G-FSH5].

13. Internal Revenue Service, *Statistics of Income – 2013 Individual Income Tax Returns* (2014), 5, www.irs.gov/pub/irs-soi/13inalcr.pdf [https://perma.cc/J5K9-KS5U].

14. Pew Research Center, November 3, 2015, "U.S. Public Becoming Less Religious," 3.

15. In fact, the interrelation between the sacred and the profane exists beyond merely the lives of believers. Jazz singer Lizz Wright, for example, "considered singing love songs on a gospel label, or singing gospel on a secular label; she asked her ministers and friends whether that was possible. She got mixed responses. Now she sees the distinction as artificial: 'I think the secular and the sacred are inseparable in nature.'" Allen Morrison, "Lizz Wright: Total Devotion," *Downbeat*, January 2016, 30.

16. Marilynne Robinson, *Gilead: A Novel* (Picador, 2006), 179.

17. Zelinksy, "Religious Exempts," 1635.

18. Louis Kaplow, *The Theory of Taxation and Public Economics* (Princeton, NJ: Princeton University Press, 2008), 397–398.

19. Liam Murphy and Thomas Nagel, *The Myth of Ownership: Taxes and Justice* (New York, NJ: Oxford University Press, 2004), 163–164.

20. Ira K. Lindsay, "Tax Fairness by Convention: A Defense of Horizontal Equity," *Florida Tax Review* 19, no. 2 (2016), 94.

21. Louis Kaplow, "Horizontal Equity: Measures in Search of a Principle," *National Tax Journal* 42, no. 2 (1989), 150. The idea that the tax law should not discriminate on the basis of race seems uncontroversial. The tax law is, naturally, written in formally race-neutral language. In spite of its apparent neutrality between races, though, Professor Dorothy Brown has demonstrated that, in actual practice, the tax law discriminates against black taxpayers. The discrimination comes, not because the tax law is somehow explicitly discriminatory, but because it treats career and lifestyle opportunities disproportionately available to white taxpayers better than it treats the career and lifestyle opportunities more likely to be available to black taxpayers. *See, e.g.*, Dorothy A. Brown, "Shades of the American Dream," *Washington University Law Review* 87, no. 2 (2009), 333; Dorothy A. Brown, "Racial Equality in the Twenty-First Century: What's Tax Policy Got to Do with It?," *University of Arkansas at Little Rock Law Review* 21, no. 4 (1999), 760–763.

22. Murphy and Nagel, *Myth of Ownership*, 170.

23. Carl H. Esbeck, "Dissent and Disestablishment: The Church-State Settlement in the Early American Republic," *Brigham Young University Law Review* 2004, no. 4 (2004), 1414.

24. Sidney E. Mead, "From Coercion to Persuasion: Another Look at the Rise of Religious Liberty and the Emergence of Denominationalism," *Church History* 25, no. 4 (December 1956), 326–327.

25. Stephanie Hoffer, "Caesar as God's Banker: Using Germany's Church Tax as an Example of Non-Geographically Bounded Taxing Jurisdiction," *Washington University Global Studies Law Review* 9 (2010), 609–611.

26. Thomas J. Curry, *The First Freedoms: Church and State in America to the Passage of the First Amendment* (New York, NJ: Oxford University Press, 1986), 107–109.

27. Kelly Olds, "Privatizing the Church: Disestablishment in Connecticut and Massachusetts," *Journal of Political Economy* 102, no. 2 (1994), 278.

28. Roger Finke, "Religious Deregulation: Origins and Consequences," *Journal of Church and State* 32, no. 3 (1990), 611; Roger Finke and Rodney Stark, "How the Upstart Sects Won America: 1776–1850," *Journal for the Scientific Study of Religion* 28, no. 1 (1989), 28.

29. Hoffer, "God's Banker," 609.

30. Sheldon D. Pollack, "The First National Income Tax, 1861–1972," *Tax Lawyer* 67 (2013), 312–314.

31. Revenue Act of 1870, ch. 255, § 8, 16 Stat. 256, 258 (1870). According to the consumer price index, a $2,000 exemption in 1870 would be worth about $37,400 in 2015 dollars, making it a relatively substantive exemption. www.minneapolisfed.org/community/teaching-aids/cpi-calculator-information/consumer-price-index-1800 [https://perma.cc/3VJ8-TPYW].

32. Ibid.

33. 41st Cong., 2d Sess. Cong. Globe 5513, 5530 (July 13, 1870).

34. Stephen C. Taysom, *Shakers, Mormons, and Religious Worlds: Conflicting Visions, Contested Boundaries*, Religion in North America (Bloomington, IN: Indiana University Press, 2011), 29, 100; Lawrence Foster, *Religion and Sexuality: Three American Communal Experiments of the Nineteenth Century* (New York, NY: Oxford University Press, 1981), 38–39.

35. Taysom, *Shakers, Mormons, and Religious Worlds*, 28; Foster, *Religion and Sexuality*, 39.

36. Revenue Act of 1870, ch. 255, § 8, 16 Stat. 256, 258 (1870).

37. Foster, *Religion and Sexuality*, 39.

38. Larry E. Ribstein, "Bubble Laws," *Houston Law Review* 40, no. 1 (2003), 78.

39. Nathan B. Oman, "The Need for a Law of Church and Market," *Duke Law Journal Online* 64, no. 14 (2015), 142.

40. The parsonage allowance was introduced in the Senate on November 2, 1921; after being read, Senator Boies Penrose accepted the amendment and, without any discussion, the Senate agreed to it. 61 Cong. Rec. S7162 (daily ed. November 2, 1921).

41. 99 Cong. Rec. A5372-A5373 (daily ed. August 3, 1953).

42. Commissioner of Internal Revenue, *Statistics of Income for 1940 pt. 1* (Washington, DC: Government Printing Office, 1943), 2.

43. *See, e.g.*, Daniel A. Lyons, "Public Use, Public Choice, and the Urban Growth Machine: Competing Political Economies of Takings Law," *University of Michigan Journal of Law Reform* 42, no. 2 (2009), 277.

44. 80 Cong. Rec. 9074 (1936) (statement of Sen. Walsh).

45. Stephanie Hoffer and Christopher J. Walker, "The Death of Tax Court Exceptionalism," *Minnesota Law Review* 99, no. 1 (2014), 222.

46. I.R.C. § 5000A (2012).

47. *Nat'l Fed'n of Indep. Bus. v. Sebelius*, 132 S. Ct. 2566, 2582–83, 2598 (2012).

48. I.R.C. § 5000A(d)(2)(A). Chapter 4 goes into more detail about Amish exemptions from general social safety net taxes.

49. Timothy Stoltzfus Jost, "Loopholes in the Affordable Care Act: Regulatory Gaps and Border Crossing Techniques and How to Address Them Implementing Health Reform: Fairness, Accountability & Competition," *Saint Louis University Journal of Health Law & Policy* 5, no. 1 (2011), 42.

50. Benjamin Boyd, "Health Care Sharing Ministries: Scam or Solution?," *Journal of Law and Health* 26, no. 2 (2013), 221.

51. I.R.C. § 5000A(d)(2)(B). Although the law defines a health care sharing ministry as a group of people with a common set of ethical or religious beliefs, not all members appear to be motivated by religious considerations. Health care sharing ministries' monthly dues are often less expensive than insurance premiums, so there is at least some incentive for individuals who do not object to insurance to nonetheless join.

4 Taxing Citizens of the Kingdom of God

1. Stephanie Hoffer, "Caesar as God's Banker: Using Germany's Church Tax as an Example of Non-Geographically Bounded Taxing Jurisdiction," *Washington University Global Studies Law Review* 9, no. 4 (2010), 601–605.

2. *See* Peter H. Serreze, "As Simple as It Can Be but Not Simpler: Science, Taxes, and Bonds," *Tax Notes* 142 (February 17, 2014), 729.

3. National Taxpayer Advocate, 2012 Annual Report to Congress, vol. 1 at 6.

4. *Comm'r v. Glenshaw Glass*, 348 US 426, 431 (1955).

5. I.R.C. § 102 (2012).

6. Randolph E. Paul, *Taxation in the United States* (Boston: Little, Brown, 1954), 61.

7. Revenue Act of 1913, § 2(B), 38 Stat. 114, 167; I.R.C. § 102.

8. *See Cesarini v. United States*, 296 F. Supp. 3 (N.D. OH, 1969); Treas. Reg. § 1.61–14 (as amended in 1993) ("Treasure trove, to the extent of its value in United States currency, constitutes gross income for the taxable year in which it is reduced to undisputed possession").

9. www.cch.com/wbot2013/factsheet.pdf [https://perma.cc/NN5M-JRLL].

10. Revenue Act of 1913 § 2(E).

11. Joseph J. Thorndike, "Original Intent and the Revenue Act of 1913," *Tax Notes* 140, no. 14 (September 20, 2013), 1490.

12. Michael M. Gleeson, "Larger Percentage of Americans to Pay Income Taxes in 2014," *Tax Notes* 140, no. 10 (September 2, 2013), 987. And the majority who did not owe taxes did not owe them because they had low earnings, were elderly, or had children at home. William G. Gale and Donald B. Marron, "5 Myths About the 47 Percent," *Washington Post*, September 21, 2012, www.washingtonpost.com/opinions/five-myths-about-the-47-percent/2012/09/21/57dc7bbe-0341-11e2-8102-ebee9c66e190_story.html [https://perma.cc/49UB-Q6XF].

13. For a broad look at many of the ways the taxation of married couples differs from the taxation of unmarried couples, see Theodore P. Seto, "The Unintended Tax Advantages of Gay Marriage," *Washington and Lee Law Review* 65, no. 4 (2008), 1529.

14. BLS CPI Inflation calculator, https://data.bls.gov/cgi-bin/cpicalc.pl?cost1=3000 &year1=191301&year2=201401. [https://perma.cc/VGZ3-6XN3].
15. Rev. Proc. 2013–35, 2013–47 I.R.B. 537.
16. http://aspe.hhs.gov/poverty/14poverty.cfm [https://perma.cc/F4JM-FGLP].
17. This fairness principal is called *vertical equity*, and is a fundamental policy consideration in enacting tax law. Essentially, vertical equity demands that, as an individual's income increases, she pay a larger percent of her income in taxes. The US federal income tax achieves vertical equity largely through two mechanisms: first, as discussed above, it exempts an initial amount from taxation. Second, it imposes progressive tax rates; as a result, taxpayers pay a higher rate of tax on higher levels of income.
18. Michael B. Lupfer, Karla F. Brock, and Stephen J. DePaola, "The Use of Secular and Religious Attributions to Explain Everyday Behavior," *Journal for the Scientific Study of Religion* 31, no. 4 (1992), 499.
19. O.D. 119, 1 C.B. 82 (1919).
20. In 1930, the Supreme Court introduced this idea with its *fruit of the tree* metaphor; it asserted that "[t]here is no doubt that the statute could tax salaries to those who earned them and provide that the tax could not be escaped by anticipatory arrangements and contracts however skilfully devised to prevent the salary when paid from vesting even for a second in the man who earned it. That seems to us the import of the statute before us and we think that no distinction can be taken according to the motives leading to the arrangement by which the fruits are attributed to a different tree from that on which they grew." *Lucas* v. *Earl*, 281 US 111, 114–115 (1930).
21. Ronald B. Flowers, "Tax Exemption and the Clergy: On Vows of Poverty and Parsonage Allowances," in *Religion and the State: Essays in Honor of Leo Pfeffer*, ed. James Edward Wood (Waco, TX: Baylor University Press, 1985), 360.
22. Ibid., 361–362.
23. Ibid., 362.
24. Treas. Reg. § 1.501(c)(3)-1(c)(2) (as amended in 2008).
25. *See, e.g., Abney* v. *Comm'r*, 39 T.C.M. (CCH) 965 (1980).
26. In spite of the IRS's clear stance on vows of poverty, some ministers continue to argue that taking a vow of poverty means that they have no tax liability. As recently as 2016, the tax court has denied that assertion. *White* v. *Comm'r*, T.C. Memo. 2016–2167.
27. Rev. Rul. 77–290, 1977–2 C.B. 26.
28. Flowers, "Tax Exemption and the Clergy," 360.
29. In order to challenge the IRS's assessment of a tax deficiency in a federal district court, a taxpayer must first pay the full assessment, then claim a refund. *Flora* v. *United States*, 362 US 145, 177 (1960).
30. *Fogarty* v. *United States*, 780 F.2d 1005 (Fed. Cir. 1986).
31. *Schuster* v. *Comm'r*, 84 T.C. 764 (1985).
32. In re Hovind, 197 B.R. 157, 159 (N.D. Fla. 1996).
33. *Good* v. *Comm'r*, 104 T.C.M. (CCH) 595 (2012).
34. David Cay Johnston, "Court Moves to Limit Tax-Avoidance Promoter," *New York Times*, February 27, 2002, sec. C.

35. DOJ press release, "Justice Department Seeks Fines and Possible Jail Time Against Florida Promoter of Tax Fraud Schemes," May 8, 2002, available at www.justice .gov/archive/tax/txdv02267.htm [https://perma.cc/RKU4-ESGS].
36. *United States* v. *Sweet*, 89 A.F.T.R.2d (RIA) 2002–2189 (M.D. Fla.2002).
37. Ibid.
38. *US* v. *Bush*, 626 F.3d 527, 529 (9th Cir. 2010).
39. *US* v. *Stoll*, 96 A.F.T.R.2d 2005–5052 (W.D. Wash. 2005).
40. Ibid.
41. *US* v. *Stoll*, 96 A.F.T.R.2d 2005–5044 (W.D. Wash. 2005).
42. Stoll, 96 A.F.T.R.2d 2005–5052.
43. *Hovind* v. *Comm'r*, 104 T.C.M. (CCH) 400 (2012).
44. *Good* v. *Comm'r*, 104 T.C.M. (CCH) 595 (2012).
45. Ibid.
46. In re Hovind, 197 B.R. at 159.
47. Treas. Reg. § 31.3121(r)-1(a) (1973).
48. *See* I.R.C. § 119 (2012). There is another provision, specifically aimed at "ministers of the gospel," that grants a broad exemption for employer-provided housing that will be discussed in the next chapter.
49. I.R.C. § 170(a)(1) (2012).
50. Kim Bloomquist et al., "Estimates of the Tax Year 2006 Individual Income Tax Underreporting Gap," in *New Research on Tax Administration:An IRS TPC Conference*, 2012, 69–78, www.irs.gov/pub/irs-soi/12rescon.pdf [https://perma.cc/JT9C-ZDS6].
51. I.R.C. § 170(b)(1)(A). Technically, the deduction cannot be for more than 50 percent of an individual's "contribution base," but the contribution base is adjusted gross income with a couple small adjustments.
52. Although the IRS does not ask whether a taxpayer is religious or not – and thus does not produce any data on the percentage of religious people who pay their taxes – it is easy enough to determine that the majority of religious people pay some or all of their taxes. In January 2012, the IRS released its estimate for the 2006 tax gap (that is, the amount by which taxpayers underpaid the taxes they owed). Individual income taxes were underreported by about 19 percent. Bloomquist *et al.*, "Estimates of the Tax Year 2006," 69. At around the same time, Pew found that about 83 percent of Americans affiliated with a religious tradition. The Pew Forum on Religion & Public Life, *U.S. Religious Landscape Survey: Religious Affiliation: Diverse and Dynamic* (2008): 5. Even if all of the people who underreported their taxes were religiously affiliated then it would be virtually impossible for all religious taxpayers to have failed to pay their taxes.
53. Timothy A. Byrnes and Mary C. Segers, "Introduction," in *The Catholic Church and the Politics of Abortion: A View From the States*, ed. Timothy A. Byrnes and Mary C. Segers (Boulder, CO: Westview Press, 1992), 2.
54. Timothy A. Byrnes, "The Politics of Abortion: The Catholic Bishops," in *The Catholic Church and the Politics of Abortion: A View From the States*, ed. Timothy A. Byrnes and Mary C. Segers (Boulder, CO: Westview Press, 1992), 15.
55. "Dissent from church teaching on abortion is not unusual within the American Catholic community." Mary C. Segers, "The Loyal Opposition: Catholics for a

Free Choice," in *The Catholic Church and the Politics of Abortion: A View From the States,* ed. Timothy A. Byrnes and Mary C. Segers (Boulder, CO: Westview Press, 1992), 169.

56. Pew Research Center, "Public Opinion on Abortion," July 7, 2017, www .pewforum.org/fact-sheet/public-opinion-on-abortion/ [https://perma.cc/684D-AZXS].

57. *Jensen v. Reno,* 75 A.F.T.R.2d 95–2416 (9th Cir. 1995).

58. Holly Fernandez Lynch, "Religious Liberty, Conscience, and the Affordable Care Act," *Ethical Perspectives* 20, no. 1 (2013), 119; *see also* Executive Order 13535 of March 24, 2010, Patient Protection and Affordable Care Act's Consistency with Longstanding Restrictions on the Use of Federal Funds for Abortion, *Code of Federal Regulations,* title 3 (2010): 15,559–15,600, www.gpo.gov/fdsys/pkg/FR-2010–03–29/pdf/2010–7154.pdf [https://perma.cc/3H8G-3KET].

59. *Pavlic v. Comm'r,* T.C. Memo. 1984–182.

60. Ibid.

61. Ibid.

62. *Martinez v. Comm'r,* 84 A.F.T.R.2d 99–6699 (5th Cir. 1999).

63. Fahy, TC Memo 1982–37.

64. Ibid.

65. John A. Hostetler, "The Amish and the Law: A Religious Minority and Its Legal Encounters," *Washington and Lee Law Review* 41, no. 1 (1984), 33.

66. Jerry Savells, "Economic and Social Acculturation Among the Old Order Amish in Select Communities: Surviving In a High-Tech Society," *Journal of Comparative Family Studies* 19, no. 1 (1988), 123.

67. Peter J. Ferrara, "Social Security and Taxes," in *The Amish and the State,* ed. Donald B. Kraybill (Baltimore, MD: Johns Hopkins University Press, 1993), 127–128.

68. 1 *Tim.* 5:8 (NSRV).

69. Ferrara, "Social Security and Taxes," 129.

70. Daniel Béland, *Social Security: History and Politics From the New Deal to the Privatization Debate,* Studies in Government and Public Policy (Lawrence, KA: University Press of Kansas, 2005), 63–64.

71. Ibid., 72.

72. Ibid., 94.

73. Joseph J. Thorndike, *Their Fair Share: Taxing the Rich in the Age of FDR,* (Washington, DC: Rowman & Littlefield Publishers, 2013), 178.

74. I.R.C. §§ 3101(a), 3102(a) (2012).

75. I.R.C. § 3111(a) (2012).

76. I.R.C. § 1401(a) (2012).

77. Thorndike, *Their Fair Share,* 180.

78. Ferrara, "Social Security and Taxes," 129.

79. *United States v. Lee,* 455 US 252, 254 (1982). In order to bring suit in a federal district court, a taxpayer must pay the full amount of taxes due, then file for a refund. Lee paid the amount he owed for the first quarter of 1973, then filed his refund suit. Ibid.

80. I.R.C. § 1402(g).

81. Ibid.

82. I.R.C. § 1402(e).
83. S. Rep. No. 89–404, reprinted in 1965 U.S.C.C.A.N. 1943, 2056.
84. Ibid.
85. *Lee v. United States*, 497 F. Supp. 180, 182 (W.D. Pa. 1980).
86. Ibid.
87. *United States v. Lee*, 455 US 252, 257 (1982).
88. Ibid., 258.
89. Ibid., 259–260.
90. Ibid., 262.
91. William C. Kashatus, *Abraham Lincoln, the Quakers, and the Civil War: "A Trial of Principle and Faith"* (Santa Barbara, CA: Praeger, 2014), 5.
92. Charles R. DiSalvo, "Saying No to War in the Technological Age - Conscientious Objection and the World Peace Tax Fund Act," *DePaul Law Review* 31 (1982), 499.
93. Kashatus, *Abraham Lincoln*, 76–77.
94. DiSalvo, "Saying 'No,'" 499–500.
95. Allen Smith, "The Renewal Movement: The Peace Testimony and Modern Quakerism," *Quaker History* 85, no. 2 (1996), 1.
96. Ibid.
97. Center on Budget and Policy Priorities, "Policy Basics: Where Do Our Federal Tax Dollars Go?," March 4, 2016, www.cbpp.org/sites/default/files/atoms/files/4-14-08tax.pdf [https://perma.cc/5CU4-NPRM].
98. Ronald B. Flowers, "Government Accommodation of Religious-Based Conscientious Objection," *Seton Hall Law Review* 24, no. 2 (1993), 715.
99. *Jenney v. United States*, 755 F.2d 1384, 1385 (9th Cir. 1985).
100. Ibid.; *see also Jenkins v Comm'r*, 483 F.3d 90, 91 (2d Cir. 2007) (Jenkins argued that the Constitution gave him the right "to retain the unpaid portion of his taxes on the basis of religious objections to military spending until such taxes can be directed to nonmilitary expenditures.").
101. Flowers, "Government Accommodation," 715.
102. *Browne v. United States*, 176 F.3d 25, 26 (2d Cir. 1999).
103. Pub. L. No. 103–141, 107 Stat. 1488 (November 16, 1993), codified at 42 U.S.C. § 2000bb through 42 U.S.C. § 2000bb-4.
104. 42 U.S.C. § 2000bb-1(b) (2012).
105. *Jenkins v Comm'r*, 483 F.3d 90, 92 (2d Cir. 2007).
106. *Browne v. United States*, 176 F.3d 25, 26 (2d Cir. 1999).
107. Hearings on the Economic Report of the President Before the Joint Economic Committee, 91st Cong., 1st. Sess. at 6 (1969) (statement of Secretary of Treasury Joseph W. Barr).
108. Michael J. Graetz, *The Decline (and Fall?) Of the Income Tax* (New York, NY: W.W. Norton, 1997), 113.
109. I.R.C. §§ 55–56 (2012).
110. Rev. Proc. 2016–55, 2016–45 I.R.B. 707.
111. Klaasen, T.C. Memo. 1998–241.
112. I.R.C. § 6702(b) (2012).
113. *McKee v. United States*, 781 F.2d 1043, 1047 (1986).
114. I.R.C. § 6673 (2012).

115. Jenkins, 483 F.3d at 94.
116. Zoe Robinson, "Rationalizing Religious Exemptions: A Legislative Process Theory of Statutory Exemptions for Religion," *William & Mary Bill of Rights Journal* 20, no. 1 (2011), 134.
117. Paul C. Cline, "Social Security and the Plain People," *West Virginia Law Review* 72, no. 3 (1970), 221.
118. Thomas L. Lehman, "The Plain People: Reluctant Parties in Litigation to Preserve a Life Style," *Journal of Church and State* 16, no. 2 (1974), 293.
119. *Hughes* v. *Comm'r*, 81 T.C. 683 (1983).
120. *Borntrager* v. *Comm'r*, 58 T.C.M. (CCH) 1242 (1990).
121. Marjorie E. Kornhauser, "For God and Country: Taxing Conscience," *Wisconsin Law Review* 1999, no. 5 (1999), 986.
122. Religious Liberty Trust Fund Act, H.R. 2483, 113th Cong. 1st Sess. § 4(a)-(b) (2013).
123. Nadia N. Sawicki, "The Hollow Promise of Freedom of Conscience," *Cardozo Law Review* 33, no. 4 (2012), 1424.
124. Robinson, "Rationalizing Religious Exemptions," 134.
125. *Cf.* Nathan B. Oman, "The Need for a Law of Church and Market," *Duke Law Journal Online* 64, no. 14 (2015), 142.

5 Housing Clergy

1. Rev. W.B. Norton, "Methodists to Dedicate Loop Temple," *Chicago Tribune*, September 26, 1924, sec. 2, http://archives.chicagotribune.com/1924/09/26/page/21/article/methodists-to-dedicate-loop-temple [https://perma.cc/CQ8Q-8GGG?type=image]; Rev. John Evans, "Pastor to Get a Home in the Sky," *Chicago Daily Tribune*, September 28, 1946, http://archives.chicagotribune.com/1946/09/28/page/1/article/pastor-to-get-a-home-in-sky [https://perma.cc/M7RN-Q6C9?type=image]; Kathryn Loring, "High Above the Bustling Loop Is a Parsonage In the Sky," *Chicago Tribune*, March 4, 1954, sec. 4, http://archives.chicagotribune.com/1954/03/04/page/37/article/high-above-the-bustling-loop-is-a-parsonage-in-the-sky [https://perma.cc/C6RJ-YBAS?type=image]; Robert Sharoff, "What's Up There?," *Chicago Tribune*, July 23, 1995, http://articles.chicagotribune.com/1995-07-23/features/9507230325_1_pyramid-trust-center-clock-tower [https://perma.cc/45JU-W7L2].
2. Devin O'Brien, "Chicago Rent Prices By Neighborhood This February," *The Zumper Blog*, March 4, 2015, www.zumper.com/blog/2015/03/chicago-rent-prices-by-neighborhood-february-2015/ [https://perma.cc/UQ5U-ZA2F].
3. To unpack this slightly: compensation is not limited to the amount of cash an employee receives. It also includes the value of other goods and services received by an employee. In the case of employer-provided housing, although the senior pastor of the First Methodist Church does not get that $65,880, the pastor also does not have to pay for housing. He can spend the money he otherwise would have spent on housing in any other way he wants.

    And why is the value of the compensation the fair rental value of the property? Had the church not provided him with a parsonage, he may have chosen more modest living arrangements. That does not change the fact, however, that he is receiving the benefit of the parsonage he lives in.

4. Matthew W. Foster, "Parsonage Allowance Exclusion: Past, Present, and Future," *Vanderbilt Law Review* 44, no. 1 (1991), 151.
5. *See, e.g.*, Erwin Chemerinsky, "The Parsonage Exemption Violates the Establishment Clause and Should Be Declared Unconstitutional," *Whittier Law Review* 24, no. 3 (2003); Eric Rakowski, "Are Federal Income Tax Preferences for Ministers' Housing Constitutional?," *Tax Notes* 95(5) (2002), 776; Gabriel O. Aitsebaomo, "Challenges to Federal Income Tax Exemption of the Clergy and Government Support of Sectarian Schools through Tax Credits Device and the Unresolved Questions after Arizona v. Winn: Is the U.S. Supreme Court Standing in the Way of Taxpayer Standing to Seek Meritorious Redress," *Akron Tax Journal* 28, no. 1 (2013).
6. Treas. Reg. § 1.61–2(d) (as amended in 2003).
7. I.R.C. § 132(a) (2012).
8. Craig A. Olson, "Do Workers Accept Lower Wages in Exchange for Health Benefits?," *Journal of Labor Economics* 20, no. S2 (2002), S113.
9. It is worth noting that the economics of excluding health insurance from taxable income may cause individuals to purchase more insurance than they objectively need to, because they get the full benefit of their overinsured state while not bearing the full cost. Jonathan Gruber and James Poterba, "Tax Incentives and the Decision to Purchase Health Insurance: Evidence from the Self-Employed," *The Quarterly Journal of Economics* 109, no. 3 (August 1, 1994), 701.
10. O.D. 265, 1919–1 C.B. 71.
11. T.D. 2992, 1920–2 C.B. 76.
12. O.D. 814, 1921–4 C.B. 84.
13. O.D. 915, 1921–4 C.B. 85.
14. O.D. 862, 1921–4 C.B. 85.
15. Revenue Act of 1921, Pub. L. No. 67–136, § 213(b)(11), 42 Stat. 227, 239 (1923).
16. Burgess J.W. Raby and William L. Raby, "Some Thoughts on the Parsonage Exemption Imbroglio," *Tax Notes* 96(11) (2002), 1499.
17. *Freedom From Religion Foundation v. Lew*, 983 F.Supp.2d 1051, 1067 (W.D. Wisc. 2013).
18. I.T. 1694, II-1 C.B. 79 (1923).
19. *See, e.g.*, *Conning v. Busey*, 127 F. Supp. 958, 959 (S.D. Ohio 1954); *MacColl v. United States*, 91 F. Supp. 721, 722 (N.D. IL. 1950); *Williamson v. Comm'r*, 224 F.2d 377, 381 (8th Cir. 1955).
20. *General Revenue Revision: Hearings on Forty Topics Pertaining to the General Revisions of the Internal Revenue Code Before the H. Comm. on Ways and Means* Part 3, 83d Cong. 1574–75 (1953) (statement of Rep. Peter F. Mack, Jr.).
21. H.R. Rep. No. 83–1337, at 15 (1954).
22. Internal Revenue Code of 1954, Pub. L. No. 83–591, § 107(2), 68A Stat. 1, 32 (1954).
23. Internal Revenue Code of 1954, Pub. L. No. 83–591, § 107(1), 68A Stat. 1, 32 (1954).
24. S. Rep. No. 83–1622, at 186 (1954).
25. Rev. Rul. 71–280, 1971–2 C.B. 92.
26. *Warren v. Comm'r*, 114 T.C. 343 (2000).
27. Chemerinsky, "Parsonage Exemption," 708.
28. *Warren v. Comm'r*, 282 F.3d 1119 (9th Cir. 2002).

29. 148 Cong. Rec. H1299 (daily ed. April 16, 2002) (statement of Rep. Ramstad).
30. Warren, 282 F.3d at 1120.
31. 148 Cong. Rec. H1299 (daily ed. April 16, 2002) (statement of Rep. Ramstad).
32. Clergy Housing Allowance Clarification Act of 2002, Pub. L. No. 107–181, § 2(a), 116 Stat. 583 (2002).
33. Ibid. § 2(b)(2).
34. Chemerinsky, "Parsonage Exemption," 709.
35. 148 Cong. Rec. H1301 (daily ed. April 16, 2002) (statement of Rep. Ramstad).
36. 148 Cong. Rec. H1301 (daily ed. April 16, 2002) (statement of Rep. Pomeroy).
37. *Warren v. Comm'r*, 302 F.3d 1012, 1013 (9th Cir. 2002).
38. I.R.C. § 107 (2012).
39. Treas. Reg. § 1.107–1(c) (as amended in 1963).
40. Rev. Rul. 83–3, 1983–1 C.B. 72.
41. I.R.C. § 265(a)(6) (2012).
42. *Driscoll v. Comm'r*, 135 T.C. 557 (2010).
43. *Comm'r v. Driscoll*, 669 F.3d 1309, 1312–13 (11th Cir. 2012).
44. David F. Shores, "Rethinking Deferential Review of Tax Court Decisions," *The Tax Lawyer* 53, no. 1 (1999), 37.
45. Revenue Act of 1921, Pub. L. No. 67–136, § 213(b)(11), 42 Stat. 227, 239 (1923); I.R.C. § 107.
46. Boris I. Bittker, "Constitutional Limits on the Taxing Power of the Federal Government," *The Tax Lawyer* 41, no. 1 (1987), 7.
47. Richard C. Schragger, "The Relative Irrelevance of the Establishment Clause," *Texas Law Review* 89, no. 3 (2011), 628.
48. Richard J. Regan, *The American Constitution and Religion* (Washington, DC: The Catholic University of America Press, 2013), 38. The Establishment Clause also prohibits the government from preferring religion to non-religion, or non-religion to religion, except under certain circumstances. The contours of these exceptions are muddy, though, given the concomitant constitutional protection of religious practice. Christopher L. Eisgruber and Lawrence G Sager, *Religious Freedom and the Constitution* (Cambridge, MA: Harvard University Press, 2007), 18.
49. Rev. Rul. 58–221, 1958–1 C.B. 53.
50. Rev. Rul. 59–270, 1959–2 C.B. 44.
51. Rev. Rul. 61–213, 1961–2 C.B. 27.
52. *Salkov v. Comm'r*, 46 T.C. 190, 199 (1966).
53. 1969–2 C.B. xxiii. When the IRS loses a case in the Tax Court, it is bound, but only with respect to that particular taxpayer. If the IRS chooses not to acquiesce to the Tax Court's ruling, it can maintain its previous position on the law as it deals with other taxpayers, even though the court has ruled against it, and even if it chooses not to appeal the ruling. Gary W. Carter, "The Commissioner's Nonacquiscence: A Case For a National Court of Tax Appeals," *Temple Law Quarterly* 59, no. 3 (1986), 879. *See also* I.R.M. 36.3.1.4(2)(C).
54. Rev. Rul. 78–301, 1978–2 C.B. 103.
55. Salkov, 46 T.C. at 194.
56. *Warnke v. United States*, 641 F.Supp. 1083, 1092 (E.D. Ky. 1986).
57. Treas. Reg. § 1.107–1(a) (as amended in 1963).

58. Rev. Rul. 70–549, 1970–2 C.B. 16.
59. Joel S. Newman, "On Section 107's Worst Feature: The Teacher-Preacher," *Tax Notes* 61no. 12 (1993), 1506.
60. Rev. Rul. 72–606, 1972–2 C.B. 78.
61. www.biola.edu/about/mission [https://perma.cc/P2EL-JJK9].
62. "Ministerial Housing Allowance," *Employee Handbook* § 9.7, available at http://offices1.biola.edu/hr/ehandbook/9.7/ [https://perma.cc/AAW5-TTFW].
63. *Warnke v. United States,* 641 F.Supp. 1083, 1088 (E.D. Ky. 1986).
64. Adrian A. Kragen and Klonda Speer, "I.R.C. Section 119: Is Convenience of the Employer a Valid Concept?," *Hastings Law Journal* 29 (1978), 924.
65. S. Rep. No. 83–1622, at 19 (1954).
66. I.R.C. § 119(a) (2012).
67. Treas. Reg. § 1.119–1(b) (as amended in 1985).
68. I.R.C. § 162(a)(1) (2012).
69. It works like this: a corporate employer is currently subject to a 35 percent rate of federal income tax. That means that ever dollar it can deduct reduces its ultimate tax by 35 cents. If it pays an employee $100,000, then, it also gets to deduct $100,000 from its gross income, which reduces its ultimate tax bill by $35,000. Essentially, then, a pre-tax salary of $100,000 costs a corporate employer $65,000 after taxes; the federal government bears the cost of the other $35,000.
70. I.R.C. § 501(c)(3) (2012).
71. Whether tax exemption represents a subsidy is a contentious issue; elsewhere, Professor David Herzig and I have argued that it does not. Rather, tax-exempt organizations do not belong in the corporate income tax base. If we are correct, then while exemption leaves churches more money with which to pay employees, it does not represent a subsidy of employee costs. David Herzig and Samuel Brunson, "Let Prophets be (Non-) Profits," *Wake Forest Law Review* 52, no.2 (forthcoming 2018), Draft September 5, 2017 at 121, https://papers.ssrn.com/sol3/papers.cfm?abstract_id=3032555.
72. I.R.C. § 172(b) (2012).
73. *Texas Monthly, Inc. v. Bullock,* 489 US 1, 15 (1989).
74. 148 Cong. Rec. H1301 (daily ed. April 16, 2002) (statement of Rep. Davis).
75. David S. Logan, "Summary of Latest Federal Individual Income Tax Data," October 24, 2011, https://taxfoundation.org/summary-latest-federal-individual-income-tax-data-0/ [https://perma.cc/4MBS-3YWM].
76. Complaint, *Freedom from Religion Foundation v. Geithner,* Case No. 11-CV-626, Doc. no. 1 (W.D. Wisc. September 13, 2011).
77. *Freedom from Religion Foundation v. Lew,* 983 F. Supp. 2d 1051, 1053 (W.D. Wisc. 2013). Earlier in the case, plaintiffs had dropped their claim that the tax-free provision of actual housing was unconstitutional, presumably because they knew they lacked standing to challenge that provision. Ibid.
78. US Const. art. III, § 2.
79. *Lujan v. Defenders of Wildlife,* 504 US 555, 560 (1992).
80. Freedom from Religion Foundation, 773 F.3d at 819–820.
81. *Vasquez v. Los Angeles Cnty.,* 487 F.3d 1246, 1250 (9th Cir. 2007).
82. *U.S. v. Richardson,* 418 US 166, 179 (1974).

83. Cynthia Brougher, "Legal Standing Under the First Amendment's Establishment Claue" (Congressional Research Service, September 15, 2009), 5, http://fas.org/sgp/crs/misc/R40825.pdf [https://perma.cc/S3WF-MV5W].
84. *Flast v. Cohen*, 392 US 83, 102 (1968).
85. Brougher, "Legal Standing," 5.
86. *Arizona Christian School Tuition Organization v. Winn*, 131 S. Ct. 1436, 1438 (2011); *see also* Linda Sugin, "The Great and Mighty Tax Law: How the Roberts Court Has Reduced Constitutional Scrutiny of Taxes and Tax Expenditures," *Brooklyn Law Review* 78, no. 3 (2013), 799.
87. *Freedom from Religion Foundation v. Lew*, 983 F. Supp. 2d 1051, 1055 (W.D. Wisc. 2013).
88. Ibid., 1066.
89. Ibid., 1056.
90. Ibid., 1068–1070.
91. Ibid., 1073.
92. *Freedom from Religion Foundation v. Lew*, 773 F.3d 815, 819 (9th Cir. 2014).
93. *Freedom from Religion Foundation v. Lew*, 773 F.3d 815, 820 (7th Cir. 2014).
94. Ibid., 821.
95. Ibid., 824.
96. *Valley Forge Christian Coll. v. Americans United for Separation of Church and State, Inc.*, 454 US 464, 476 (1982).
97. Freedom from Religion Foundation, 773 F.3d at 821 n.3.
98. Complaint, *Gaylor v. Lew*, Docket No. 3:16-cv-00215 (W.D. Wis. April 6, 2016).
99. *Gaylor v. Mnuchin*, Docket No. 3:16-cv-00215 (W.D. Wis. October 6, 2017).
100. Ibid., *42.

6 Neither a Borrower nor a Lender Be

1. Micheline Maynard, "On Paying for Cars With Cash," *New York Times*, July 28, 2007, www.nytimes.com/2007/07/28/business/yourmoney/28money.html [https://perma.cc/7S93-XS8L].
2. Elizabeth Rhodes, "Home Prices' Long Rise: Is the End Near?," *Seattle Times*, September 3, 2006, http://old.seattletimes.com/html/businesstechnology/2003241541_appreciation03.html [https://perma.cc/N26V-BR2V]; http://seattletimes.nwsource.com/ABPub/2006/09/02/2003241651.pdf [https://perma.cc/5ZNC-RRYP].
3. Lornet Turnbull, "Faith and Finance Collide for Muslim Home Buyers," *Seattle Times*, March 21, 2005, www.seattletimes.com/seattle-news/faith-and-finance-collide-for-muslim-home-buyers/ [https://perma.cc/SF3G-SQVP].
4. Mehrsa Baradaran, *How the Other Half Banks: Exclusion, Exploitation, and the Threat to Democracy* (Cambridge, MA: Harvard University Press, 2015), 102–105.
5. Eric Johnson, "Dodging DOMA: The State of the Mortgage Interest Deduction for Same-Sex Couples after *Sophy v. Commissioner*," *Tax Lawyer* 66, no. 3 (2013), 789.
6. Pew Research Center, "America's Changing Religious Landscape," (May 12, 2015), 4.

7. Karen Armstrong, *Fields of Blood: Religion and the History of Violence* (New York, NY: Alfred A. Knopf, 2014), 197.
8. Paul S. Mills, *Islamic Finance: Theory and Practice* (New York, NY: St. Martin's Press, 1999), 1.
9. Roberta Mann, "Is Sharif's Castle Deductible: Islam and the Tax Treatment of Mortgage Debt," *William and Mary Bill of Rights Journal* 17, no. 4 (2009), 1140.
10. Abdullah. Saeed, *Islamic Banking and Interest: A Study of the Prohibition of Riba and Its Contemporary Interpretation*, Studies in Islamic Law and Society, v. 2 (New York, NY: EJBrill, 1996), 20–21.
11. Mills and Presley, *Islamic Finance*, 7.
12. Ibid., 17.
13. Amr Mohamed El Tiby, *Islamic Banking: How to Manage Risk and Improve Profitability*, Wiley Finance Series (Hoboken, NJ: Wiley, 2011), 3.
14. Saeed, *Islamic Banking and Interest*, 49.
15. Timur Kuran, "The Economic System in Contemporary Islamic Thought: Interpretation and Assessment," *International Journal of Middle East Studies* 18, no. 2 (1986), 135.
16. Mann, "Sharif's Castle," 1140.
17. National Association of Realtors, "Home-Price Growth Slightly Accelerates in Fourth Quarter of 2014," www.realtor.org/news-releases/2015/02/home-price-growth-slightly-accelerates-in-fourth-quarter-of-2014 [https://perma.cc/MJ36-MWQN].
18. Richard Fry and Rakesh Kochhar, "America's Wealth Gap Between Middle-Income and Upper-Income Families is Widest on Record," www.pewresearch.org/fact-tank/2014/12/17/wealth-gap-upper-middle-income/ [https://perma.cc/ML2S-74AQ].
19. National Association of Realtors, "2014 Profile of Home Buyers and Sellers," 7, www.realtor.org/sites/default/files/reports/2014/2014-profile-of-home-buyers-and-sellers-highlights.pdf [https://perma.cc/Y6UF-T5YC].
20. Jennifer Murray, "Of Note: Home Ownership the Islamic Way: Sharia-Compliant Mortgages in the United States," *SAIS Review of International Affairs* 27, no. 2 (2007), 93.
21. Ibid.
22. Ibid.; Mann, "Sharif's Castle," 1149.
23. Murray, "Home Ownership the Islamic Way," 93–94; Mann, "Sharif's Castle," 1150.
24. Tavia Grant, "Banks Give Sharia a Second Look," *The Globe and Mail*, May 25, 2007, www.theglobeandmail.com/report-on-business/banks-give-sharia-a-second-look/article17996067 [https://perma.cc/9Z48-PFBX]; Huma Qureshi, "Sharia-Compliant Mortgages Are Here – and They're Not Just for Muslims," *The Guardian*, June 28, 2008, sec. Money, www.theguardian.com/money/2008/jun/29/mortgages.islam [https://perma.cc/NJ5C-EHR7].
25. I.R.C. § 163(a) (2012).
26. Ibid. § 163(h).
27. Ibid. Of that $1.1 million, not more than $100,000 can be used for purposes other than acquiring, constructing, or substantially improving the residence that secures the loans.

28. Treas. Reg. § 1.163–10(T)(p)(3)(ii) (1987).
29. Samuel D. Brunson, "Repatriating Tax-Exempt Investments: Tax Havens, Blocker Corporations, and Unrelated Debt-Financed Income," *Northwestern University Law Review* 106, no. 1 (2012), 225–272, 239.
30. *White v. United States*, 305 US 281, 292 (1938).
31. Jacob Goldstein and Sally Helm, "A Bank Without Interest." Podcast. *Planet Money*, 2016. www.npr.org/templates/transcript/transcript.php?storyId=477956675 [https://perma.cc/J7G2-69KZ].
32. News release, Treas. JS-1706 (Dept. Treas.), 2004 WL 1206118.
33. *See, e.g.*, Robert W. Wood and Rafi W. Mottahedeh, "Taxation of Islamic Finance: Part I, Ijara and Sukuk Al-Ijara," *Tax Notes* 144 no. 3 (2014), 353.
34. Mann, "Sharif's Castle," 1154.
35. Treas. Reg. § 1.6664–4(b)(1) (as amended in 2003).
36. Ibid.
37. The expected penalty is the nominal penalty she would pay, discounted by the probability of the sanctions being imposed. Alex Raskolnikov, "Crime and Punishment in Taxation: Deceit, Deterrence, and the Self-Adjusting Penalty," *Columbia Law Review* 106, no. 3 (2006), 576.
38. Saeed, *Islamic Banking and Interest*, 77.
39. Ibid., 62.
40. Rebel A. Cole, "What Do We Know about the Capital Structure of Privately Held US Firms? Evidence from the Surveys of Small Business Finance," *Financial Management* 42, no. 4 (December 1, 2013), 807.
41. Amy S. Elliott, "New Data Quantify Tax Code's Debt Financing Distortion," *Tax Notes* 146 no. 7 (2015), 857.
42. Devon Bank has offered Islamic financing since 2003. www.devonbank.com/faith-based-financing/ [https://perma.cc/8EBM-45HP].
43. Tenn. Code Ann. § 67–5–212(b)(3)(B) (2015).
44. In re: Islamic Center of Nashville, Claim of Exemption, Property ID 114 00 0 146.00, Exempt No. 80212, Tennessee State Board of Equalization.
45. National Conference of State Legislatures, "Real Estate Transfer Taxes," www.ncsl .org/research/fiscal-policy/real-estate-transfer-taxes.aspx [https://perma.cc/X3VZ-MGTQ].
46. Wojciech Kopczuk and David J. Munroe, "Mansion Tax: The Effect of Transfer Taxes on the Residential Real Estate Market" (National Bureau of Economic Research, May 1, 2014), 5, www.nber.org/papers/w20084.pdf [https://perma.cc/QJA3-GX8V].
47. Habib Ahmed, "Islamic Banking and Shari'ah Compliance: A Product Development Perspective," *Journal of Islamic Finance* 3, no. 2 (November 30, 2014), 24.
48. New York Tax Law § 1402(a) (McKinney 2014).
49. N.Y. ADC Law § 11–2102 (2015).
50. State of New York TSB-A-08(2)R (April 28, 2008), available at 2008 WL 2081105 (N.Y.Dept.Tax.Fin.).
51. State of New York TSB-A-10(3)R (June 16, 2010), available at 2010 WL 2639627 (N.Y.Dept.Tax.Fin.).

52. City of New York FLR-024790–021 (April 9, 2002), available at 2002 WL 1575755 (N.Y.C.Dept.Fin.).
53. City of New York FLR 034811–021 (January 13, 2004), available at 2004 WL 1590343 (N.Y.C.Dept.Fin.).
54. Michael A. Helfand and Barak D. Richman, "The Challenge of Co-Religionist Commerce," *Duke Law Journal* 64, no. 5 (2015), 805.
55. 19 RNCY § 16–05(a) (2015) (finance letter rulings are "binding upon the Department of Finance only with respect to the person to whom the ruling is rendered); 20 NYCRR 2376.4 (effective 2009) ("An advisory opinion…is binding upon the commissioner only with respect to the petitioner and only about the facts described in the advisory opinion.").
56. *US v. Phellis*, 257 US 156, 168 (1921).
57. *Frank Lyon Co. v. US*, 435 US 561, 573 (1978).
58. Bret Wells, "Economic Substance Doctrine: How Codification Changes Decided Cases," *Florida Tax Review* 10, no. 6 (2010), 412.
59. Jeffrey C. Glickman and Clark R. Calhoun, "The States of the Federal Common Law Tax Doctrines," *Tax Lawyer* 61, no. 4 (2008), 1191.
60. Ibid., 1197.
61. *Cornelius v. Comm'r*, 494 F.2d 465, 471 (5th Cir. 1974).
62. Emily Cauble, "Rethinking the Timing of Tax Decisions: Does a Taxpayer Ever Deserve a Second Chance," *Catholic University Law Review* 61, no. 4 (2012), 1036.
63. For instance, when a borrower sells a bond at less than its stated redemption price, the tax law treats some portion of the excess as if it were interest. I.R.C. § 1273(a) (2012). Similarly, where a lender makes a loan with a below-market interest rate, the tax law treats the lender as making a gift of the forgone interest to the borrower. The borrower, in turn, is treated as paying that amount – as interest – to the lender, even though the money never trades hands. Ibid. § 7872(a) (2012). And US taxpayers who invest in certain foreign corporations are required to treat certain "interest equivalent amounts" as though they were, in fact, interest. Treas. Reg. § 1.954–2(h)(2)(i) (as amended in 2016).
64. Eddy S. Fang and Renaud Foucart, "Western Financial Agents and Islamic Ethics," *Journal of Business Ethics* 123, no. 3 (2014), 475.
65. The Supreme Court of the United States explained in 1994 that, "whatever the limits of permissible legislative accommodations may be," singling out a single religion for special treatment violates the Constitution. *Board of Educ. of Kiryas Joel Village School Dist. v. Grumet*, 512 US 687, 706–07 (1994).
66. This kind of financing is similar to various mutual loan clubs. See, e.g., Howard L. Jones, "Chinese Mutual Savings and Loan Clubs," *The Journal of Business* 40, no. 3 (1967), 336.
67. I.R.C. § 6601(a) (2012).
68. This concept is known as the "time value of money" principal. If, for example, the country is facing 2 percent inflation, what I could purchase today for $100 will cost me $102 in a year. If I can wait to pay that $100 for a year, it only costs me the equivalent of $98.04 today.

69. Alice G. Abreu, "Distinguishing Interest from Damages: A Proposal for a New Perspective," *Buffalo Law Review* 40 (1992), 377–378.
70. *Cf.* Andrew Haughwout, Christopher Mayer, and Joseph Tracy, "Subprime Mortgage Pricing: The Impact of Race, Ethnicity, and Gender on the Cost of Borrowing," *Brookings-Wharton Papers on Urban Affairs* 2009, no. 1 (August 6, 2009), 41.
71. I.R.C. §§ 6601(a), 6621(a)(2) (2012).
72. I.R.C. § 6621(a)(2).

7 Deductible Contribution or Purchase of Religious Benefit?

1. J. Gordon Melton, "Birth of a Religion," in *Scientology*, ed. James R. Lewis (New York, NY: Oxford University Press, 2009), 17, 19–21.
2. Ibid., 21.
3. Ibid., 22.
4. Ibid., 23.
5. Ibid., 23–24.
6. *Church of Scientology of California v. Comm'r*, 83 T.C. 381, 404 (1984).
7. Hugh B. Urban, *The Church of Scientology: A History of a New Religion* (Princeton, NJ: Princeton University Press, 2013), 157.
8. 83 T.C. at 405.
9. *Founding Church of Scientology v. United States*, 188 Ct. Cl. 490 (1969).
10. Urban, *Church of Scientology*, 157.
11. Ibid., 167–168.
12. Lawrence Wright, *Going Clear: Scientology, Hollywood, and the Prison of Belief* (New York, NY: Vintage, 2013), 280.
13. Richardson, "Scientology in Court," 289.
14. *Giving USA 2014: The Annual Report on Philanthropy for the Year 2013* (Chicago, IL: Giving USA Foundation, 2014), 26, 35.
15. Population statistics are from the US Census Bureau. In 2013, the United States had a population of approximately 316 million people. https://factfinder.census.gov/faces/tableservices/jsf/pages/productview.xhtml?pid=PEP_2016_PEPANNRES&src=pt [https://perma.cc/6WJ5-8SKN?type=image]. Those 316 million people lived in about 122 million households. www.census.gov/hhes/families/files/hh1.xls [https://perma.cc/X7MG-DHAR]. In 2013, Americans had a median household income of $52,250. www.census.gov/content/dam/Census/library/publications/2014/acs/acsbr13-02.pdf [https://perma.cc/6LM4-VXAD].
16. *Giving USA 2014*, 16.
17. I.R.C. § 170(a) (2012).
18. Lilian V. Faulhaber, "Charitable Giving, Tax Expenditures, and Direct Spending in the United States and the European Union," *Yale Journal of International Law* 39, no. 1 (2014), 95; HM Revenue and Customs, "Tax Relief When You Donate to a Charity," www.gov.uk/donating-to-charity/gift-aid [https://perma.cc/2XY7-KYUS].
19. www.irs.gov/uac/SOI-Tax-Stats-Tax-Stats-at-a-Glance [https://perma.cc/HJP4-PR4Z].

20. *Giving USA 2014*, 27. It is also worth noting that not all itemizers make charitable donations. In fact, in 2010, only 86 percent of itemizers (or 27 percent of taxpayers) claimed a charitable deduction. Statement of Sen. Max Baucus, Hearing Before the Senate Committee On Finance: Tax Reform Options: Incentives for Charitable Giving (October 18, 2011), 2.
21. *Giving USA 2014*, 39.
22. Ibid., 107.
23. Samuel D. Brunson, "Reigning in Charities: Using an Intermediate Penalty to Enforce the Campaigning Prohibition," *Pittsburgh Tax Review* 8, no. 2 (2011), 132–133.
24. Professor Lilian Faulhaber dubs this phenomenon the hypersalience of the charitable deduction. *See generally* Lilian V. Faulhaber, "The Hidden Limits of the Charitable Deduction: An Introduction to Hypersalience," *Boston University Law Review* 92 (2012), 1318–1328.
25. Statement of Orrin G. Hatch, Hearing Before the Senate Committee On Finance: Tax Reform Options: Incentives for Charitable Giving (October 18, 2011), 3.
26. Testimony of Dallin H. Oaks, Hearing Before the Senate Committee On Finance: Tax Reform Options: Incentives for Charitable Giving (October 18, 2011), 9.
27. I.R.C. § 170(b)(1)(A), (d)(1).
28. *See US* v. *Am. Bar Endowment*, 477 US 105, 116–117 (1986).
29. Treas. Reg. § 1.170A-1(h)(2) (as amended in 2008).
30. http://shop.npr.org/products/classic-npr-tote [https://perma.cc/WA9J-BUDA].
31. Treas. Reg. § 1.170A-1(h)(4).
32. Robin Pogrebin, "Gift by Geffen to Be Writ Large at Avery Fisher," *New York Times*, March 5, 2015, sec. A.
33. Ibid.
34. William A. Drennan, "Where Generosity and Pride Abide: Charitable Naming Rights," *University of Cincinnati Law Review* 80, no. 1 (2011), 66–67.
35. John D. Colombo, "The Marketing of Philanthropy and the Charitable Contributions Deduction; Integrating Theories for the Deduction and Tax Exemption," *Wake Forest Law Review* 36 (2001), 663.
36. Craig Harline, *Sunday: A History of the First Day from Babylonia to the Super Bowl* (New York, NY: Yale University Press, 2011), 34.
37. Rev. Rul. 78–366, 1978–2 C.B. 241.
38. Conde B. Pallen, *The New Catholic Dictionary* (Universal Knowledge Foundation, 1929), 752, https://archive.org/stream/TheNewCatholicDictionary#page/n1/mode/2up [https://perma.cc/AGX2-BWDN].
39. Rev. Rul. 70–47, 1970–1 C.B. 49.
40. James R. Lewis, "Introduction," in *Scientology*, ed. James R. Lewis (New York, NY: Oxford University Press, 2009), 3, 5.
41. Urban, *Church of Scientology*, 46–47.
42. Ibid., 135–136.
43. *Hernandez* v. *Comm'r*, 490 US 680, 685 (1989).
44. Rev. Rul. 78–189, 1978–1 C.B. 68.
45. *Hernandez* v. *Comm'r*, 490 US 680, 685 (1989).
46. I.R.C. § 7141(a) (2012).

47. Carolyn D. Wright, "Release of Exemption Closing Agreements Gets Mixed Reviews," *Tax Notes* 78 no. 4 (1998), 403.
48. James T. Richardson, "Scientology in Court: A Look at Some Major Cases from Various Nations," in *Scientology*, ed. James R. Lewis (New York, NY: Oxford University Press, 2009), 283, 288; Urban, *Church of Scientology*, 3; Janet Reitman, *Inside Scientology: The Story of America's Most Secretive Religion* (Boston, MA: Mariner Books, 2013), 170.
49. Although the closing agreement was – and continues to be – private, the IRS did not operate entirely in the shadows here. In 1978, it had issued a revenue ruling explicitly stating that Scientologists' fixed donations for auditing were not deductible. Rev. Rul. 78–189, 1978–1 C.B. 68. In 1993, it publicly obsoleted that ruling. Rev. Rul. 93–73, 1993–2 C.B. 75.
50. While closing agreements are private contracts between the IRS and a taxpayer, somebody leaked a closing agreement that purports to be the scientology agreement. Tax Analysts published the leak in its publication *Tax Notes Today*. 97 TNT 251–24. Although *Tax Notes Today* is available both on Lexis and at www.taxnotes .com, both require subscriptions to access. The alleged agreement has also been posted online at a personal website titled "Scientology versus the IRS." www.cs .cmu.edu/~dst/Cowen/essays/agreemnt.html [https://perma.cc/B3AM-U8N5].
51. This agreement not to contest taxpayer positions is not unique to the scientology closing agreement. For example, the IRS has similarly announced that it will not assert a deficiency against taxpayers who do not include in their gross income frequent flier miles received from business travel. I.R.S. Announcement 2002–18, 2002–1 C.B. 621. In the same way the scientology closing agreement does not assert that payments for auditing are, in fact, deductible, the announcement does not claim that frequent flier miles are not income. Instead, both provide an administrative safe harbor for taxpayers. Rather than asserting that the law is taxpayer favorable in these ways, they merely say that the IRS will not enforce the law in a way that it could.
52. Treas. Reg. § 1.170A-13(f)(8)(i)(B) (as amended in 1996).
53. I.R.C. § 170(i); Kristin Balding Gutting, "Relighting the Charitable Deduction: A Proposed Public Benefit Exception," *Florida Tax Review* 12, no. 6 (2012), 484–485.
54. Quoted in Urban, *Scientology*, 173.
55. Richardson, "Scientology in Court," 289.
56. It is worth noting that as part of the Revenue Reconciliation Act of 1993, Congress added section 6115 to the Internal Revenue Code. Section 6115 requires tax-exempt organizations to provide a written statement to donors where donors receive something of value in return from the tax-exempt organization. Congress provided an exception, though, where the only thing the donor received was "an intangible religious benefit that generally is not sold in a commercial transaction outside the donative context." I.R.C. § 6115(b) (2012). The legislative history of this carve out for intangible religious benefits does not explicitly mention the *Hernandez* case, but the Supreme Court's decision was almost certainly the impetus behind its enactment. Jacob L. Todres, "Internal Revenue Code Section 170: Does the Receipt by a Donor of an Intangible Religious Benefit Reduce the Amount of the Charitable Contribution Deduction? Only the Lord Knows for Sure," *Tennessee Law Review* 64, no. 1 (1996), 152.

Unfortunately, if Congress intended to reverse the Supreme Court, it failed. Section 6115 is not a substantive tax provision. That is, it does not affect a tax-payer's tax liability, nor does it determine whether a charitable donation is fully deductible, partially deductible, or not deductible at all. All it does is carve out an exception from tax-exempt organizations' general obligation to inform donors who receive a quid pro quo that their donation is not fully deductible. To the extent section 6115 is an accommodation, then, it is one to lessen the administrative burden on religions, not to permit taxpayers to ignore intangible religious benefits they receive in exchange for their donations. That accommodation remains the result of various IRS rulings and, for scientologists, the IRS closing agreement.

57. Church of Scientology, *Updated Information on Taxes and Your Dona-tions, 2008/2009* (2008), 7, 12, www.scribd.com/doc/28618681/08-09-Updated-Information-on-Taxes-and-Your-Donations-2008-2009.
58. Rev. Rul. 54–580, 1954–2 C.B. 97.
59. *Sklar v. Comm'r*, 549 F.3d 1252 (9th Cir. 2008).
60. *Sklar v. Comm'r*, 125 T.C. 281, 288 (2005).
61. Sklar, 549 F.3d at 1260.
62. *Sklar v. Comm'r*, 282 F.3d 610, 620 (9th Cir. 2002).
63. *Oppewal v. Comm'r*, 30 T.C.M. (CCH) 1177 (T.C. 1971).
64. *Oppewal v. Comm'r*, 468 F.2d 1000 (1st Cir. 1972); *see also* Rev. Rul. 83–104, 1983–2 C.B. 46.
65. *Winters v. Comm'r*, 468 F2d 778 (2d Cir. 1972); *DeJong v. Comm'r*, 309 F2d 373 (9th Cir. 1962).
66. Rev. Rul. Rev. Rul. 83–104, 1983–2 C.B. 46.
67. I.R.S. Priv. Ltr. Rul. 90 – 04–030 (January 26, 1990).
68. Joseph J. Thorndike, "The Love-Hate Relationship With the Standard Deduc-tion," *Tax Notes* 142 (2012), 1394.
69. I.R.C. § 170(b)(1) (2012).
70. Edwin S. Cohen, *A Lawyer's Life: Deep in the Heart of Taxes* (Arlington, VA: Tax Analysts, 1994), 368–369.
71. Treas. Reg. § 1.170A-13(a)(1) (as amended in 1996).

8 A Right to Tithe?

1. In fact, American Protestants are split on whether tithes are still required, or whether they are part of the law that Jesus claimed to fulfill. While Protestants discovered that the tithe, with its biblical precedent, was an "unappealable" law, in the twentieth century, it began to fall out of favor with some Protestants. James Hudnut-Beumler, *In Pursuit of the Almighty's Dollar: A History of Money and American Protestantism* (Chapel Hill, VA: The University of North Carolina Press, 2007), 216–217.
2. Adam S. Chodorow, "Maaser Kesafim and the Development of Tax Law," *Florida Tax Review* 8, no. 1 (2007), 155, 165–167.
3. Nur Barizah Abu Bakar, "A Zakat Accounting Standard (ZAS) for Malaysian Companies," *The American Journal of Islamic Social Sciences* 24, no. 4 (2007), 76–77; Russell Powell, "Zakat: Drawing Insights for Legal Theory and Economic Policy from Islamic Jurisprudence," *Pittsburgh Tax Review* 7, no. 1 (2009), 43–44;

Mohamed Nimer, *The North American Muslim Resource Guide: Muslim Community Life in the United States and Canada* (Oxford: Routledge, 2014), 6.

4. "How Do You Interpret Tithing?," *Christianity Today*, December 2012, 56.
5. Phillip B. Jones, *Southern Baptist Congregations Today* (Research, North American Mission Board, SBC, 2001), 42.
6. Gordon B. Dahl and Michael R Ransom, "Does Where You Stand Depend on Where You Sit? Tithing Donations and Self-Serving Beliefs," *The American Economic Review* 89, no. 4 (1999): 703–727, 704; Stewardship Ministries, General Conference of Seventh-Day Adventists, "Frequently Asked Questions," www.adventiststewardship.com/article/4/frequently-asked-questions#7 [https://perma.cc/XQ7F-DF7B].
7. David A. Skeel Jr., "When Should Bankruptcy Be an Option (for People, Places, or Things)," *William & Mary Law Review* 55, no. 6 (2014), 2222.
8. Kenneth N. Klee, "Tithing and Bankruptcy," *American Bankruptcy Law Journal* 75, no. 2 (2001), 157–158.
9. Donald R. Price and Mark C. Rahdert, "Distributing the First Fruits: Statutory and Constitutional Implications of Tithing in Bankruptcy," *U.C. Davis Law Review* 26, no. 4 (1993), 878–879.
10. Klee, "Tithing and Bankruptcy," 159–160, 162–163.
11. 11 U.S.C. § 548(a)(2) (2012).
12. Ibid. § 548(d)(4).
13. I.R.C. § 170(c)(2) (2012).
14. 11 U.S.C. § 548(a)(2), (d)(3).
15. I.R.C. § 6159 (2012).
16. Treas. Reg. § 1.6159–1(f) (as amended in 2009).
17. Shu-Yi Oei, "Who Wins When Uncle Sam Loses: Social Insurance and the Forgiveness of Tax Debts," *U.C. Davis Law Review* 46, no. 2 (2012), 438; Marion E. Wynne, "Helping Clients With Tax Debts," *Alabama Lawyer* 60 (September 1999), 325–326.
18. IRS Form 433-A (2012).
19. Treas. Reg. § 301.7122–1(b) (2002).
20. Ibid., § 301.7122(d)(1).
21. I.R.S. Chief Couns. Mem. 200102001 (January 12, 2001) ("Should the taxpayer fail to keep [the] promise [to comply], the Service may terminate the compromise and take action to collect the full balance of the unpaid tax liabilities covered by the compromise."); I.R.C. § 6159(b)(4) (2012).
22. Wynne, "Helping Clients," 326.
23. I.R.M. 5.15.1.7 (October 2, 2012).
24. I.R.M. 5.15.1.10 (November 17, 2014).
25. *See Lemann* v. *Comm'r*, T.C. Memo. 2006–37.
26. *Pixley* v. *Comm'r*, 123 T.C. 269 (2004).
27. I.R.C. § 6671(b) (2012).
28. *Thompson* v. *Comm'r*, 140 T.C. 173 (2013).

9 Without Purse, Scrip, or Taxes

1. "U.S. Court Rules Missionary Work is Tax-Deductible," *Ensign* (April 1984), 80.

2. Interview with Idaho State Senator Bart Davis, September 3, 2015.
3. 725 F.2d 1269 (10th Cir. 1984).
4. Email from Robert P. Lunt, September 9, 2015.
5. Originally, the case was assigned to Judge Marion J. Callister, himself a practicing Mormon. The Department of Justice attorney asked him to recuse himself, arguing that, as a Mormon, he could not be impartial. Judge Callister refused. Shortly after, though, Judge Callister did recuse himself, and the case went to Idaho's other district court judge. Judge Ryan, who was not Mormon, ultimately heard the case. Later, Bart learned that between when Judge Callister refused to recuse himself and when he did, in fact, recuse himself, he had a relative who was called on a Mormon mission, and whom he was expected to help support. At that point, he could benefit economically from his ruling, and determined that he needed to recuse himself.
6. Stephen Neill, *A History of Christian Missions* (New York, NY: Penguin Books 1964), 21–22.
7. Rosalind I.J. Hackett, "Revisiting Proselytization in the Twenty-First Century," in *Proselytization Revisited: Rights Talk, Free Markets and Culture Wars,* ed. Rosalind I.J. Hackett (Oxford: Routledge, 2014), 1.
8. I.R.C. § 102(a) (2012).
9. *Comm'r v. Duberstein,* 363 US 278, 285 (1960).
10. I.R.C. § 102(c). The only way that an employer gift qualifies as a tax gift is where the employer and employee have a relationship outside of work. So, for example, if an individual works in the family business and his mother is also his employer, she can still give him gifts for tax purposes, as long as those gifts are given in her capacity as mother, not as employer.
11. Rev. Rul. 68–67, 1968–1 C.B. 38.
12. Michael J. Graetz and Michael M. O'Hear, "The 'Original Intent' of U. S. International Taxation," *Duke Law Journal* 46, no. 5 (1997), 1054.
13. I.R.C. § 911(a)(1) (2012).
14. Revenue Act of 1926, H.R. 1, 69th Cong. § 213(b)(14), 44 Stat. 26 (1926).
15. H.R. Rep. No. 69–1, at 7.
16. Maina Chawla Singh, *Gender, Religion, and the Heathen Lands: American Missionary Women in South Asia, 1860s-1940s* (Routledge, 2016), 52–55.
17. Johannes Aagaard, "The First Furlough," *International Review of Mission* 56, no. 224 (October 1, 1967), 439–440.
18. Rev. Rul. 55–464, 1955–2 C.B. 291.
19. Rev. Rul. 76–191, 1976–1 C.B. 201.
20. Rev. Proc. 2014–61 § 3.32, 2014–47 I.R.B. 860.
21. www.bls.gov/oes/current/oes212099.htm [https://perma.cc/5XYD-BSSD].
22. I.R.C. § 1402(e). By opting out of paying social security taxes, a minister also forfeits the right to receive social security payments.
23. Rev. Rul. 55–471, 1955–2 C.B. 615.
24. I.R.C. § 1401(a) (2012).
25. Staff of the Joint Committee on Taxation, "Overview of the Federal Tax System as In Effect for 2015," March 30, 2015, www.jct.gov/publications .html?func=startdown&id=4763 [https://perma.cc/DMV5-J6JT]; *see also* Howard Gleckman, "For Most Households, It's About the Payroll Tax, Not the Income

Tax," TaxVox (April 2, 2015), www.taxpolicycenter.org/taxvox/most-households-its-about-payroll-tax-not-income-tax [https://perma.cc/3KLP-6UUS].

26. For example, many volunteer mission trips involve a small number of adolescents traveling with a youth pastor to perform a discrete service task for one to two weeks. These short-term mission trips tend to focus more on providing service than they do on proselytizing. For example, Jenny Trinitapoli and Stephen Vaisey, "The Transformative Role of Religious Experience: The Case of Short-Term Missions," *Social Forces* 88, no. 1 (December 10, 2009), 132.

27. Rodney Stark, "The Rise of a New World Faith," *Review of Religious Research* 26, no. 1 (1984), 19.

28. Richard L. Jensen, "Without Purse or Scrip? Financing Latter-Day Saint Missionary Work in Europe in the Nineteenth Century," *Journal of Mormon History* 12 (1985), 4–5.

29. Even into the twentieth century, there were occasional flirtations with the traditional method of funding one's missionary work, but "the realities of a cash-based economy and the decline of hospitality for itinerant preachers usually made the old way impractical in the long run." Ibid., 12–13.

30. Stark, "New World Faith," 21.

31. Mario S. De Pillis, "The Persistence of Mormon Community into the 1990s," *Sunstone*, October 1991, 49 n.56.

32. Rev. Rul. 62–113, 1962–2 C.B. 10.

33. See *Aeroquip-Vickers, Inc.* v. *Comm'r*, 347 F.3d 173, 181 (6th Cir. 2003).

34. *Davis* v. *US*, 664 F.Supp. 468, 469–70 (D. Idaho 1987).

35. Ibid., 470; *Davis* v. *US*, 495 US 472, 479 (1990).

36. I.R.C. § 170(c) (2012).

37. Davis, 495 US at 475.

38. Treas. Reg. § 1.170A-1(g) (as amended in 2008).

39. Davis, 664 F. Supp. at 472; *Davis* v. *US*, 861 F.2d 558, 562 (9th Cir. 1988).

40. Davis, 664 F. Supp. at 471–472; Davis, 861 F.2d at 563–564.

41. In 1980 and 1981, the standard deduction for an unmarried individual was $2,300. Tax Policy Center, *Standard Deduction Amount, 1970–2015*, www.taxpolicycenter.org/taxfacts/Content/PDF/historical_standard_deduct.pdf [https://perma.cc/WC9G-RR3Q]. Admittedly, in both years, the Davises deposited more than $2,300 in Benjamin's bank account, and he apparently spent more than that. However, under the tax law, his tax home would have been in New York, where he was performing his missionary work, meaning that his food and housing expenses would not be deductible in any event. Davis, 861 F.2d at 564. Although the courts' opinions do not break down Benjamin's expenses, presumably housing and food costs constituted a significant percentage of his expenses. It is unlikely that his non-food and housing-related expenses exceeded $2,300 in either year.

42. *White* v. *US*, 514 F.Supp. 1057, 1058 (D. Utah 1981).

43. *Brinley* v. *Comm'r*, 782 F.2d 1326, 1328–1329 (5th Cir. 1986).

44. Ibid. 1336; *White* v. *US*, 725 F.2d 1269, 1272 (10th Cir. 1984); email from Robert P. Lunt, October 14, 2015.

45. See Erwin N. Griswold, "The Need for a Court of Tax Appeals," *Harvard Law Review* 57, no. 8 (1944), 1164.

46. David Laro, "The Evolution of the Tax Court as an Independent Tribunal Panel Discussion," *University of Illinois Law Review* 1995, no. 1 (1995), 23.
47. Richard L. Revesz, "Specialized Courts and the Administrative Lawmaking System," *University of Pennsylvania Law Review* 138, no. 4 (1990), 1134.
48. *Davis v. US*, 493 US 953, 953 (1989).
49. *Davis v. US*, 495 US 472, 481–485 (1990).
50. Ibid., 487–488.
51. Trent Toone, "The Challenges and Blessings of Financing a Mormon Mission," *Deseret News*, March 31, 2015, www.deseretnews.com/article/865625379/The-challenges-and-blessings-of-financing-a-Mormon-mission.html [https://perma.cc/9S69-TU9Y].
52. "Policy Equalizes Mission Expenses," *Church News*, December 1, 1990, www.ldschurchnewsarchive.com/articles/19765/Policy-equalizes-mission-expenses.html [https://perma.cc/YBV8-MDMK].
53. Wilkes v. Comm'r, T.C. Summ. Op. 2010–2053.
54. I.R.C. § 61 (2012).
55. *Comm'r v. Glenshaw Glass*, 348 US 426, 431 (1955); *see* Alice G. Abreu and Richard K. Greenstein, "Defining Income," *Florida Tax Review* 11, no. 5 (2011), 296.
56. Treas. Reg. § 1.62–2(c)(4) (as amended in 2003).
57. Treas. Reg. § 1.62–2(d)(1) (as amended in 2003).
58. Rev. Rul. 62–113, 1962–2 C.B. 10.
59. Dallin H. Oaks, "Sacrifice," www.lds.org/general-conference/2012/04/sacrifice?lang=eng [https://perma.cc/ZMG6-D39A].
60. https://web.archive.org/web/20141018141130/http://www.mormon.org/values/missionary-work [https://perma.cc/ST3B-NXB6].
61. I.R.C. § 170(a) (2012).
62. Treas. Reg. § 1.170A-1(g) (as amended in 2008).
63. The *Missionary Handbook*, given to all Mormon missionaries, explains that the amounts missionaries receive from the mission are "sacred"; as a result, they should use their money almost exclusively for basic needs, and should return any leftover money to the mission. *Missionary Handbook* (Salt Lake City, UT: Church of Jesus Christ of Latter-day Saints 2006), 43–44, www.lds.org/bc/content/ldsorg/topics/missionary/MissionaryHandbook2006Navigate.pdf.
64. *See, e.g.*, Barbara Ehrenreich, *Nickel and Dimed: On (Not) Getting By in America* (New York, NY: Picador, 2011), 197–199.
65. Rev. Rul. 68–67, 1968–1 C.B. 38.
66. In certain circumstances, treating the monthly mission allowances could result in a missionary receiving additional money from the government, instead of paying taxes, if the missionary were eligible for the earned income tax credit. If the qualifying missionary earned income within a certain (inflation-adjusted) range, she would actually *receive* money from the government. In 2015, an unmarried individual with no children could receive up to $503; the amount would depend on how much income she earned, but she would receive money back from the government if she earned between $6,580 and $14,820. Rev. Proc. 2014–61 § 3.06, 2014–47 I.R.B. 860. Most Mormon missionaries would not qualify, though: to qualify, an individual with no children must live in the United States, be at least

25 years old, and not be a dependent for tax purposes. I.R.C. § 32(c)(1)(A)(ii) (2012).

10 Religious Communitarians

1. Joel Hawkins and Terry Bertolino, *House of David Baseball Team* (Mount Pleasant, SC: Arcadia Publishing, 2000), 18.
2. Ibid., 7.
3. *Acts* 2:44–45.
4. *Acts* 4:34–35.
5. *Acts* 5:1–10.
6. See, e.g., Matthew Bowman, "Primitivism in America: Restorationism, Revitalization, and Renewal," *Oxford Research Encyclopedia of Religion*, August 5, 2016, http://religion.oxfordre.com/view/10.1093/acrefore/9780199340378.001.0001/acrefore-9780199340378-e-416 [https://perma.cc/S9E7-C3UQ].
7. Lawrence Foster, "Sex and Conflict in New Religious Movements: A Comparison of the Oneida Community under John Humphrey Noyes and the Early Mormons under Joseph Smith and His Would-Be Successors," *Nova Religio: The Journal of Alternative and Emergent Religions* 13, no. 3 (February 1, 2010), 36.
8. Stephen C. Taysom, *Shakers, Mormons, and Religious Worlds: Conflicting Visions, Contested Boundaries*, Religion in North America (Bloomington, IN: Indiana University Press, 2011), 101.
9. Ibid.
10. Lawrence Foster, *Religion and Sexuality: Three American Communal Experiments of the Nineteenth Century* (New York, NY: Oxford University Press, 1981), 220–223.
11. Ibid., 109.
12. Ibid., 30–31.
13. Samuel Brunson, "Taxing Utopia," *Seton Hall Law Review* 47, no. 1 (2016), 139.
14. Leonard J. Arrington, Feramorz Y. Fox, and Dean L. May, *Building the City of God: Community and Cooperation Among the Mormons* (Salt Lake City, UT: Desert Books, 1976), 15–16.
15. Edwin Brown Firmage and Richard Collin Mangrum, *Zion in the Courts: A Legal History of the Church of Jesus Christ of Latter-Day Saints, 1830–1900* (Urbana, IL: University of Illinois Press, 1988), 62–63.
16. Brunson, "Taxing Utopia," 159.
17. Simon M. Evans and Peter Peller, "Hutterite Colonies and the Cultural Landscape: An Inventory of Selected Site Characteristics," *Journal of Plain and Anabaptist Studies* 4, no. 1 (2016), 54.
18. Hanna Kienzler, "Communal Longevity. The Hutterite Case," *Anthropos* 100, no. 1 (2005), 202.
19. Karl Peter et al., "The Dynamics of Religious Defection among Hutterites," *Journal for the Scientific Study of Religion* 21, no. 4 (1982), 327.
20. Pierre L. van den Berghe and Karl Peter, "Hutterites and Kibbutzniks: A Tale of Nepotistic Communism," *Man* 23, no. 3 (1988), 532.
21. Brunson, "Taxing Utopia," 157–158.

22. Ran Abramitzky, "Lessons from the Kibbutz on the Equality–Incentives Trade-Off," *The Journal of Economic Perspectives* 25, no. 1 (2011), 185.

23. Richard Sosis and Bradley J. Ruffle, "Religious Ritual and Cooperation: Testing for a Relationship on Israeli Religious and Secular Kibbutzim," *Current Anthropology* 44, no. 5 (2003), 714.

24. Tsilly Dagan and Avital Margalit, "Tax, State, and Utopia," *Virginia Tax Review* 33, no. 4 (2014), 551.

25. Ajay K. Mehrotra, *Making the Modern American Fiscal State: Law, Politics, and the Rise of Progressive Taxation, 1877–1929* (Cambridge: Cambridge University Press, 2014), 3.

26. Roy G. Blakey, "The New Income Tax," *The American Economic Review* 4, no. 1 (1914), 35–36.

27. Mehrotra, *Modern American Fiscal State*, 138.

28. Joseph J. Thorndike, *Their Fair Share: Taxing the Rich in the Age of FDR* (Washington, DC: Rowman & Littlefield Publishers, 2013), 5.

29. Brunson, "Taxing Utopia," 182.

30. Paul Arnsberger et al., "A History of the Tax-Exempt Sector: An SOI Perspective," *SOI Bulletin* 27, no. 3 (2008), 106–107.

31. *Israelite House of David* v. *Holden*, 14 F.2d 701 (W.D. Mich. 1926).

32. *Hofer* v. *United States*, 64 Ct. Cl. 672 (1928).

33. *Hutterische Bruder Gemeinde* v. *Comm'r*, 1 B.T.A. 1208 (1925).

34. *See, e.g.,* Clare E. Adkin, *Brother Benjamin: A History of the Israelite House of David* (Berrien Springs, MI: Andrews University Press, 1990), 46.

35. Brunson, *Taxing Utopia*, 161; Jeffrey L. Kwall, "Subchapter G of the Internal Revenue Code: Crusade without a Cause," *Virginia Tax Review* 5 (1985), 235.

36. I.R.C. § 501(d) (2012).

37. 80 Cong. Rec. 9074 (1936) (statement of Sen. Walsh).

38. *Twin Oaks Community, Incorp.* v. *Comm'r*, 87 T.C. 1233, 1247 (1986).

39. *Ibid.*, 1248–1249.

40. I.R.C. § 501(d).

41. David M. Schizer, "Between Scylla and Charybdis: Taxing Corporations or Shareholders (or Both)," *Columbia Law Review* 116, no. 7 (2016), 1894.

42. Melford E. Spiro, *Kibbutz: Venture in Utopia* (New York, NY: Schocken Books, 1963), 12–20.

43. Zvi D. Altman, "Survey of Israeli Tax System," *Tax Notes International* 24 (2001), 1017.

44. Dagan and Margalit, "Tax, State, and Utopia," 567–568.

45. I.R.C. § 11(b) (2012).

46. Rev. Proc. 2016–55 § 3.01, 2016–45 I.R.B. 707. For individuals, the tax brackets are indexed to inflation, so every year, the IRS releases the new dollar amounts that trigger a rise in the next tax bracket.

47. Tax Policy Center, "Household Income Quintiles," www.taxpolicycenter.org/statistics/household-income-quintiles [https://perma.cc/EN3F-UNGY].

48. *Internal Revenue Service Data Book, 2015* (2016), 58, www.irs.gov/pub/irs-soi/15databk.pdf [https://perma.cc/XG6R-5U6S].

49. Brunson, "Taxing Utopia," 181–195.

11 A Framework for Religious Tax Accommodation

1. Steven G. Gey, "Why Is Religion Special: Reconsidering the Accommodation of Religion under the Religion Clauses of the First Amendment," *University of Pittsburgh Law Review* 52, no. 1 (1990), 75.

2. *McDaniel* v. *Paty*, 435 US 618, 639 (1978) (Brennan, J., concurring).

3. Hillel Y. Levin, Allan J. Jacobs, and Kavita Shah Arora, "To Accommodate or Not to Accommodate: (When) Should the State Regulate Religion to Protect the Rights of Children and Third Parties," *Washington and Lee Law Review* 73 no. 2 (2016), 917.

4. Zoe Robinson, "Rationalizing Religious Exemptions: A Legislative Process Theory of Statutory Exemptions for Religion," *William & Mary Bill of Rights Journal* 20, no. 1 (2011), 138–139.

5. *Zubick* v. *Burwell*, 136 S.Ct. 1557, 1560 (2016).

6. *W. Virginia State Bd. of Educ.* v. *Barnette*, 319 US 624, 642 (1943).

7. *Palmer* v. *Board of Ed. of City of Chicago*, 466 F. Supp. 600, 602 (N.D. IL 1979).

8. Dallan F. Flake, "Bearing Burdens: Religious Accommodations That Adversely Affect Coworker Morale," *Ohio State Law Journal* 76, no. 1 (2015), 170–171.

9. *United States* v. *Lee*, 455 US 252, 260 (1982); *Nelson* v. *United States*, 796 F.2d 164, 168 (6th Cir. 1986).

10. Christopher L. Eisgruber and Lawrence G. Sager, *Religious Freedom and the Constitution* (Cambridge, MA: Harvard University Press, 2007), 83.

11. Michael W. McConnell, "Accommodation of Religion," *The Supreme Court Review* 1985 (1985), 18.

12. Brian Leiter, *Why Tolerate Religion?* (Princeton, NJ: Princeton University Press, 2013), 63.

13. McConnell, "Accommodation," 18.

14. David Little, "Does the Human Right to Freedom of Conscience, Religion, and Belief Have Special Status International Law and Religion Symposium," *Brigham Young University Law Review* 2001 no. 2 (2001), 604.

15. Camden Hutchinson, "The Historical Origins of the Debt-Equity Distinction," *Florida Tax Review* 18, no. 3 (2015), 101–102.

16. 28 U.S.C. §2201(a) (2012).

17. I.R.C. § 7421(a) (2012).

18. It is not just in the Establishment Clause standing setting that courts ignore the economic identity between direct spending and tax expenditures. In fact, that artificial difference is salient to courts in both the United States and the European Union. Lilian V. Faulhaber, "Charitable Giving, Tax Expenditures, and Direct Spending in the United States and the European Union," *Yale Journal of International Law* 39, no. 1 (2014), 89.

19. Samuel D. Brunson, "Dear IRS, It Is Time to Enforce the Campaigning Prohibition. Even Against Churches," *University of Colorado Law Review* 87, no. 1 (2016), 161–163.

20. Samuel A. Donaldson, "The Easy Case against Tax Simplification," *Virginia Tax Review* 22 no. 4 (2003), 650.

21. Richard C. Schragger, "The Relative Irrelevance of the Establishment Clause," *Texas Law Review* 89, no. 3 (2011), 609.

22. Ira C. Lupu and Robert W. Tuttle, *Secular Government, Religious People* (Grand Rapids, MI: Eerdmans, 2014), 218–219.
23. www.pewforum.org/religious-landscape-study/ [https://perma.cc/X833-DRW2].
24. I.R.C. § 163(h) (2012).
25. *Id.* § 1(a)-(d) (2012).
26. Ira K. Lindsay, "Tax Fairness by Convention: A Defense of Horizontal Equity," *Florida Tax Review* 19, no. 2 (2016), 99.
27. *Jacobellis* v. *State of Ohio*, 378 US 184, 197 (1964) (Stewart, J. concurring).
28. Andrew Koppelman, *Defending American Religious Neutrality* (Cambridge, MA: Harvard University Press, 2013), 7–8; Andrew Koppelman, "How Could Religious Liberty Be a Human Right?," Draft August 11, 2016, at 36–37. https://papers.ssrn.com/sol3/papers.cfm?abstract_id=2995605.
29. *US* v. *Meyers*, 906 F. Supp. 1494, 1502–04 (D. Wyo. 1995).
30. 42 U.S.C. § 2000cc-5(7)(A) (2012).
31. *See* Richard W. Garnett, "A Hands-off Approach to Religious Doctrine: What Are We Talking About?," *Notre Dame Law Review* 84, no. 2 (2009), 848–849.
32. *Sossamon* v. *Lone Star State of Texas*, 560 F.3d 316, 332 (5th Cir. 2009), aff'd sub nom. *Sossamon* v. *Texas*, 563 US 277 (2011).
33. More technically, Henry Simons explains that one determines the quantity of consumption by determining "the value of rights exercised in a certain way (in destruction of economic goods)." Henry Calvert Simons, *Personal Income Taxation: The Definition of Income as a Problem of Fiscal Policy*, (Chicago, IL: University of Chicago Press, 1965), 49–50.
34. I.R.C. § 170 (2012).
35. Until now, I have focused on tax disadvantage to the religious taxpayer. Theoretically, the religiously mandated form could produce advantageous tax consequences. In those cases, the government could, of course, do a kind of reverse accommodation, where it increases the taxes on the religiously motivated form to make them equivalent to the standard transactional form. I consider this unlikely, though: in most cases, if the religious form provides advantageous tax results, non-religious taxpayers will also adopt the form, meaning that horizontal equity considerations will be met. Congress may still want to close such a loophole, but the loophole closing would have nothing to do with religious accommodation.
36. Professor David Weisbach illustrates the effects of this discontinuity in rules through the example of mixing bowl transactions. A typical partnership transaction (where a partner contributes assets to the partnership) is typically tax free. A typical sale or exchange is taxable. Between these two extremes are a series of possible transactions that involve transferring property to a partnership, and from the partnership to another partner. The tax law generally applies to the extremes, though, so it had to draw sometimes arbitrary lines classifying this middle transactions as either sales or partnership transactions. David A. Weisbach, "Formalism in the Tax Law," *University of Chicago Law Review* 66, no. 3 (1999), 872. In this middle range is the opportunity to arbitrage, but this middle range exists all over the tax law.
37. Victor Fleischer, "Regulatory Arbitrage," *Texas Law Review* 89, no. 2 (2010), 229–230.
38. *US* v. *Lee*, 455 US 252, 260 (1982).

39. Professor Adam Chodorow explains that, irrespective of the "right" theoretical answer, "the rules must be designed so that taxpayers can comply with them and tax authorities can effectively enforce them." Adam S. Chodorow, "Bitcoin and the Definition of Foreign Currency," *Florida Tax Review* 19, no. 6 (2016), 381–382.

40. Linda Sugin, "Tax Expenditure Analysis and Constitutional Decisions," *Hastings Law Journal* 50, no. 3 (1999), 408.

41. In 2013, the IRS dealt with nearly 147.4 million individual income tax returns (that is, IRS Forms 1040, 1040A, and 1040EZ). IRS, "Statistics of Income – 2013 Individual Income Tax Returns," www.irs.gov/pub/irs-soi/13inalcr.pdf [https://perma.cc/QPW3-R9BD].

42. National Taxpayer Advocate *Annual Report to Congress* vol. 1 (2015), xiv.

43. Joel Slemrod and Jon Bakija, *Taxing Ourselves: A Citizen's Guide to the Debate over Taxes* (Cambridge, MA: The MIT Press, 2008), 10.

44. State ex rel. *Singleton v. Woodruff*, 153 Fla. 84, 87, 13 So. 2d 704, 705 (1943).

45. *See* John Rawls, *A Theory of Justice*, Revised (Cambridge, MA: The Belknap Press, 1999), 181.

46. *See* Leiter, *Why Tolerate Religion?*, 63.

47. It is worth noting that this financial bind is not limited to taxpaying; the Supreme Court has held that requiring businesses whose owners object to birth control on religious grounds to provide contraceptive coverage as part of their employees' health insurance impermissibly burdens their free exercise rights. *Burwell* v. *Hobby Lobby Stores, Inc.*, 134 S. Ct. 2751, 2779 (2014). This line of reasoning does not bear on religious objections to paying taxes, however, because of the Court's determination that taxes never unreasonably burden free taxpayers' exercise rights.

48. I.R.C. § 119(a) (2012).

49. Even if the parsonage allowance were to meet the first two prongs of the test, moreover, there may be extrinsic reasons to not grant it in any event. As currently designed, the Treasury Department estimates that the parsonage allowance will reduce federal revenue by about $9.3 billion between 2016 and 2025. Department of Treasury, Tax Expenditures Fiscal Year 2017 at 23, www.treasury.gov/resource-center/tax-policy/Documents/Tax-Expenditures-FY2017.pdf [https://perma.cc/YE78–8RJP]. Of course, during that same period, the Congressional Budget Office estimates that the federal income tax will raise about $20.6 *trillion* in revenue. Congressional Budget Office, "The Budget and Economic Outlook: 2016–2026" (2016), 149, www.cbo.gov/publication/51129 [https://perma.cc/UPX9–2YVU]. The revenue the government gives up from the parsonage allowance, while a significant absolute number, represents less than 0.05 percent of the expected total revenue. If the potential accommodation were to reach the third prong, Congress would need to use its judgment to determine whether this represented an extrinsic argument against the allowance.

50. Complaint, *Gaylor v. Lew*, No. 16-CV-215 (W.D. Wisc. April 6, 2016).

51. *Gaylor v. Mnuchin*, Docket No. 3:16-cv-00215 (W.D. Wis. October 6, 2016).

52. In 2015, according to the National Association of Realtors, the median price of an existing single-family home in the United States was $223,900, while the median family income was $67,507. National Association of Realtors, "Housing Affordability Index," https://perma.cc/F9H7–3HG7. Even if the median family could save all

of its income to buy a house, it would have to save for more than three years to buy the median home.

53. I.R.C. § 163(h) (2012).

54. Pew Research Center, May 12, 2015, "America's Changing Religious Landscape," 4.

55. Treas. Reg. § 1.8611–2(a)(7) (as amended in 1997).

56. *Hernandez* v. *Comm'r*, 490 US 680, 709 (1989).

57. S. Rep. No. 1622, 83d Cong., 2d Sess., 196 (1954); H.R. Rep. No. 1337, 83d Cong., 2d Sess., A44 (1954).

58. *Hernandez* v. *Comm'r*, 490 US 680, 690 (1989).

59. Although there is a range of prices for various bags on the NPR website, as of this writing, the Classic NPR Tote costs $32. http://shop.npr.org/products/classic-npr-tote [https://perma.cc/WA9J-BUDA].

60. www.artic.edu/join-and-give/members/membership-levels [https://perma.cc/F449-LTEA].

61. www.artic.edu/visit?qt-reference_nodes=1#quicktabs-reference_nodes [https://perma.cc/WQR9-PDQQ].

62. www.artic.edu/join-and-give/members/member-faq#membership-tax-deductible [https://perma.cc/BWY7-9WLR].

63. www.fieldmuseum.org/file/116906 [https://perma.cc/XRP3-CBN8].

64. The Internal Revenue Code explicitly lists corporations organized for "education purposes" as qualifying for tax exemption. I.R.C. § 501(c)(3) (2012). As long as they meet the other requirements for tax exemption, private schools can clearly qualify.

65. *Fogarty* v. *US*, 780 F.2d 1005, 1008 (Fed. Cir. 1986).

66. Even structuring the religious entity as a partnership would not resolve this double-taxation problem. While true that a partnership is not a taxpaying entity, partners must pay taxes on their share of partnership income. The way most communitarian organizations are structured, members are not equity owners; even if the partnership did not pay taxes on its income, its owners would, and then the communitarians would pay taxes when they received money from the partnership.

67. 1 Cor. 7:8 NSRV.

68. There is an extensive literature detailing and analyzing the tax consequences of marriage. For a broad overview of those consequences, *see, e.g.*, Thedore P. Seto, "The Unintended Tax Advantages of Gay Marriage," *Washington and Lee Law Review* 65, no. 4 (2008), 1529; Stephanie Hunter McMahon, "To Have and to Hold: What Does Love (of Money) Have to Do with Joint Tax Filing," *Nevada Law Journal* 11, no. 3 (2011), 718.

69. In practice, of course, the accommodation would initially exist as elective for a couple. Nothing in an individual's tax return asks her religion, so the IRS would have no way of knowing whether an individual belonged to the Paulite religion or not. And there would be no public record of marriage, given that the couple did not marry civilly. A couple for whom the accommodation would prove expensive, then, could choose not to file as married.

The accommodation would not always be elective, though: once a couple filed as married, they would have to continue to file as married unless and until they uncoupled in a religious equivalent of a divorce. That would prevent them from essentially harvesting the accommodation during good years and giving it up during bad years. And if the couple tried to claim strategic uncoupling (that is, uncoupling during years when the tax was lower unmarried, and recoupling in years when it was lower married), the IRS could ignore their claimed uncouplings. *See* Rev. Rul. 76–255, 1976–2 C.B. 40; *Boyter* v. *Comm'r*, 74 T.C. 989 (1980).

70. Samuel Brunson, "Taxing Polygamy," *Washington University Law Review* 91, no. 1 (2013), 145–167.

Index